Lives of the Wits

BIOGRAPHIES BY
HESKETH PEARSON

Doctor Darwin (Erasmus Darwin)
The Smith of Smiths (Sydney Smith)
The Fool of Love (William Hazlitt)
Gilbert and Sullivan
Labby (Henry Labouchere)
Tom Paine
The Hero of Delhi (John Nicholson)
Bernard Shaw
A Life of Shakespeare
Conan Doyle
The Life of Oscar Wilde
Dickens
Dizzy (Benjamin Disraeli)
The Man Whistler (James McNeill Whistler)
Walter Scott
Beerbohm Tree
Gilbert (W. S. Gilbert)
Johnson and Boswell
Charles II
The Pilgrim Daughters
Lives of the Wits
With Malcolm Muggeridge:
About Kingsmill (Hugh Kingsmill)

HESKETH PEARSON

Lives of the Wits

HEINEMANN

LONDON MELBOURNE TORONTO

William Heinemann Ltd
LONDON MELBOURNE TORONTO
CAPE TOWN AUCKLAND
THE HAGUE

First published in Great Britain 1962

© HESKETH PEARSON, 1962

Printed in Great Britain
by The Windmill Press Ltd
Kingswood, Surrey

To
My Friend
Frank MacGregor

Contents

Illustrations

Introducing the Wits

'No pecuniary embarrassments equal to the embarrassments of a professed wit,' wrote Sydney Smith to a friend: 'an eternal demand upon him for pleasantry, and a consciousness on his part of a limited income of the facetious; the disappointment of his creditors – the importunity of duns – the tricks, forgeries and false coin he is forced to pay instead of gold. Pity a wit . . .'

He needs to be pitied, being the only person in an atmosphere of social relaxation who cannot relax. Whatever his profession by day, he must make people laugh round the dinner-table at night; though no one expects a clergyman to preach, a politician to debate, a barrister to plead, an actor to perform, a doctor to prescribe, or a stockbroker to give tips off-duty. The man who is famous for witty flings is never off-duty. People wait for his *mots* and are disappointed if he does not oblige, calling him overrated or unsociable or a charlatan. If therefore he is not in the vein for wit or humour, he must take comfort from his fame in other directions. A brilliant churchman or statesman can keep silent without sacrificing a jot of his reputation; and it so happens that the greatest wits were famous for something more than their clever repartees or pithy sayings.

At its best wit does not consist of sparkling retorts or ingenious apothegms spoken by anyone with a quick intelligence. It is the expression of personality, and there are as many kinds of wit as there are characters to give it utterance. The three most consistently and spontaneously witty men in English, both oral and scriptorial, were Sydney Smith, Oscar Wilde and Bernard Shaw, all with strongly marked individualities. Wit was a part of their being, a mental habit; they could scarcely open their mouths or take up their pens without being witty, and even their gravity was frequently upset by their levity. They were endowed with two fertile qualities usually withheld from wits, good nature and good humour, but in each case the wit has a tang that reveals its creator; and this last feature is manifested in all fourteen wits here presented to the reader. Broadly speaking, and allowing for qualifications, the wit of Swift was that of hate, of Johnson argument, of Sheridan ridicule, of Smith gaiety, of Disraeli epigram, of Labouchere detachment, of Whistler malice, of Gilbert absurdity, of Tree smartness, of Wilde frivolity, of Shaw criticism, of Belloc pugnacity, of Beerbohm urbanity, of Chesterton analogy. And all these men were notable as personalities or creative artists or both, their wit being merely an aspect of their characters as expressed in various spheres of activity and thought.

It may be said that my list of wits does not contain the names of certain prominent practitioners of the past; but I have discovered that many of these lived largely on their reputations for liveliness, not on the record of their witticisms, and that the rest should have been described as wags or punsters or jesters or mimics, rather than as wits. I will briefly run through the more obvious omissions.

The earlier wits have to be taken on trust. We may be sure that Shakespeare and Ben Jonson were as keenly intelligent in their conversation as in their works, but the evidence for their verbal sallies is slight; indeed the authentic record of first-rate wit in table or tavern talk practically begins with Swift, for there is scarcely any of that quality in the conversation of Selden recorded by Milward, of Ben Jonson by Drummond, or of Pope by Spence. We have a few isolated examples in the seventeenth century, such as Edmund Waller's reply to Charles II, who asked why his panegyric on Cromwell was better than his poem welcoming the King's restoration: 'Please, your Majesty, we poets always excel in fiction.' But the second Earl of Rochester, supposedly the 'star' wit of Charles's Court, seems to have relied on practical joking for his best efforts, while Charles himself was more of a humourist than a wit, and Congreve's reputation rests solely on the brilliant dialogue of his plays. Going further back, George Buchanan, the eminent Scottish scholar who became tutor to James VI (the First of England), was renowned for his pleasantries, but most of his recorded jokes were apochryphal and rabelaisian, implying that he relied for laughter on smut for smut's sake. In the latter part of the eighteenth century a number of Scottish judges were reputed to shine on the bench; but judicial wit is too easy, for the person at whom it is directed cannot answer back with safety, and the justice has a lot of time in which to crystallise his comments. I question if any judge qualifies for inclusion among the great wits on account of his bright observations outside the law courts.

But I cannot pass over one of the Scottish law-lords, because of his outburst, clearly spontaneous and straight from the heart, against the judgment of his brethren. His name was George Fergusson and he became Lord Hermand, a tall, thin, passionate man with a long neck and a long face; not a temperance reformer. He and his brethren sat on a case in which a young man had accidentally murdered a friend with whom he had passed a summer night over a bowl of punch. Convicted of culpable homicide, the fellow was treated leniently, being sentenced to a short term of imprisonment, to the indignation of Hermand, who demanded transportation and addressed the other judges with heat: 'We are told that there was no malice, and that the prisoner must have been in liquor. In liquor! Why, he was drunk! And yet he murdered the very man who had been drinking with him! They had been carousing the whole night; and yet he stabbed him, after drinking a whole bottle of rum with him. Good God, my Laards, if he will do this when he's drunk, what will he not do when he's sober?'

With Swift we are on firm ground, and most of the social records of the eighteenth century can be relied upon. Yet, in spite of their contemporary fame, the majority of wits in that age cannot hold a candle to Johnson and Sheridan. To take the best examples from the artistic world of Johnson and the social world of Sheridan: there was Samuel Foote, actor, dramatist, droll and mimic, who made Johnson laugh but depended wholly on his oddities of manner to arouse mirth, for he hardly ever said a thing worth remembering; and there was George Augustus Selwyn, famous in fashionable circles for the gravity of his countenance while delivering wisecracks, and who deserved the laugh he got when someone met him leaving the Commons in a hurry and asked whether the House was up : 'No, but Burke is!' Incidentally Selwyn's macabre taste for public executions and the sight of dead bodies inspired a good remark by his friend Lord Holland, who during an illness was told that George had been to inquire after his health: 'If Mr Selwyn calls again, show him into my room. If I am alive I shall be glad to see him; if I am dead he will be glad to see me.'

Perhaps the two wittiest men in the second half of the eighteenth century, apart from Johnson and Sheridan, were the famous demagogue John Wilkes, who was expelled from Parliament, outlawed, exiled, imprisoned, and elected Lord Mayor of London, and John Philpot Curran, who eloquently defended the leaders of the Irish rising in 1798 and became Master of the Rolls in Ireland. Yet their surviving facetiae do not justify their fame. Wilkes certainly made a few good cracks. When his friend Lord Sandwich told him that he would die either of the pox or on the gallows, he saw the possibilities: 'That depends, my Lord, on whether I embrace your mistress or your principles.' During an election campaign a citizen frenziedly declared that he would rather vote for the Devil than Wilkes, who instantly asked: 'And if your friend is not standing ?' His great enemy was George III, and on one occasion the Prince of Wales, surprised to observe him drinking the loyal toast, asked how long he had been concerned over his Majesty's health. 'Since I had the honour of your Royal Highness's acquaintance', replied Wilkes. Curran, too, must have added to the gaiety of his nation, but few of his scintillations bear repetition and we are forced to conclude that he carried them off with an exceptional charm of manner, his gestures being as pointful as his jokes. His light-heartedness is best recalled by a suggestion he made when fighting a duel with a fellow-barrister, John Egan, whose body was huge while Curran's was minute. Egan complained that he might as well fire at a razor's edge as at Curran, whereas his opponent could hit him as easily as a turfstack. Curran at once provided a solution: 'I'll tell you what, Mr Egan. I wish to take no advantage of you whatever. Let my size be chalked upon your side, and I am quite content that every shot which hits outside that mark should go for nothing.' They exchanged shots without harming one another.

Entering the nineteenth century, we have Samuel Rogers, the banker-poet, who was more the cause of wit in others than witty himself; Henry Luttrell, a genial diner-out, who paid for his dinners with pleasantries that passed muster over the wine; Charles James Fox, whose remarkable personality made his comments sound more pregnant than they were; Byron, many of whose japes were thought inimitable on account of his peerage; and Theodore Hook, more of a wag than a wit, whose puns, impromptus and bursts of mimicry convulsed his audiences, but who is chiefly remembered today for the question he put to a self-important person strutting down the Strand as if he owned it: 'Pray, sir, may I ask if you are anybody in particular?' On being faced with a really great wit, Sydney Smith, Hook dried up completely, and Sydney had to do all the talking.

Until the literary movement of the nineties killed that form of humour, puns were the stock-in-trade of many men of letters throughout the century. Puns can be poetic as in Thomas Hood's

> Like the sweet blossoms of the may
> Whose fragrance ends in must,

and they can also aid wit, as in some of Charles Lamb's comical eruptions. But most of Lamb's puns were lamentable (usually as bad as that) and his amusing trifles, helped by a stammer, were not imaginative enough to give him a place among the leading wits. Yet he could be very funny and sometimes perceptive. On Wordsworth's statement that he would experience little difficulty in writing like Shakespeare if he had a mind to try it, Lamb remarked: 'N-nothing w-wanting but the m-mind.' At the East India House, where he was employed, the head of the office reproved him for the irregularity of his attendance: 'Really, Mr Lamb, you come very late!' 'Y-yes, b-but c-consider how ear-ly I g-go!' After Coleridge had impressed the company with the intensity of his religious beliefs, Lamb consoled one of them: 'N-never m-mind what Coleridge says; he's f-full of f-fun.' Leaving Gillman's house in Highgate, where Coleridge lived, Lamb, having dined well, took his place in the coach with a party of friends. An outside passenger called from the top: 'All full inside?' Lamb interpreted the general feeling: 'W-well, that last p-piece of Gillman's p-pudding did the business for me.' A lugubrious acquaintance drew this from the gentle Charles: 'He'd throw a d-damp upon a f-funeral.' One of his observations touched the core of human nature: 'The greatest p-pleasure I know is to do a g-good action by stealth, and to have it f-found out by accident.' But on the whole Lamb was more of a clown than a wit, and just as most men are liable to become pious as they become impotent so do most comedians become buffoons as they grow older. Carlyle's picture of Lamb towards the end of his life is distressing.

There was one wit in the nineteenth century, an Irishman named William Connor Magee, of whom we should like to hear more; but his elevated position in the Church of England made the Victorian circles in which he moved more cautious than usual. Fortunately a public impromptu when he was Bishop of Peterborough has survived. While consecrating a cemetery he had been mobbed and insulted by a crowd of rioters. The matter was raised in the House of Lords, and his spiritual brethren were indignantly sympathetic; but he calmed them with an explanation of how he had dealt with the brawlers: 'I inflicted on them the ignominy of an episcopal benediction, and dismissed them from my mind.'

The first half of the twentieth century was illuminated by the genius of Bernard Shaw, described by Desmond MacCarthy as 'surely the most prolifically witty writer since Voltaire'. This is undoubtedly true, though the conversation of Shaw and Voltaire lacked the rich imaginative quality of Sydney Smith's and Oscar Wilde's. As a wit, G.B.S. was incomparable, and even his younger contemporaries, Hilaire Belloc and G. K. Chesterton, great as they were, could not compete with him either viva voce or in print. With the other wits of this period we do not feel that their clever sayings sprang from something fundamental in their natures: they were the squibs of exhibitionism, let off for effect or to discomfort an opponent. Such were the sparks emitted by F. E. Smith (later Lord Birkenhead) who sometimes made M.P.s roll in their seats. But a wit in Parliament is an oasis in a desert of verbiage, the thinnest trickle of fun creating an appreciative hubbub. The best specimen of his ironic manner was given me by Stanley Baldwin. While he was staying at Wilton House, his host Lord Pembroke showed F. E. Smith the family portraits, explaining that whenever one of his ancestors had an illegitimate child he received the name of Montgomery. F.E. pondered on this for a moment, and then delivered judgment: 'If such an untoward event should happen to me, God forbid that I should deny my child the name of Smith.'

It will be noticed that I have given much more space to Swift and Sheridan than to my other wits. This is because I found their characters more complicated, their careers more involved, than the rest. I had already written full-length biographies of nine of my present subjects, and had therefore understood their natures to the limit of my comprehension; but Swift and Sheridan, though I had been keenly interested in them from youth, were new to me as themes for biography, and so I took longer to indicate their essential characteristics. It may be objected that as I had dealt in detail with nine of my wits, there was not much point in reducing their bulk. I had two motives: firstly, a collection of Lives of men related by a similar gift is bound to be interesting in itself, and I have always taken a special delight in studying the wits; secondly, the experiment of reducing a full-length portrait to the size of a miniature was fascinating, and I attempted in prose what many artists have essayed in paint. The difficulty was to keep the salient features of my subjects clear within the limit imposed, and this I discovered to be, in the words of Sir Thomas Browne, 'no easy matter'.

Jonathan Swift

Mystery envelops the origin and early years of Jonathan Swift. The story, partly written by himself and amplified by his biographers, is a strange one, and in certain respects may be questioned; but we must follow the record before suspicion is released.

The family of Swift were of Yorkshire descent, and one of them, Thomas, became Vicar of Goodrich near Ross in Herefordshire. Though a clergyman, he actively participated as a Royalist in the Civil War of the seventeenth century, his doughty deeds earning him the violent hostility of the Parliamentarians: he was ruined, maltreated, imprisoned, and died two years before the Restoration of the monarchy could repair his misfortunes. Five of his sons crossed to Ireland in the hope of obtaining a livelihood, the eldest, Godwin, becoming Attorney-General of the Palatinate of Tipperary, marrying four times, collecting a dowry from each of his wives, and accumulating considerable wealth. One of the Rev. Thomas's younger sons, born in 1640, was named Jonathan and did not possess the acquisitive ability of his elder brother. Arriving in Ireland at the age of eighteen, he got odd jobs about the courts with the help of Godwin, and married Abigail Erick, whose family, though notable in Leicestershire, were unable to provide her with a dowry. He begat a daughter, and died in the early spring of 1667, some eight months before his widow gave birth to a son, who inherited his patronymic and his poverty.

The future Dean of St Patrick's, Jonathan Swift, was born in

Hoey's Court, Dublin, on St Andrew's Day, 30 November, 1667. His mother, largely dependent on charity, nevertheless had a nurse for her children, and when Jonathan was a year old an event occurred that seemed 'very unusual', as he afterwards related. Expecting a legacy from a dying relative, the nurse travelled to Whitehaven in England, stealing Jonathan and secreting him on the boat without his mother's knowledge. But apparently his mother raised no objection when apprised of the theft, because she instructed the nurse not to attempt the return-journey until the child was in a fit condition to undertake it. Baby Jonathan remained at Whitehaven for three years, and having been taught to spell he made such good progress that by the age of five he could read any chapter in the Bible. Returning to Ireland, he perceived that he would henceforth be dependent on the charity of Uncle Godwin, who was not the sort of man to bestow bounty with anonymity, and Jonathan was made to feel his position acutely. At the age of six his uncle sent him to the grammar school of Kilkenny, where he remained for eight years; and as his mother had returned to her relations in Leicestershire we may surmise that Jonathan's holidays were spent either in the solitude of the school or in the grudging discomfort of his uncle's guardianship.

All we know of his schooldays at Kilkenny is that he must have been ambitious to shine among his fellows and that he had a certain amount of pocket-money. Anxious to own a horse on which he could parade before the other youths, he bought a mangy, emaciated specimen from a poor man who was about to sell it for the price of its hide. Able to offer rather more than that would fetch, Jonathan's appearance on the animal's back won the envy of some, the ridicule of others. But the horse soon collapsed, and, having no money to feed or stable it, he felt relieved when it died, while weeping bitterly for the loss of his cash. Incidentally one of his companions at Kilkenny school was the future dramatist William Congreve, with whom he formed a close friendship in after years.

He entered Trinity College, Dublin, at the age of fourteen.

There are many dubious accounts of his behaviour there, from which our knowledge of his character enables us to compose a fairly accurate picture. His extreme individuality made him rebel against the curriculum, whilst his uncle's niggardliness and lack of sympathy drove him in upon himself. He tried to escape from it all by reading novels, plays and poetry. Being intensely sensitive, he hated the position of a poor relative dependent on doles from a man he despised; and like many intelligent youths he had a poor opinion of those pedagogues who thought erudition more important than imagination. In the examination preceding the disputation which decided the grant of degrees, he failed in two subjects out of three; but owing no doubt to some influence he obtained a B.A. degree by 'special indulgence'. Late in life he explained his failure as due to dullness, describing himself as a dunce; but that was merely his way of excusing a dislike of enforced knowledge and a disposition to laziness when faced with labour for which he had no taste. However, he began to study for his M.A. degree, which with any diligence he would have won, but before he could take the final examination the revolution which unseated James II from the English throne broke out, and as the Irish army, as well as the Viceroy, were Roman Catholics, there was a sudden exodus of Protestants from Ireland to England, Jonathan Swift among them.

Uncle Godwin had recently died; Jonathan had received a sum of money from one of his merchant-cousins in Lisbon; and this enabled him to visit his mother in Leicestershire with enough in his pocket to be idle for a while. He was fond of his mother, who appears to have been a cheerful, easy-going soul with sufficient means to face life without qualms. She may have lived on an allowance, the source of which will shortly be conjectured. The first use Swift made of his money was to dally with a maiden named Betty Jones. Ignorant of his nature, his mother suspected him of meditating matrimony and reminded him that he had nothing to marry on. But he was content with dalliance, and soon after his departure the girl married a publican at Loughborough.

Having spent several months in the company of his mother and

the tattling social world of Leicester, he left to obtain employment in the household of Sir William Temple, who had been a
notable diplomatist in the reign of Charles II, having effected the
Triple Alliance between England, Holland and Sweden, and
arranged the marriage between William of Orange and Mary.
Temple had married Dorothy Osborne, whose letters during their
long courtship were to become famous, and in 1677 had refused
the King's offer to be Secretary of State. He now lived in scholarly
ease at Moor Park near Farnham in Surrey, and at the request of
Swift's mother he engaged Jonathan as a secretary. It is quite
possible that the retired diplomatist and his young employee
were half-brothers, a relationship that explains much of Swift's
later behaviour. The Temple and Swift families had known each
other well in Ireland. Sir John Temple, father of Sir William, had
been Master of the Rolls in that country, had formed a close
intimacy with Godwin Swift, and had been, in Jonathan's words,
'a great friend to the family'. The theory that Jonathan Swift was
the natural son of Sir John Temple is supported by the im-
probability of his putative father being in a condition to propagate
a child within a few weeks of his death, by the stinginess of
Godwin Swift, whose allowance for the lad's upkeep may have
been restricted after his friend Sir John's decease and who never
displayed the least affection for Jonathan, by the strangely
detached attitude of the boy's mother when the nurse took him to
Whitehaven and her indifference to his future welfare, by the fact
that she was able to live in relative comfort at Leicester without
any known means of subsistence, by Sir William's unquestioning
employment of Jonathan in a confidential capacity, and by Swift's
subsequent conduct to a girl who was probably Sir William
Temple's natural daughter.[1]

Swift did his duties at Moor Park efficiently. He read to Sir
William, wrote letters for him, and kept his accounts. But
Temple was a man with a very high opinion of himself and would
scarcely have recognised the peculiar merits of his secretary. Also
the household was run not by Lady Temple but by Lady Giffard,

1. See *In Search of Swift* by Denis W. Johnston, 1959.

the widowed sister of Temple, and, as she had an arbitrary nature, it is likely that Swift felt uncomfortable between a man who thought himself perfect and a woman who loved to dwell on the imperfections of others. Swift began to suffer from giddiness, indigestion and deafness, which he attributed to eating too many apples at a sitting, but which were probably due to the nervous condition of a sensitive young man conscious of his genius, placed in a position of inferiority, and treated at one moment with aloof restraint, at another with unrestricted rudeness. At any rate he soon tired of his situation and persuaded Temple to write a letter recommending him to the notice of Sir Robert Southwell, then with William III in Ireland as Secretary of State. But Southwell was too busy at the moment with a crisis which was about to terminate in the Battle of the Boyne, and the letter was merely added to his collection of papers. Perceiving that there was nothing for him in the land of his birth, Swift again visited his mother in Leicestershire and once more indulged in a certain amount of mild flirtation with women, finding that such an occupation soothed an unemployed mind. He was not the kind of man to lose his mental balance over any woman. He may at one time have wanted to marry, and as a preliminary to the choice of a wife he sought as much feminine society as possible, experimenting with the affections of those who enjoyed playing at love. But his real passion was devoted to ambition, and 'household thoughts', as he admitted, always drove matrimony out of his mind.

For a year or so he frittered away his time, but by the close of 1691 he was back with Temple, who had doubtless missed him and now made up for an earlier coolness by forming a more intimate relationship with the young man. With his patron's assistance, Swift went to Oxford and took his degree as Master of Arts, working at Latin and Greek for the purpose but asserting that he would 'rather die in a ditch' than study philosophy. Temple also encouraged his poetic muse and exposed to his view:

The wily shafts of state, those juggler's tricks,
Which we call deep designs and politics.

But after writing several odes of no particular merit, he was told
by Dryden that he would never be a poet and dropped verse-
making for a while, taking up instead the study of humanity in the
eminent specimens thereof who visited Temple at Moor Park.
Among them was King William III, who not only explained to
Swift the Dutch method of cutting and eating asparagus but
offered him a captaincy of dragoons. How Swift managed to
evade the offer we do not know, but he benefited from the advice
about asparagus, for many years afterwards when Dean of St
Patrick's he gave dinner to an alderman who asked for a second
helping of that vegetable. 'Sir, first finish what you have upon
your plate,' said the Dean. 'What, sir, eat my stalks?' 'Ay, sir,
King William always ate the stalks.' In telling this story to a
friend, the alderman was asked, 'Were you blockhead enough to
obey him?' to which he rejoined, 'Yes, and if you had dined with
Dean Swift, *tête à tête*, you would have been obliged to eat your
stalks too!'

Temple gave proof of the trust he now reposed in Swift by
sending the young man to Kensington, where he placed before the
King strong arguments in support of the Bill for triennial
Parliaments then being debated. But the King was not convinced.
This was the first time Swift had come into contact with Courts,
and he told his friends that it helped to cure him of vanity. While
becoming indispensable to Temple, he began to grow restless.
Ambition was stirring within him, and his present employment
seemed a dead end. The Church offered possibilities of advancement, though he did not care to take holy orders solely for
mercenary motives. Aware no doubt that he would refuse it,
Temple offered him a job as clerk in the office of the Rolls at
Dublin, the salary being £120 a year. Swift promptly turned it
down, but used the offer to his advantage by saying that as it
would have given him financial freedom he could now enter the
Church without the reproach of being driven into the priesthood

for a living. When he decided to leave Moor Park, Temple was extremely angry and they parted on bad terms; but Swift was now twenty-six years old and had resolved to be independent. Leaving Temple in May 1694, he stayed for a short while with his mother, and then went on to Dublin with the intention of being ordained. But the Archbishop of Dublin was unhelpful, demanding a certificate of his good behaviour during the years of his absence from Ireland. This could only be obtained from Sir William Temple, and he had to eat humble pie in a letter to his former patron, putting it off as long as possible: 'The sense I am in how low I have fallen in your honour's thoughts has denied me assurance enough to beg this favour till I find it impossible to avoid.' To show his lack of resentment, or to prove his indifference, Temple sent the necessary certificate, and Swift's ordination as deacon took place in October 1694. In January of the following year he became a priest, and the same month managed to obtain the prebend of Kilroot, near Belfast, where his congregation was scant, his income £100 a year.

A neighbouring rector named Waring had a daughter, Jane, and Swift kept boredom at bay by making love to her, giving her the fanciful name of Varina. Indeed he actually ¦proposed marriage, but that was probably a poetic gesture, for when he heard that Temple was anxious to have him back as a guest he made up his mind to leave Kilroot, where the waters of Belfast Lough were a poor substitute for the company at Moor Park. All the same he was anxious to test the strength of Varina's feelings before going and took the risk of writing: 'I am once more offered the advantage to have the same acquaintance with greatness that I formerly enjoyed, and with better prospect of interest. I here solemnly offer to forgo it all for your sake. I desire nothing of your fortune; you shall live where and with whom you please till my affairs are settled to your desire, and in the meantime I will push my advancement with all the eagerness and courage imaginable, and do not doubt to succeed.' But he probably knew the risk was slight, and Varina played the game according to the rules. He managed to transfer the prebend to a friend, and left for England in May 1696.

His third period at Moor Park was on a different footing from his previous residences there. His one-time patron welcomed him as a friend and collaborator, because he was helping to put Sir William's papers in order; he was free to do as much reading and writing as he liked, free to come and go whenever he pleased, and treated as a guest of honour. 'I live in great state,' he announced, 'and the cook comes in to know what I please to have for dinner: I ask very gravely what is in the house, and accordingly give orders for a dish of pigeons, or &c.' He polished off a book which, when published, would make his reputation as a writer and kill his chances of preferment as a clergyman. He took violent exercise, riding, walking and running. Sometimes he walked all the way to Leicester or Oxford, spending the nights in cheap lodgings but always paying twopence extra for clean sheets. Every day at Moor Park he ran up a neighbouring hill, both before and after dinner, under the impression that it was good for his health. Whatever he did was done with the whole of his energy, whether mental or physical; and, although he cannot have been greatly interested in the controversy, he wrote with considerable vigour *The Battle of the Books*, a defence of the attitude taken by Temple in the current disputation concerning the ancient and modern writers, a controversy started in France, where many scribes wished to believe that the reign of Louis XIV was the greatest in history and therefore marked the apogee of literature as well as of conquest and civilisation. Temple took the side of the ancients against the moderns, and there was 'great argument about it and about', Swift's view being determined by that of Temple, who however made a point that his antagonists would not have admitted: 'God be thanked, man has this one felicity to comfort and support him, that, in all ages, in all things, every man is always in the right.'

Meanwhile Swift had been engaged in a recreation suited to his peculiar constitution. He was teaching a girl in the Moor Park household. Temple's sister, Lady Giffard, later to be described by Swift as a 'beast', employed a widow named Mrs Johnson, whose husband had been one of Temple's favourite servants. Mrs Johnson had two daughters, the elder named Hester having been about eight years old when Swift first went to Moor Park; but she had now reached the age of fifteen. From his first residence he had taken the child's education in hand and had soon engaged her affection. It may be that her early mispronunciation of words had appealed to him and started the baby-talk or 'little language' which they kept up to the end of her days, a form of endearment common among lovers and spouses. Openly stated by some people at the time, it is probable that she was Temple's natural daughter, which, if Swift were Sir John Temple's natural son, would mean that he was her uncle. But even if aware of this afterwards, it is unlikely that he knew it in the Moor Park days. At the age of fifteen she was, in Swift's remembrance, 'one of the most beautiful, graceful, and agreeable young women in London, only a little too fat. Her hair was blacker than a raven, and every feature of her face in perfection.' As time went on, he declared, she developed 'a gracefulness somewhat more than human in every motion, word, and action', and at social gatherings 'she never failed before we parted of delivering the best thing that was said in the company'. Later he called her Stella, by which she is known to posterity. She accompanied the family whenever they went to London, was treated by Temple with as much affection as he was capable of showing, and inherited £1,500 at his death in January 1699, by which time Swift had completely captivated her, while her admiration and adoration appealed strongly to his vanity and need for affection, though his queerly twisted nature or some grave physical impediment prevented him from acting as most normal men in his situation would have done.

Over the next few years Swift worked on Temple's papers and arranged their publication, but did not earn much money by the labour. After Sir William's death he went to London and petitioned the King for a prebend of Canterbury or Westminster, which his Majesty had promised to give him. The Earl of

Romney, who 'professed much friendship', agreed to second the petition, but, wrote Swift, 'as he was an old vicious, illiterate rake, without any sense of truth or honour, said not a word to the King', and after dancing attendance at Court for a long time Swift went to Ireland as chaplain and private secretary to the Earl of Berkeley, who had been appointed one of the Lord Justices.

In 1699 Swift reached the age of thirty-two and began to analyse his nature, listing a number of things he must be on his guard against 'when I come to be old'. First of all he determined 'not to marry a young woman', and then went on to enumerate the various failings of old age to be avoided, such as covetousness, intolerance of youthful follies, dirtiness, garrulity, repetitiveness, overbearingness; but the list was so long that he felt bound to add that he should not 'set up for observing all these rules, for fear I should observe none.' But since he was a keenly ambitious man the one quality of all others that should have aroused his immediate vigilance was his tendency to outspokenness, which caused him more trouble and vexation of spirit than all the weaknesses he could have named.

On arrival in Dublin a fellow named Bushe managed to persuade Lord Berkeley that a chaplain should not also be a secretary, and got the latter job himself. Berkeley made Swift a feeble apology and implied that as soon as a good church vacancy occurred he would obtain it. Soon afterwards the deanery of Derry was at the Earl's disposal, and Swift heard that if he cared to bribe Bushe with a thousand guineas he would get the vacancy. Swift was furious, cursed both Berkeley and Bushe, called them a couple of scoundrels, and a more pliable man became Dean. For some months thereafter the Earl and his secretary were subjected to satirical verses from Swift's pen, which no doubt they tried to laugh off, but which made them feel so uncomfortable that when the chance arose the satirist was fobbed off with three church livings, Laracor, Agher and Rathbeggan, in County Meath, the combined income from which scarcely equalled a third of the rich deanery of Derry. Nevertheless, as the Earl's chaplain, he still passed most of his time at Dublin Castle, where he was popular with the ladies, especially Berkeley's two daughters, and where he had leisure to observe the peculiarities of the domestic staff, his advice to some of them being written at a later date. In two of his hints to servants he seems to have anticipated the principles laid down by modern trade unions:

'Never submit to stir a finger in any business but that for which you are particularly hired. For example . . . if a corner of the hanging wants a single nail to fasten it, and the footman be directed to tack it up, he may say he doth not understand that sort of work but his honour may send for the upholsterer.'

'You may quarrel with each other as much as you please, only bear in mind that you have a common enemy, which is your Master and Lady.'

Butlers in particular attracted his notice:

'If you are curious to taste some of your master's choicest ale, empty as many of the bottles just below the neck as will make the quantity you want; but then take care to fill them up again with clean water, that you may not lessen your master's liquor.'

'You need not wipe your knife to cut the bread for the table, because in cutting a slice or two it will wipe itself.'

It may have been a memory of something served up at a Castle dinner that inspired this direction to cooks:

'If a lump of soot falls into the soup, and you cannot conveniently get it out, stir it well in, and it will give the soup a high *French* taste.'

We do not know whether a verse on Lord Berkeley's proneness to break wind in company earned Swift an increase of income, but in 1700 he was given the prebend of Dunlaven in St Patrick's and soon afterwards he obtained a Doctor's degree at Trinity College. He was clearly going up in the world and Jane Waring, his Varina, reopened negotiations, doubtless feeling that union with a canon would be more agreeable than marriage with a curate. But Swift had got over his mood of flirtation and sent her a letter which cannot have encouraged her to pursue the subject. After saying that he had never entertained thoughts of marriage to anyone but herself, he went on to define the necessary qualifications for his wife: 'Have you such an inclination to my person and humour as to comply with my desires and way of living, and endeavour to make us both as happy as you can? Will you be ready to engage in those methods I shall direct for the improvement of your mind so as to make us entertaining company for each other, without being miserable when we are neither visiting nor visited? . . . Have you so much good nature as to endeavour by soft words to smooth any rugged humour occasioned by the cross accidents of life? Shall the place wherever your husband is thrown be more welcome than courts or cities without him?' She could not answer these questions in the affirmative, and their correspondence ceased.

At about this period Swift had some trouble with his sister, who wished to marry a currier named Fenton. Something about the fellow evoked Swift's dislike and he fiercely opposed the match; but his sister resented his attitude and the marriage took place, with the result that he never spoke to her again, though when her husband died leaving her in poverty Swift supported her for the rest of her life.

Berkeley was superseded in 1701 and Swift accompanied him to London, where he soon became embroiled in politics. In those days political passions were more violent than they have ever been since, both Church and State being torn with factions. The Whigs, who had brought William III to power and represented the forces of religious dissent, were against the authority of the Church upheld by the Tories, who were suspected of favouring the restoration of the Stuart dynasty. The fight between them was therefore a life and death struggle for power, place and pelf, the leaders of the displaced party being in danger of losing life or freedom by impeachment for high treason or corruption. Swift was wholly opposed to party government, hating the tyranny of the powerful over the dispossessed, and, when the Tories, recently returned to office, were in process of impeaching William's chief Whig advisers, Lords Halifax, Somers, Portland and Orford, he wrote an anonymous pamphlet entitled *On the*

Dissensions at Athens and Rome in which the folly of the Tory action was exposed in classical guise. It was a blow struck for the Whigs; and, though the writer as a clergyman of the Established Church was Tory in sentiment, he hated the bitterness of these party squabbles and temporarily took the side that was about to suffer for its opinions. The pamphlet appeared at an opportune moment, for it happened that James II died at St Germain in September 1701, and the French King Louis XIV acknowledged James's son as King of England. Instantly England bubbled over with national indignation, rallied to William, and the Tories were swept out of office. When the leading Whigs discovered the name of the man who had written this timely pamphlet they were all over him, desiring his acquaintance 'with great marks of esteem and professions of kindness. . . . They were very liberal in promising me the greatest preferments I could hope for, if ever it came in their power . . . I grew domestic with Lord Halifax, and was as often with Lord Somers as the formality of his nature . . . made it agreeable to me.'

Swift must have visited Moor Park while in England, because he persuaded Stella to reside henceforth in Ireland, not only on the ground that it would be 'very much for my own satisfaction' but also on account of cheap living, some of her legacy of £1,500 from Temple being in Irish land. A friend, Rebecca Dingley, who had a small income, accompanied her and remained with her to the end of her life. According to report, Swift always saw them both together and they only lived in his house during his absences. Though it may appear incredible to an age grown careless of appearances, Swift and Stella were never left alone in the same building, though when in Ireland he saw her almost daily. This arrangement was made by him for the sake of her reputation as an unmarried woman, and possibly as a check to his own feelings. When he was at Laracor they had lodgings at Trim, when at Dublin in rooms nearby; but whenever he stayed in England they occupied one or other of his houses in Ireland, and he wrote them a regular journal of his doings. It happened that a clergyman named Tisdall fell in love with Stella. Swift knew him well and wrote to say that 'if my fortunes and humour served me to think of that state I should certainly among all persons on earth make your choice, because I never saw that person whose conversation I entirely valued but hers', yet he would not on that account stand in the other's way. He probably felt safe in making this assurance, since he knew that Stella preferred his friendship to marriage with anyone else, and in due course Tisdall was made to share his knowledge.

From 1701 to 1709 Swift spent his time partly at Laracor and partly in London. The rectory at Laracor as well as the church badly needed repair, owing to the fact that many clergy in those days took no further interest in their livings than to draw their incomes and to pay a small part thereof to the curates who performed the duties. Swift changed that in his own parish. He built a new parsonage, added to the glebe, erected walls for the garden, planted fruit trees, made a pond, and dammed a small stream which he turned into a canal and fringed with willows. He made essential repairs to the church and announced that prayers would be read every Wednesday and Friday. His Sunday services seldom drew more than a dozen persons, and the prayer-meetings could only depend on a congregation of one, his clerk and bell-ringer Roger Cox. It is recorded that at the first of these he commenced the exhortation: 'Dearly beloved Roger, the Scripture moveth you and me in sundry places . . . .'

In London his main job was to obtain certain financial remissions for the relief of the Irish clergy, but he received no encouragement from the Whig Ministers. In 1704 his satire *The Tale of a Tub*, written about seven years earlier, was published anonymously, but the author was quickly identified. It delighted the wits but alarmed the authorities. William III had died in March 1702, and Queen Anne was now on the throne, but, though inclined to Toryism, she could not swallow such an irreverent defence of the established religion, and it was commonly reported in the years ahead that the work had wrecked Swift's chances of a bishopric. In effect it satirised the Roman Catholic faith as well as the beliefs of the Dissenters and the disbeliefs of the freethinkers; but Swift had about as little of the mystic in him as any man that ever lived, and the rollicking or detached treatment of sacred subjects was more than anyone but a severely rational Christian could bear; indeed Voltaire said that Swift had 'soused the Christian religion all over with ridicule'. He also dealt with the assumptions of science, the futility of human reason and the limitless idiocy of mankind with a divine, or diabolical, disregard of human feeling.

The tale, though it lost him a diocese, won him a reputation, and all the leading wits of Will's Coffee-House in Bow Street and the St James's Coffee-House were eager to know him. Addison inscribed one of his books 'To Dr Jonathan Swift, the most agreeable companion, the truest friend, and the greatest genius of his age'. The two men used to talk far into the night, so engrossed in their conversation that they had no need of a companion. Steele, Congreve, Vanbrugh, Prior, Gay and Dr Arbuthnot, the Court physician, clustered around a man who won the admiration due to his brains and the affection inspired by his honesty and kindness. No one ever produced literary work so much at variance with the warmth of his personal relationships. But this was because, as he told Alexander Pope, 'I hate and detest that animal called Man, although I heartily love John, Peter, Thomas, and so forth,' and therefore in all his literary labours he wished 'to vex the world rather than divert it'. There was in fact a canker in his heart: 'I remember, when I was a little boy, I felt a great fish at the end of my line, which I drew up almost on the ground, but it dropt in, and the disappointment vexes me to this very day.' The loss of the fish may have prefigured his ensuing disappointments, but what he felt with the utmost keenness was the obscurity of his birth and social position, confiding in Pope that 'All my endeavours from a boy to distinguish myself were only for want of a title and fortune, that I might be used like a Lord by those who have an opinion of my parts, whether right or wrong it is no great matter; and so the reputation of wit or great learning does the office of a blue riband or of a coach and six horses.' Yet such was the perversity

c

of his nature that all his works were published anonymously and he never made a penny out of them until, through Pope's insistence, he received something for the copyright of *Gulliver's Travels*.

He still hoped for a Church preferment from the Whig leaders, Somers and Halifax, but though their words were friendly their deeds were negligible. 'Pray, my Lord,' he addressed Halifax, 'desire Dr South to die about the fall of the leaf, for he has a prebend of Westminster which will make me your neighbour, and a sinecure in the country . . . which my friends have often told me would fit me extremely.' But Dr South did not oblige him by dying and he hoped Halifax would move Somers, then Lord President, to consider him for the bishopric of Cork. All to no avail. The Whig peers were frightened of his pen, or more concerned over remaining in power than acknowledging literary merit. All through those years Marlborough's victories on the continent kept the Whigs in the ascendant; but by the close of the first decade of the eighteenth century people were tiring of victories that brought no obvious benefits, and the indifference of the Whigs to the established religion decreased their popularity. The Queen's chief confidante was Mrs Masham, whose influence greatly helped the Tory element, and, when the feeling in the country seemed to favour a change, the famous Whig Minister Godolphin was sacked and Robert Harley, an ex-Whig now supported by the Tories, was made Chancellor of the Exchequer.

At this moment Swift came over from Ireland to appeal once more for the grant of Queen Anne's Bounty to the Irish Church, and he found Harley not only in favour of his mission but extremely friendly to himself, receiving him 'with the greatest marks of kindness and esteem'. Harley introduced him to Henry St John, the new Secretary of State for foreign affairs, who fully appreciated the importance of attaching him to their interest, and Swift found that he was in the peculiar position of being courted by men who were being courted by the rest of the world. His wishes were granted, his whims gratified, his advice was sought, and he was admitted to the intimacy of the two most powerful men in the state. He perceived that *The Tale of a Tub* had gained him their friendship. 'If it had not been for that,' he wrote to Stella, 'I should never have been able to get the access I have had; and if that helps me to succeed, then that *same thing* will be serviceable to the Church.' Nevertheless he did not put too much trust in politicians; he remained watchful and wary.

The picture of Swift at this period, painted by his friend Jervas, is that of a man satisfied with himself and content with the world, which he regards with an amused toleration. Though it does not show his real character, it gives us an impression of how he appeared to the world when in a position of authority. His eyes, said Pope, were 'quite azure as the heavens, with a very uncommon archness in them', but his thick black eyebrows were rather fearsome. Slightly above middle height, he was beginning to put on weight in his early forties, and this was one of the reasons that he walked so incessantly, sometimes breaking into a run. He had an odd, abrupt way of speaking, as of one who wished to shock or surprise his auditors, and his remarks were sufficiently individual to have that effect. In conversation he never laughed, though the suddenly compressed mouth and the expression of his eyes implied that he was secretly amused. Many years later he confessed that he could not remember laughing more than twice in his life: once at some trick a mountebank's merry-andrew played, the other time when Tom Thumb killed the Ghost in Fielding's play. He was at times arrogant, sometimes reserved, never submissive, frequently agreeable. His attacks of giddiness, headache, vertigo and deafness, occasionally made life almost insupportable, but during periods of good health he was excellent company and capable of arousing the lasting love of his friends. As he became more and more identified with the Tories, he saw less and less of the Whiggish writers such as Congreve, Addison and Steele, but the only man who behaved spitefully to him was the one to whom he had been most useful, having given invaluable aid in the launching and consequent success of Steele's paper *The Tatler*.

All his life Swift detested party politics. 'Party is the madness of many for the gain of a few,' he declared. He could not help liking certain politicians, but he was under no illusions concerning their ability: 'I never yet knew a minister who was not earnestly desirous to have it thought that the art of government was a most profound science; whereas it requires no more in reality than diligence, honesty, and a moderate share of plain natural sense.' Having a responsive nature, he could not resist the blandishments of Harley and St John, though he made it perfectly clear to both of them that he would not be patronised by either. St John soon became Viscount Bolingbroke, and Harley the Earl of Oxford, but their ennoblement did not make them more important in the eyes of Swift, who told Oxford that he would never allow quality or station to make any difference between men, and in after years wrote to him: 'I loved you just so much the worse for your station. In your public capacity you have often angered me to the heart, but as a private man never. I was too proud to be vain of the honour you did me. I was never afraid of offending you . . .' When Oxford sent him £50 for services rendered by his pen, he returned it and refused an invitation to dine with the Chancellor, insisting on a written apology. Again, when Bolingbroke treated him a little frigidly, he wrote to say that he would not stand a cool manner of countenance or behaviour from a crowned head, and 'no subject's favour is worth it'. Bolingbroke apologised, excusing himself on the ground that much business had kept him up for several nights and much drinking on another, and begged Swift to dine with him; but Swift declined because he would not encourage a second offence by too easily passing over the first; moreover he had another engagement. 'If we let these great ministers pretend too much, there will be no governing them,' he reported, and he wrote to Bolingbroke 'that if the Queen gave you a dukedom and the Garter tomorrow, with the Treasury at the end of it, I would regard you no more than if you were not worth a groat.' This independent attitude displeased Dr Samuel Johnson, who wrote in his Life of Swift: 'No man can pay a more servile tribute to the great than by suffering his liberty in their presence to aggrandise him in his own esteem.' This might be true of the generality of men, but Swift felt, rightly, that a man of genius or talent was a character superior to one who was merely 'a Lord in High Station'.

Though he constantly obtained jobs for his old Whig friends, he complained that he was 'worse used by that party than any man', but this was due to the power of his pen. Articles, pamphlets, lampoons poured from him, and he was generally regarded by the other side as a renegade; but he was a clergyman, and the Tories were strong for the Established Church, while the Whigs favoured Presbyterianism and other forms of Dissent. Another aspect of the political situation jarred upon him. The long war had bred profiteers, chief among them Marlborough and his favourite officers, and it was a Whig war from which no one benefited except politicians, soldiers and stockjobbers. In the autumn of 1711 he wrote a pamphlet known as *The Conduct of the Allies*, which had a more immediate and potent effect on public affairs than any treatise in English history. Its particular appeal to the nation was due to the manner in which Swift showed that the war was being fought solely for the advantage of the Dutch, that the victories of Marlborough had been of no use to anyone else, for 'when our armies take a town in Flanders, the Dutch are immediately put into possession and we at home make bonfires', and that after ten glorious campaigns England was just 'expiring with all sorts of good symptoms.' This remarkable piece of satire exposed the absurdity of war as no previous writer had done, and led to the downfall of Marlborough, the close of the campaign and the Treaty of Utrecht. It also gave Swift an extraordinary prestige. The Whigs would have liked to burn him alive, not being in a mood to appreciate the truth of his statement that 'a man should never be ashamed to own he has been in the wrong, which is but saying in other words that he is wiser today than he was yesterday'. He now occupied a position unique in English politics, no man of letters before or since his time having achieved his authority and influence. Hints of his renown appear in the Journal to Stella, who is told of his invitations to dine or stay with all the notabilities who sought his acquaintance. 'I suppose I have said enough in this and a former letter how I stand with new people, ten times better than ever I did with the old; forty times more caressed.' He tried hard to maintain the old relationship with Addison, Congreve and the rest, for he hated to think that political partisanship should impair friendship, but they became cool. As for the gang of Whigs who were merely concerned with intrigue and personal profit, 'Rot 'em, for ungrateful dogs; I'll make them repent their usage before I leave this place.' The only drawback to his intimacy with Oxford and Bolingbroke was that they expected him to drink as much as they did. His refusal did not help them to keep sober.

At first he had lodgings in Bury Street, St James's; then, for the sake of his health, he moved to Chelsea, just beyond the church, where he bathed in the river at night with the chance of being knocked senseless by a boat. When the Court went to Windsor he went too, witnessing the hunts in the park which were followed by the Queen, who drove herself furiously in a one-horse chaise. He became friendly with the great Earl of Peterborough, but a poem he wrote aroused the animosity of the Duchess of Somerset, Mistress of the Robes, who had considerable influence with the Queen. He was the chief figure of the Scriblerus Club, a semi-literary, semi-political organisation, the members of which included Pope, Gay, Arbuthnot, the Lord Treasurer (Oxford), the Duke of Ormond, and the Secretary of State (Bolingbroke). Sometimes Swift stayed with Peterborough at Parson's Green, but mostly he was in London, moving his lodgings from Bury Street to Suffolk Street, then to St Martin's Street, then to Panton Street. At St James's Palace, in the Mall, at his own lodgings, wherever he was to be seen, people besieged him with requests. Dukes and duchesses asked for his acquaintance, and he made it clear that he was granting them a favour. At Court, he told Stella, he was 'so proud I make all the lords come up to me', and 'I affect to turn from a lord to the meanest of my acquaintance'. The Duke of Hamilton and Lord Abercorn begged him to obtain French dukedoms for them. Even men in high office like the Duke of Ormond solicited his influence. Having a passion for power, he loved it all and forgot his own advancement in forwarding that of others. Once he did remind Oxford that the Dean of Wells had just died, the implication being that there would be no difficulty in filling his place, and Bolingbroke wrote to assure 'dear Jonathan' that he too had mentioned the matter to the Lord Treasurer, adding that he would 'never neglect any opportunity . . .' etc., etc. But as a rule Swift was more anxious to display his power than to take personal advantage of it, one of his chief pleasures being to collect money from Oxford, Bolingbroke and others, and distribute it to any poor author; though the necessity of providing for the future was never out of his thoughts.

While basking in the glory of his favoured position, he wrote continually to Stella, or rather to the two friends living at his Irish vicarage. Even in correspondence he did not care to compromise Stella, and his Journal was addressed both to her and her friend Rebecca Dingley. 'God Almighty bless poor dear Stella,' he wrote to them on her birthday, 'and send her a great many birthdays, all happy and healthy and wealthy, and with me ever together, and never asunder again, unless by chance.' He told them of his walks to Chelsea, 'just five thousand seven hundred and forty-eight steps,' of his longing to be with them, 'all together, now and forever all together', of his bad temper in hot weather, of his giddiness, which he still attributed to the eating of fruit, of breaking his shin in the Strand one night over a tub of sand left in the way, of the grief exhibited by her relations on Lady Asburnham's death ('People will pretend to grieve more than they really do, and that takes off from their true grief'), and of the difficulty he experienced in keeping Oxford and Bolingbroke from quarrelling. He loved Oxford, liked and admired Bolingbroke, and was placed in a very tricky position while trying to reconcile them. Bolingbroke wished to take Oxford's place as Prime Minister, and his fiery licentious spirit was at odds with the other's dilatoriness and domestic content. Swift did not know that both the Ministers constantly negotiated with the Pretender,

though he was aware that Bolingbroke would have preferred a
Stuart to a Hanoverian succession, and he felt convinced that if
they did not sink their differences and co-operate their power
would collapse. A bad attack of shingles gave him 'miserable
torture', and the moment he recovered he found that the relationship between the two Ministers had deteriorated, but could
report some six months later that 'I have helped to patch up these
people together once more. God knows how long it may last . . .'
It was an exhausting business, and 'if I had not a spirit naturally
cheerful, I should be very much discontented at a thousand
things'.

He would have left them to settle their own troubles and gone
off to his canal and willow trees at Laracor if he had not still
hoped for preferment, telling Stella that 'all the days I have passed
here have been dirt to those' which he had spent riding with her in
Ireland. But 'to return without some mark of distinction would
look extremely little, and I would likewise gladly be somewhat
richer than I am.' Since he had ventured all his credit in trying to
clear up the misunderstandings between Oxford and Bolingbroke, he felt that he 'ought to have the merit of it'. Above all he
wished to get an appointment that would enable him to make life
easy for Stella and secure his independence. 'A wise man,' he
once wrote to Bolingbroke, 'ought to have money in his head but
not in his heart.' He lived up to the maxim, being prudent to the
point of penuriousness in his own affairs, generous to others.

Naturally he did not tell his friends at Laracor that he was
privily seeing a great deal of a girl twenty years younger than
himself. Esther Vanhomrigh was the eldest child of a Dutch
merchant who had made money in Ireland after the Battle of the
Boyne, died in 1703, and left the fortune to his widow and four
children. When Swift arrived in London the family were living
in Bury Street and his lodgings were only five doors off. He soon
made himself at home with them, telling Stella of the many
occasions when he dined there. While living at Chelsea he kept
his best gown and periwig at their house, where a room was
placed at his disposal. He sent them venison, wine, etc., usually

spent rainy days under their roof, always felt quite at ease in their company, and gave lessons to Esther. With slight variations the pattern of his relationship with Stella was copied in the case of Esther, whom he soon called Vanessa, by which name we know her. Although his complexion was described as muddy, his facial expression sour or severe, the tone of his voice high and sharp, his manner brusque, there was something about Swift that appealed to both sexes. He inspired an affection from his male friends that was expressed in an extreme form by Pope, who wrote, 'You have made it impossible for me to live at ease without you,' while many women found him irresistible. One who signed herself 'Sacharissa' sent him what she rightly termed a 'distracted scroll' from which it appeared that his writings had first aroused her passion, causing her to suffer anguish 'even before I saw your godlike form'. She begged him to 'lighten the insupportable burden of my love by generously bearing a part. When I consider to whom I speak, that 'tis to the divine, immortal Swift, I am confounded at my vanity; but alas! the malignity of my disorder is so great that my love soon gets the better of the regard and homage I render even to his name.' Such missives probably pleased him more than a letter from 'The White Perruke' in Maiden Lane wherein the writer declared that he owed to Swift the love he bore to the English language and signed himself 'Voltaire'. There was a great deal more conceit than vanity in Swift, who once remarked that 'every man has just as much vanity as he wants understanding', but every man, however impervious to the opinion of the world, is susceptible to female flattery, and male vanity is touched to the quick by an attractive woman's admiration or adoration.

Swift has been reproved for not telling Vanessa about Stella and for keeping Stella in the dark about Vanessa, but those who blamed him have not been in his situation. From being Vanessa's teacher, he found himself being taught:

> *Ideas* came into her Mind
> So fast, his Lessons lagg'd behind.

In a poem he wrote some three years after their first meeting, entitled *Cadenus*[1] *and Vanessa*, we learn that she began to lose interest in the education he tried to impart, displacing it with an interest in himself. It may have been while she was visiting him at Windsor that she declared her passion:

> It was an unforeseen Event,
> Things took a Turn he never meant.

While trying to reason her out of the feelings he had aroused, he made her more enamoured, and his verses show that he was not displeased:

> *Cadenus*, to his Grief and Shame
> Cou'd scarce oppose *Vanessa's* Flame;
> But though her Arguments were strong,
> At least cou'd hardly wish them wrong.
> Howe'er it came, he cou'dn't tell,
> But, sure, she never talk'd so well.
> His Pride began to interpose,
> Preferr'd before a Crowd of Beaux . . .
> 'Tis Merit must with her prevail,
> He never knew her Judgment fail.
> She noted all she ever read,
> And had a most discerning Head.

The poet's vanity makes him leave the outcome uncertain:

> But what Success *Vanessa* met,
> Is to the World a Secret yet.

We who can guess at his nature have the key to the secret. He was a man for whom the preliminary excitation of love is more satisfactory than its fulfilment, the skirmish than the engagement; and, while he was relishing their excursions to Windsor and Kingston, their cosy chats in what he called the Sluttery in Ryder Street, St James's, to which her family moved from Bury Street, she was trying to suppress her feelings in order to keep him in a

1. An anagram of Decanus (Dean).

good temper, comforting herself with such phrases in his letters as: 'Adieu till we meet over a pot of coffee or an orange and sugar in the Sluttery, which I have so often found to be the most agreeable chamber in the world.' Naturally she shared, or pretended to share, his interests, and they often talked politics, he telling her many secrets which it flattered her to know.

At last, after much pretence and evasion on the part of the Chief Minister, Swift had his reward. He would have been a great deal sillier than he was if he had ever believed that a politician would recompense merit and genius when accompanied by an independent spirit, and Oxford was a typical politician, who had not the guts to oppose an eddy of alarm in Court and ecclesiastical circles. Swift's enemy, the Duchess of Somerset, got the backing of the Archbishop of York, who assured the Queen that the man who wrote *The Tale of a Tub* was unfit to be a bishop and hardly the right person for a prebend at Windsor. It was generally felt that he would be safer at a distance, and he received the deanery of St Patrick's, Dublin, being installed on 13 June 1713, an unlucky date for a future English Government.

As a rule Swift spent a short time with his mother in Leicestershire on his journeys to and from Ireland, but she had died in 1710 ('I have now lost my barrier between me and death', he reflected), and he went straight to Dublin on his appointment, riding to Chester in six days, thence to Holyhead, and so to the Irish capital. The deanery needed much repair, and for many expenses of the kind he had been promised £1,000, which he never got. His view being that 'no man is thoroughly miserable unless he is condemned to live in Ireland', it is needless to say that he thought he 'should have died with discontent' on arrival, and that he felt 'horribly melancholy' during the ceremony of installation. He dashed off to Laracor, where he exchanged discontent for dullness, and while in the neighbourhood of Stella he had the discomfort of receiving letters from Vanessa. On his journey across England he had written to her: 'Pray God preserve you and make you happy and easy – and so adieu, brat.'

He hoped that would close the correspondence, but she heard that he was ill from Erasmus Lewis, a devotee of Swift and Oxford, and then that he was well, which made her write: 'If you are very happy, it is ill-natured of you not to tell me so, except it is what is inconsistent with mine.' Now was the moment for Swift to break the news about Stella, but he had not the hardihood. Instead he tried to put Vanessa off with: 'I told you when I left England I would endeavour to forget everything there, and would write as seldom as I could', assuring her that he was now 'fitter to look after willows and to cut hedges than meddle with affairs of state'. But the wire-pullers in politics thought otherwise, and so apparently did he, for on receiving a message from Oxford that his presence was urgently needed in London he left the willows and hedgerows of Laracor and was back in London within three months of leaving it.

Bolingbroke and Oxford were again at enmity, a condition spasmodically mitigated at the meetings of the Scriblerus Club when they were inebriated. But Bolingbroke hankered for Oxford's place and gave all the reasons for his greater fitness in the post. Swift was again in the awkward position of appeasing the two, his loyalty to Oxford preventing him from taking the other side in their dispute, though Bolingbroke tried hard to win him. At last his patience gave way and he left them to fight it out. 'Weary to death of Courts and Ministers and business and politics', he went as a paying-guest to stay with a clerical friend who held the living of Letcombe Bassett near Wantage in Berkshire. 'I care not to live in storms when I can no longer do service in the ship and am able to get out of it,' he wrote. He spent his time reading, writing and walking. His friends Pope and Parnell visited him, and they discussed the affairs of the world.

The crisis he had feared came at the end of July 1714. Following a noisy scene between the two Ministers during a conference with the Queen, Oxford was dismissed and Bolingbroke was triumphant. At this moment Swift showed his mettle. Bolingbroke promised to pay the £1,000 for the cost of making the deanery of St Patrick's habitable and said that Swift would shortly receive a good appointment in England. But Swift announced his intention of staying with the fallen Oxford, who had retired to Herefordshire, explaining his action thus: 'His personal kindness to me was excessive. He distinguished and chose me above all other men while he was great.' Swift was making arrangements to visit Oxford when Queen Anne, who had never got over the scene she had witnessed, died a few days after its occurrence. The country did not want the Stuarts back and went Whig-mad. As a result Oxford was sent to the Tower to await trial, and Bolingbroke decided that the climate of France would be preferable to that of England while the political atmosphere remained unsettled. Swift, back in Dublin, wrote to offer Oxford his 'poor service and attendance' at the Tower, but Oxford declined the offer, no doubt on sound political grounds. Swift again proved that he was not a fair-weather friend by writing to sympathise with Lady Bolingbroke and the Duchess of Ormond, whose husband had also fled the country.

Vanessa had visited Swift in Berkshire and had declared her intention to live thenceforth on her Irish property. Swift thought her action in coming to see him indiscreet and afterwards wrote words of warning, hoping to put her off by saying that he might not stay in Ireland for long: 'If you write to me, let some other direct it, and I beg you will write nothing that is particular, but what may be seen; for I apprehend letters may be opened, and inconvenience will happen. If you are in Ireland while I am there, I shall see you very seldom. It is not a place for any freedom, but where everything is known in a week, and magnified a hundred degrees . . . I would not answer your questions for a million, nor can I think of them with any ease of mind.'

With the Whigs again in power Swift too had to exercise discretion. He was assailed in pamphlets, speeches and lampoons, one hostile piece of invective being entitled *The Hue and Cry after Dean Swift*. An early biographer avers that he was mobbed and pelted by the populace on his return to Dublin after the death of Queen Anne, and, since mobs have a habit of insulting unpopular figures, we can believe it; but apart from his own admission that he lit a bonfire to celebrate the coronation of George I in order to save his windows, he does not seem to have been affected by the behaviour of 'the mutable rank-scented many'; though he suffered from the rudeness and brutality of those who should have known better and so behaved worse, and he petitioned the Irish House of Lords to restrain one of their number, Lord Blaney, from trying to unhorse him on the public road. He had no hope now of getting the £1,000 promised by Oxford and granted by Bolingbroke for repairs to the deanery, and, though he soon came into collision with his Chapter as well as the Archbishop of Dublin, William King, he walked warily for a time and cultivated his garden at Laracor. Matters were made no easier for him when Bolingbroke was reported to have joined the Pretender, which brought an accusation of Jacobitic sympathies on the Dean, who thereupon wrote to the Archbishop that he regarded 'the coming of the Pretender as a greater evil than any we are likely to suffer under the worst Whig Ministry that can be found'. Ireland soon suffered from the worst Whig Ministry that could be found when the new Prime Minister Sir Robert Walpole decided to stamp out national feeling by giving all the good jobs to Englishmen, or to Irishmen with strong Anglican sympathies. Swift described the Irish bishops appointed by Walpole: 'Excellent and moral men have been selected on every occasion of vacancy. But it fortunately has uniformly happened that as these worthy divines crossed Hounslow Heath on their way to Ireland to take possession of their bishoprics, they have been regularly robbed and murdered by the highwaymen frequenting that common, who seized upon their robes and patents, came over to Ireland, and are consequently bishops in their stead.'

Life for Swift was difficult enough in these first years of his exile or banishment from what he always considered his own country. But his anxieties took a new form when Vanessa, after the death of her mother, brought her sister over to Ireland and settled on her inheritance, Marlay Abbey near Celbridge, about eleven miles from Dublin. She wrote asking him to see her, but he replied that he would not have gone to her house for all the world: 'I ever told you you wanted discretion.' She then begged for his advice in all her financial worries, 'a wretch of a brother, cunning executors and importunate creditors of my mother's', and reminded him of a maxim of his own, 'to act what was right, and not mind what the world said.' His frowns, she added, made her life insupportable. He promised to see her soon, 'and believe me it goes to my soul not to see you oftener. I will give you the best advice, countenance, and assistance I can . . . I did not imagine you had been under difficulties. I am sure my whole fortune should go to remove them.' And he declared that his delay was 'not want of friendship or tenderness, which I will always continue to the utmost.' At length they met again, but the interview cannot have soothed her, for she wrote: 'It is impossible to describe what I have suffered since I saw you last; I am sure I could have borne the rack much better than those killing, killing words of yours.' Sometimes she resolved to die without seeing him again, but the contrary desire was stronger and she implored him to come 'and speak kindly to me, for I am sure you would not condemn anyone to suffer what I have done, could you but know it. The reason I write to you is because I cannot tell it you . . . for when I begin to complain, then you are angry, and there is something in your look so awful that it strikes me dumb. Oh! that you may but have so much regard for me left, that this complaint may touch your soul with pity . . . Did you but know what I thought, I am sure it would move you.'

Swift was now in the unenviable position of being loved by two women, for both of whom he had a deep affection, but he lacked the strength of mind or the power of discrimination to give up one for the other. Vanessa took lodgings in Dublin and Swift saw as much of her as he dared. But he was too well known for his actions to be unobserved, and no doubt the social world was buzzing with scandalous gossip long before Stella heard of her rival. Human nature being what it is, and malice being a prominent part of it, there can be little doubt that Vanessa soon got to know as much about Stella as Stella eventually did about Vanessa, though neither would have dared to tackle the Dean openly on the subject. As we have seen, his was a paralysing frown. Vanessa had the lesser hold on him, his sentimental life being concentrated on Stella, but the sexual allure of Vanessa was stronger because fresher and more flattering. The oddity in his sexual make-up has caused much controversy and disagreement, but its cause is not beyond all conjecture.

As already suggested, he was a man whose emotions demanded constant flirtation with women, but whose mind shrank from fornication. In his personal tastes and habits he was excessively fastidious, and it is clear from his writings that he was repelled by certain physiological features of the human animal which more normal natures accept without uneasiness. The coarseness of his expressions illustrates one of his remarks: 'A nice man is a man of nasty ideas.' He constantly dwelt on the excretory and expulsive stinks of the human body, and he was disgusted by the association of the organs of desire and pollution. Had he been involved in passion he would have overcome this state of nausea, but his mental faculty was too strong to be in harmony with his physical constitution. In his description of Gulliver's return home from the country of the Houyhnhnms we have a not wholly fanciful picture of his own feelings: 'And when I began to consider that, by copulating with one of the Yahoo-Species, I had become a Parent of more, it struck me with the utmost Shame, Confusion and Horror. As soon as I entered the House, my Wife took me in her Arms, and kissed me; at which, having not been used to the Touch of that odious Animal for so many Years, I fell in a Swoon for almost an Hour . . . At the Time I am writing, it is five Years since my last Return to England . . . Yet the smell of a Yahoo continuing very offensive, I always keep my Nose well stopt with Rue, Lavender, or Tobacco-Leaves . . .' Swift's failure to conquer his aversion from sexual intercourse expressed itself in the grossness of his imagery, his narrow humour being that of one who hates life, unlike the broad humour of Shakespeare and Rabelais, which reveals their love of life, except when the former is in Timonic mood and erupts in a loathing which is the obverse of his natural felicity. Swift's insufficiency made him say: 'No woman ever hates a man for being in love with her, but many a woman hates a man for being a friend to her', and he once spoke of love as 'that ridiculous passion which has no being but in play-books or romances'.

One of the strangest stories about this strangest of clergymen is that, to set Stella's mind at rest, he agreed to marry her and that the marriage took place in the garden of the deanery in 1716, the ceremony being conducted by the Bishop of Clogher. According to this story, Swift imposed upon Stella the condition that they should never live together, and that their marriage should be kept secret from the world. But as the sole object of such a marriage was to establish Stella's worldly reputation as a moral woman, the rite was so futile that we would have to assume the participants were insane. The entire episode was founded on hearsay and has been accepted by Swift's biographers on evidence that could only have imposed on quidnuncs. Enough to say here that Stella made her will many years later and signed it 'Esther Johnson, Spinster', and that long after her death her most intimate friend Rebecca Dingley, who was present whenever Swift and Stella were together, dismissed the story with a laugh 'as an idle tale founded on suspicion'. On the other hand, an incident described by a clergyman, Swift's friend Patrick Delany, is probably true. Delany called on Archbishop King, and as he was about to enter the library Swift rushed out distractedly, passing him without a word. The Archbishop was in tears and said to Delany: 'You have just met the most unhappy man on earth; but on the subject of his wretchedness, you must never ask a question.' No doubt the relationship between Swift and Stella had caused much scandalous gossip in clerical circles, and Swift had explained the position to King. The inference is either that the Dean had discovered a blood relationship which made marriage impossible or that he was haunted by the spectre of madness which his fits of dizziness, deafness and depression had called up and which made the thought of procreation horrible to him. Aware of his peculiar sexual organisation, he must have known that marriage with Stella would spoil an

D

otherwise delightful companionship, but we may doubt whether this aspect of the matter would have been disclosed to the Archbishop.

There can be no question that Swift loved Stella as he loved no other human being, but for reasons already given he did not wish for carnal intercourse. After his death a lock of her hair was discovered in an envelope on which he had written 'Only a woman's hair', his deeply-felt emotion being characteristically dismissed with apparent indifference. It is easy therefore to believe the account of his behaviour when Vanessa, tired of his attempts to get her married to certain clergymen of his acquaintance, brought matters to a crisis. She left Dublin for Celbridge about the year 1717 'to nurse her hopeless passion in seclusion from the world', as Sir Walter Scott put it. She continued to write, telling Swift that it was not in the power of time or accident to lessen her inexpressible passion, that the whole of her body and soul were given up to the emotion, that if religion could comfort her 'you'd be the only deity I should worship', and that 'Sometimes you strike me with that prodigious awe, I tremble with fear; at other times a charming compassion shines through your countenance which revives my soul.' His replies consisted of words which could please no woman in her condition, such as 'esteem', 'honour' and 'value', but he maintained their earlier feelings by referring to memorable episodes in their London excursions, and his letters had the playfulness of love without the feeling.

In 1721 her sister died and he wrote sympathetic words, adding counsel with which she could have dispensed: 'Nothing now is your part but decency.' At last her passion got the better of her judgment and she wrote either to Swift insisting on marriage or to Stella asking whether she was his wife. The versions differ, but a letter was sent to one or the other, and if to Stella it was handed to Swift. In a violent temper he rode to Marlay Abbey, dashed in, flung the letter down in front of Vanessa, and left without speaking a word. The blow probably killed her. She died within a year, on 2 June 1723, leaving instructions that her correspondence with Swift, together with his poem on their relationship *Cadenus and Vanessa*, written solely for her own eyes, should be published. His friends prevented the appearance of the correspondence, but copies of the poem were passed round and quotations from it were soon in everyone's mouth. Swift meanwhile had left Dublin and gone to remote parts of Ireland such as Cork and Galway. The shock of what had happened kept him away for four months, during which Stella and Rebecca Dingley were also absent from the capital. After their return Stella went to a social gathering where one of the guests remarked that Vanessa must have been an extraordinary woman to inspire such a fine poem. But Stella did not agree, saying it was well known that the Dean could write finely on a broomstick.

On Swift's reappearance in Dublin he continued to give regular dinners to his acquaintances, and Stella did the honours, if not exactly as the hostess. His position as Dean of Ireland's chief Cathedral gave him a distinguished social station; but soon he attained a new and unprecedented position. The Irish were being bullied and starved by the English Government, and no one had risen to assert the rights, let alone the independence, of the people; at least no one had successfully opposed the imposition of English interests over Irish liberties, and anyone who spoke a word about the wrongs of Ireland was considered a Jacobite. The country was ruled despotically by the English Viceroy from Dublin Castle, the Irish Parliament took its orders from the English authorities, and the laws were made to support English power and privilege. Swift, though he loved England and hated Ireland, loved justice and hated oppression still more, and fought with the whole of his ability and enthusiasm for the people he contemptuously called slaves. His friends thought him a republican, which, in the literal sense of one who placed the interest of the commonwealth before that of party and prerogative, he certainly was. But he did not see himself in the light of a liberator, and when in 1728 Pope wrote to praise his patriotism he replied: 'I do profess without affectation that your kind opinion of me as a Patriot (since you call it so) is what I do not deserve, because what I do is owing to perfect rage and resentment, and the mortifying sight of slavery, folly and baseness about me, among which I am forced to live.'

His first considerable blow was delivered in 1720, his pamphlet being called *A Proposal for the Universal Use of Irish Manufactures*. The English Government since the time of Charles II had prevented the Irish from selling their cattle in England, and later had ruined the Irish woollen trade by prohibiting exportation. It happened that the weavers lived in the 'Liberties of St Patrick's Cathedral', where Swift was a magistrate, and their families numbered some 6,000, most of whom were starving. In his pamphlet Swift advised the Irish to retaliate and 'burn everything that comes from England except the coal'. With searing sarcasm he exposed the wretched condition of their country and the tyrannical treatment of its inhabitants. The Government regarded this as an attack on themselves, as indeed it was, and the printer Waters was arrested. The Lord Chief Justice Whiteshed did his best to browbeat the jury into a verdict against the printer, and even swore that the object of the pamphlet was to restore the Pretender, but the jury refused to be bullied. He sent them back eight times and at last tired them down, their verdict making it possible for the case to continue. But when a new Lord Lieutenant arrived on the scene the prosecution was abandoned. Most people knew that Swift was the author; and when he wrote an epilogue to a play for the benefit of the weavers, his exhortation that everyone in the country should only wear clothes made of Irish material was received with a deafening roar of assent. He also set aside £500 of his own money to be lent in small sums to those in need at an interest just sufficient to pay a fee to the accountant. The scheme worked successfully as long as Swift was able to supervise it.

From that moment Swift became the hero of the poor within his jurisdiction, and his next public action gave him a position unique in the history of Ireland. A shortage of copper coins in that country was to be made good by one William Wood, who had paid George I's German mistress, the Duchess of Kendal, £10,000 to get him the patent for coining over a hundred thousand pounds' worth of halfpence and farthings. Previously the coinage had been made in Ireland, and this was another encroachment on the part of the English Government, which wanted all the profit it could wring out of a poverty-stricken province. The two Houses of the Irish Parliament were not consulted, and though normally subservient to their English masters they were sufficiently aroused to present memorials against the patent. While a Committee of Inquiry was sitting in London, Swift made articulate the national grievance by writing a pamphlet, supposedly the work of a shopkeeper named M. B. Drapier, which appeared in April 1724. He cunningly pretended that the new coinage would be debased and argued his point with much ingenuity; but his real case was that Ireland should assert her independence and cease to be the slave of a detestable tyrant. The sensation caused by the first Drapier letter increased steadily when the second and third appeared within a few months, and mounted to hysteria when the fourth came out in October. By this time the shopkeeper had been dropped, and every reader knew that only one man could be Drapier, who now defied the English dictatorship while pretending that his attack was confined to Wood and his copper coins. 'For in reason all government without the consent of the governed is the very definition of slavery', he wrote, 'but in fact eleven men well armed will certainly subdue one single man in his shirt.' Ireland had been subdued by well-armed men, but it looked as if Drapier would rouse the nation to valour, even though most of the population had pawned their shirts.

The Government, feeble and corrupt, had no answer, and acted in the usual futile way by arresting the printer and proclaiming a reward of £300 for the discovery of the author of the wicked, malicious, seditious, scandalous pamphlet signed M. B. Drapier. If anyone had moved a step in the direction of naming Swift as the author, he would have been torn to pieces by the common people, in whose eyes the Dean was now deified. A new Viceroy was appointed to deal with the situation, Lord Carteret, who had been friendly with Swift in England and knew perfectly well that no one but he could have written the Drapier pamphlets. Soon after his arrival the two men met and had a sparring match. Carteret was clever enough to earn the suspicion of all parties, and at one point in their dispute he got the better of Swift, who lost his temper and shouted: 'What the vengeance brought you among us? Get you gone, get you gone! Pray God Almighty send us our boobies back again.' But Carteret had a proper appreciation of Swift's genius, and often made appointments on his advice.

Again the farcical business of prosecuting the printer was set on foot, and again Lord Chief Justice Whiteshed bullied the jury, once more without effect. He discharged it and called another, which proved openly rebellious, and the case was dropped. Dublin was now in a state of wild excitement. Whiteshed was ridiculed in lampoons and caricatures, Swift was lauded in broadsheets and ballads. A fifth Drapier letter completed the Government's discomfiture, the copper coinage was withdrawn, and Wood received about £24,000 in compensation, though it is unlikely that the Duchess of Kendal disgorged her bribe. At one moment during the turmoil Walpole meditated the arrest of Swift, but, on being told that 10,000 soldiers would be necessary to effect it, he meditated on something else. Swift's triumph was somewhat marred by a new appointment. Prime Minister Walpole did not trust Carteret, and when the Primacy of Ireland fell vacant he filled it with a serviceable tool, Dr Hugh Boulton, who thenceforward became the Archbishop of Armagh and real governor of Ireland. Allowing for the fact that he was the guardian of purely English interests, he did his job honestly, efficiently and unselfishly, indulged in no rancour, and was a loyal friend; but, as their outlooks were radically dissimilar, he and Swift were constantly at daggers drawn. It cannot have pleased Boulton to see innumerable inns throughout the country with fresh signs, 'The Drapier's Head', and the knowledge that one clergyman had united a nation, beaten the power of an English Government and set the law at naught, was excessively vexing to the new Primate. In fact, by pamphlets and sermons, Swift had, single-handed, kindled rebellion and commenced the long struggle for Irish independence.

Carteret, however, remained friendly with him and asked him to dinner at the Castle. The Dean liked Lady Carteret, and showed her a field near the deanery which he had bought as a paddock for his horses but was now turning into a garden which he called 'Naboth's Vineyard'. Through Swift's interest with the Viceroy two of his younger friends were promoted. The Rev. Thomas Sheridan, a pleasant, volatile schoolmaster with whom the Dean spent his lighter hours composing pasquinades, and whose chief fault, according to Swift, was 'a wife and four children', received a living near Cork; while the Rev. Patrick Delany, a shrewd and soothing companion, was started on a career which ended in a deanery. Swift sometimes stayed at Quilca, Sheridan's country residence, and was there for a few months in 1725 with Stella and Rebecca Dingley. Every year Stella received verses from Swift on her birthday, one of his contributions revealing their relationship:

> Thou, Stella, wert no longer young,
> When first for thee my harp was strung,
> Without one word of Cupid's darts,
> Of killing eyes, or bleeding hearts;
> With friendship and esteem possest,
> I ne'er admitted Love a guest.

He frequently praised her qualities of heart and mind, and drank toasts to her never-failing courage, especially noteworthy being the occasion when she and Rebecca occupied a lonely house and a gang of armed blackguards attempted to break in. The only male in the house was a boy, and while the female staff were cowering with fear Stella quietly raised the dining-room window, took careful aim with a pistol, blazed at the nearest ruffian, and killed him. The rest quickly dispersed.

While they were at Quilca in the summer of 1725 Swift was polishing off *Gulliver's Travels* and considering a visit to England, where he had made his true friendships and left his real desires. He had been in Ireland for twelve years without a break, and the thought of returning to it after seeing his English friends 'would be a mortification hard to support'. But Oxford died in May 1724, and when Swift heard that Dr Arbuthnot had been very ill he determined to make the journey, for he wrote to Pope: 'Oh! if the world had but a dozen Arbuthnots in it, I would burn my Travels', which, as he admitted, were founded on misanthropy. Pope wrote begging him to come over and saying that 'there is no one living or dead of whom I think oftener or better than yourself'. Swift reached London in March 1726 and received a warm welcome from his friends. He stayed much with Pope, saw a lot of Bolingbroke, and spent some weeks with Gay, to whom he had suggested the idea for *The Beggar's Opera*. He received several invitations to visit the Princess of Wales, who admired his wit, and when at last he consented to go he did his best to interest her in the sufferings of the Irish. She promised that when she became Queen she would use all her credit to relieve their distresses, but the promises of people without power bear little relation to their performances when in possession of power. Swift dined with Walpole at Chelsea, but in a later interview between them it became clear that they could never reach an agreement, since they held contrary views on the subject of liberty. Walpole would no doubt have tried to bribe Swift with an English bishopric if the Dean's attitude to the Government's Irish policy, implemented by Archbishop Boulton, had shown the least sign of weakening.

While enjoying himself in the society of his companions, Swift heard that Stella was seriously ill, indeed at the point of death, and he wrote in great agitation to several Irish friends. 'I would not for the universe be present at such a trial of seeing her depart', he confessed, though his despair was not so great as to extinguish his sense of propriety. 'In case the matter should be desperate', he wrote to his Sub-Dean, 'I would have you advise, if they come to town, that they should be lodged in some airy healthy spot, and not in the deanery, which, besides, you know, cannot but be a very improper thing for that house to breathe her last in. This I leave to your discretion, and I conjure you to burn this letter immediately, without telling the contents of it to any person alive.' He assured another correspondent that 'violent friendship is much more lasting, and as much engaging, as violent love'. Unburdening himself to Sheridan, he said: 'I look upon this to be the greatest event that can ever happen to me; but all my preparations will not suffice to make me bear it like a philosopher, nor altogether like a Christian . . . Nay, if I were now near her, I would not see her; I could not behave myself tolerably, and should redouble her sorrow . . . I have been long weary of the world, and shall for my small remainder of years be weary of life, having forever lost that conversation which could only make it tolerable.'

But Stella got better, and Swift left for Ireland in the middle of August. Some idea of the pleasure his company gave to his friends is conveyed in a letter he received from Pope, who on the day of his departure 'walked about like a man banished, and when I came home found it no home. It is a sensation like that of a limb lopped off . . .' The Dean's return was celebrated with royal honours. Flags were hung on the quayside; church bells rang; wherries took the civic authorities to meet his ship; and the population cheered him through the streets. He must have smiled grimly at the thought of what he had left behind in London: the manuscript of a book in which mankind were flayed with a frigid loathing unequalled in literature.

From Swift's declaration that he never made money from any of his works except *Gulliver's Travels*, for which Pope obtained two or three hundred pounds, we may infer that Pope left the pseudonymous manuscript of that work at the publisher's office. It appeared in November 1726 and was instantaneously successful, being devoured and discussed by everyone who could read and reason. Pope and Gay reported that 'from the highest to the lowest it is universally read, from the cabinet council to the nursery', and Swift said that it had made the publisher 'almost rich enough to be an alderman'. The satire throughout was too generalised to hurt individuals; moreover, as its author said, 'Satire is a sort of glass, wherein beholders do generally discover everybody's face but their own.' All the same the military profession, the leading politicians and the House of Lords cannot have been vastly amused by such passages as these:

'A soldier is a *Yahoo* hired to kill in cold blood as many of his own species, who have never offended him, as possibly he can.'

'A First or Chief Minister of State . . . makes use of no other passions but a violent desire of wealth, power and titles . . . he applies his words to all uses, except to the indication of his mind . . . The worst mark you can receive is a promise, especially when it is confirmed with an oath; after which every wise man retires, and gives over all hopes.'

'That a weak diseased body, a meagre countenance and sallow complexion, are the true marks of noble blood; and a healthy robust appearance is so disgraceful in a man of quality that the world concludes his real father to have been a groom or a coachman. The imperfections of his mind run parallel with those of his body, being a composition of spleen, dullness, ignorance, caprice, sensuality and pride.'

The voyage to Laputa was generally regarded as the least successful of the travels, but since it satirises science it is more applicable to our own age. The King of Brobdingnag's view of the human race accords with that of Swift: 'I cannot but conclude the bulk of your natives to be the most pernicious race of little odious vermin that nature ever suffered to crawl upon the surface of the earth.'

Satire is often a boomerang which hits the man who uses it, and, though Swift in his more tranquil moments might have perceived the poetic justice of a work founded on hatred becoming a popular story, nothing in life could have enraged him so much, since his main object was to vex mankind. 'To be angry is to revenge the faults of others upon ourselves,' he said; yet he could not help his fury, telling Bolingbroke that he was dying in Ireland in a rage 'like a poisoned rat in a hole'. Christianity could not help him, and his favourite reading in the Bible was the book of *Job*. He asked Delany whether the corruptions and villainies of men in power did not eat his flesh and exhaust his spirits. 'No', said the clergyman. 'Why – why – how can you help it, how can you avoid it?' fumed Swift. 'Because I am commanded to the contrary – "Fret not thyself because of the ungodly".' But Swift fretted himself until he could fret no more and his body lay 'where rage and resentment can no longer eat into the heart', as he noted in Latin for his tombstone.[1] Constantly expressed wrath against others is largely due to self-dissatisfaction, and Swift's anger was that of the ambitious man who, because his aims were thwarted, turned against the world and railed at it. Bolingbroke acutely wrote to him: 'If you despised the world as much as you pretend and perhaps believe, you would not be so angry with it.' But Swift's rage was too much a part of himself to be caused by other people's imperfections. Just as his nature deprived him of a normal sexual outlet and resulted in an excremental terminology, so did his baffled ambition feed his hatred and drive him into an almost insane scorn of mankind. *Gulliver's Travels* contain a perfectly truthful account of the behaviour of human beings when actuated by self-interest, as they usually are. 'Life', said Swift, 'is not a farce; it is a ridiculous tragedy, which is the worst kind of composition.' If this were the whole truth, Gulliver would be the last word on the subject of human life, instead of which his Travels have become favourite fairy-tales in the nursery. Yet they faithfully represent the despair and misery of Swift, who at no period could have been happy, though the present age might have given him glimpses of felicity because for the first time in history there is a distinct possibility of mankind being blotted out. The really interesting question for us is whether Gulliver would have described his travels if Swift had been given a mitre.

The enormous success of the book drew Swift again to England in April 1727. He stayed with Pope, saw all his friends, and appeared to be pleased when George I died because it would mean the end of Walpole. But the power of Caroline, George II's wife, proved stronger than that of his mistress, Mrs Howard, and Walpole again became Prime Minister. Swift toyed with the notion of going to Aix-la-Chapelle, thinking the waters might cure his recurring fits of dizziness, but was dissuaded from the

1. *ubi saeva indignatio ulterius cor lacerare nequit.*

journey by his friends, who wished him to benefit from his favour
with the new Queen. But he took no steps to that end on account
of deafness and giddiness. Then he heard that Stella was dying,
and this made everything else seem insignificant. For her birthday that year he had written:

> Me, surely me, you ought to spare,
> Who gladly would your sufferings share;
> Or give my scrap of life to you,
> And think it far beneath your due;
> You, to whose care so oft I owe
> That I'm alive to tell you so.

Dreading the event, he lingered on, but left Pope's house at
Twickenham abruptly without explanation, driven to sorrow and
solitude in London. He sent an apology to the Queen for not
being able to see her, as she had desired him to do, and departed
for Ireland in September, being delayed by contrary winds for a
week at Holyhead, where he wrote these lines:

> I never was in haste before,
> To reach that slavish hateful shore.
> Before, I always found the wind
> To me was most malicious kind,
> But now the danger of a friend,
> On whom my hopes and fears depend,
> Absent from whom all Climes are curst,
> With whom I'm happy in the worst,
> With rage impatient makes me wait
> A passage to the Land I hate.

Stella was dying of consumption, and Swift suffered months of
agony before her death on 28 January 1728. To keep his mind
from 'thinking too precisely on the event' he started on the night
she died to describe her life and character, continuing on the 29th
until his head ached. Beginning again on the 30th, he wrote:
'This is the night of the funeral, which my sickness will not suffer
me to attend. It is now nine at night, and I am removed into an-

other apartment, that I may not see the light in the church, which is just over against the window of my bed-chamber.' He went on writing, and finished the description at intervals thereafter. His future loneliness was mitigated by the production of many pamphlets on the condition of the Irish people. He denounced the rack-renting absentee landlords, the pitiable dens in which the poor lived, the general filth, starvation and naked misery of the natives. One of his productions must be mentioned, a *Modest Proposal for Preventing the Children of Poor People from being a Burden to their Parents or the Country, and making them Beneficial to the Public*. With devastating irony he suggested that they should be fattened and cooked: 'I have been assured by a very knowing American of my acquaintance in London that a young healthy child well nursed is at a year old a most delicious, nourishing, and wholesome food, whether stewed, roasted, baked or boiled, and I make no doubt that it will equally serve in a fricassee or a ragout . . . I grant this food will be somewhat dear, and therefore very proper for landlords, who, as they have already devoured most of the parents, seem to have the best title to the children . . . Those who are more thrifty (as I must confess the times require) may flay the carcass, the skin of which, artificially dressed, will make admirable gloves for ladies, and summer boots for fine gentlemen.' He could not concern himself about the vast number of old, diseased and maimed people because they were 'every day dying and rotting, by cold and famine and filth and vermin, as fast as can be reasonably expected'; but one argument greatly in favour of infant-eating was that 'it would greatly lessen the number of Papists, with whom we are yearly over-run, being the principal breeders of the nation, as well as our most dangerous enemies . . .' His complete disinterestedness in the scheme was proved by the fact that 'I have no children by which I can propose to get a single penny'. In another pamphlet he declared: 'What we want is depopulation. Make Ireland a desert, and all will be well', for there would be nothing left to tempt the plunderers.

In 1729 Swift received the freedom of the city, but it did not restrict his freedom of speech, and he was once reproved by Archbishop Boulton for inciting the populace to disobedience. 'If I were but to lift my finger', said the Dean, 'they would tear you to pieces', a plain statement of fact, for by this time Swift could scarcely stir abroad without being followed by the people's benedictions, and even when he visited other towns he received regal honours. He was the uncrowned King of Ireland. In 1730 the representative of the crowned King of England left his post. Lord Carteret as Viceroy somehow managed to retain the liking of Swift, who was on jocular terms with Carteret's wife. One day she remarked that the air of Ireland was very good, at which the Dean fell on his knees and uttered a prayer: 'For God's sake, madam, don't say so in England, for if you do they will certainly tax it.' In after years the ex-Viceroy confessed: 'When people ask me how I governed Ireland, I say that I pleased Dr Swift.'

In spite of increasing age and infirmities Swift's pen became active whenever some cause he favoured was imperilled; and when it appeared that the clergy would lose and the landlords gain from the suppression of certain tithes, he headed a petition, which was opposed by an eminent Serjeant-at-law, against whom Swift wrote a broadside ridiculing 'the booby Bettesworth'. In a drunken rage the Serjeant swore he would cut off the Dean's ears, called at the deanery, found his enemy was at a friend's house, followed him there, and demanded an interview. Swift left the company, went into the room where the Serjeant was raging, and asked what he wanted. 'I am Serjeant Bettesworth', announced the visitor, knowing perfectly well that his name would explain his business. 'Of what regiment, pray?' innocently inquired the Dean. Bettesworth wanted to know whether Swift had written the verses on him and threatened retaliation if he admitted it. 'Sir', replied Swift, 'when I was a young man I had the honour of being intimate with some great legal characters, particularly Lord Somers, who, knowing my propensity to satire, advised me, when I lampooned a knave or a fool, never to own it. Conformably to that advice, I tell you I am not the author.' This did not content the Serjeant, who left the room vowing vengeance, upon which some thirty of the 'nobility and gentry' of the Liberty of St Patrick's formed themselves into a bodyguard to defend their Dean against the Serjeant and his gang of 'ruffians and murderers.' Bettesworth became the butt of further lampoons, and his legal practice dwindled.

The deaths of Gay and Arbuthnot intensified Swift's gloom and lessened his desire to revisit England. His popularity in Ireland spread, his birthdays being celebrated with feasts, bonfires, flags, domestic illuminations, the firing of guns and the ringing of bells; but he was out of favour with the governing class, and he assured Pope that the affection he aroused was 'wholly confined to the common people, who are more constant than those we miscall their betters. I walk the streets, and so do my lower friends, from whom, and from whom alone, I have a thousand hats and blessings upon old scores, which those we call the gentry have forgot. But I have not the love, or hardly the civility, of any one man in power or station', and he felt depressed by the 'execrable corruptions' in every branch of public management. When asked at a Sheriff's banquet to drink a toast to the Trade of Ireland, he answered 'Sir, I drink no memories.' Again and again Pope invited him to Twickenham, but he replied that he 'would rather be a free man among slaves than a slave among free men', and in 1733 he explained why he preferred Dublin to London: 'I am one of the governors of all the hackney-coaches, carts and carriages round this town, who dare not insult me like your rascally waggoners and coachmen, but give me the way; nor is there one Lord or Squire for a hundred of yours to turn me out of the road, or run over me with their coaches and six. Then I walk the streets in peace without being justled, nor ever without a thousand blessings from my friends the vulgar. I am Mayor of 120 houses. I am absolute Lord of the greatest Cathedral in the Kingdom, am at peace with the neighbouring Princes, the Lord Mayor of the City and the Archbishop of Dublin . . . These advantages contribute to my ease, and therefore I value them.' Nevertheless, some two years later, he intimated that when dead 'my flesh and bones are to be carried to Holyhead, for I will not lie in a country of slaves'. He continued to ride a dozen miles or so three times a week and to walk three or four miles every day. He was content to return to his own bed at night, but added a revealing sentence in a letter to Pope: 'My best way would be to marry, for in that case any bed would be better than my own.' His sense of life's dreariness deepened with the years: 'I never wake without finding life a more insignificant thing than it was the day before.'

Like so many misanthropes, he became more miserly with age. 'When we are young,' he once wrote, 'we are slavishly employed in procuring something whereby we may live comfortably when we grow old, and when we are old we perceive it is too late to live as we proposed.' From an early age he had recognised the importance of money as a means to good health, good humour and independence. 'Wealth is liberty', he said, 'and liberty is a blessing fittest for a philosopher.' Though generous to those in need, he had always been over-prudent on his own account; and, fearing that the habit might become unpleasant, he asked Sheridan to watch for signs of this and to caution him if his stinginess were developing into a vice. Unfortunately Sheridan failed to perceive that the sort of man who wishes to be warned when losing his sense of proportion is not the sort of man whose sense of proportion will enable him to bear the warning with equanimity; and, when Swift heard that what he had feared had come to pass, he dismissed Sheridan as an idiot and brought their friendship to an end.

In these later years too his natural bluntness of expression had changed to the vice of rudeness; his more intelligent acquaintances began to drop away, and he had to make the best of new ones. Among these were a newly-married couple, the Rev. Matthew Pilkington and his wife Letitia, who had been introduced to Swift by Delany. These two, especially the wife, amused him, and her memories give a more vivid picture of the Dean in his relaxed moments than we can find elsewhere. On their early acquaintance he described Matthew as 'a little young poetical parson', Letitia as 'a little young poetical wife'. Some five years later he called Matthew a rogue and Letitia a whore; but at first

Jonathan Swift: *from a portrait by Charles Jervas*

Samuel Johnson: *from a portrait
by Joshua Reynolds*

he helped the parson and treated the wife with affectionate playfulness, addressing her in a manner that would have made Dr Johnson frown: 'Pox on you, you slut!' At a dinner-party he daubed her face with the pitch and rosin which secured the corks on his wine bottles, and made her take off her shoes in the hope, as he said, of being able to expose her dirty toes. She asked him to stand godfather to her unborn child. 'If it be a boy, I don't much care if I do', he said, 'but if it be a little bitch, I'll never answer for her.' It happened to be a boy, and on the Dean's return to Dublin after a short absence he called to make inquiries. On being told that the baby had died, he exclaimed: 'The Lord be praised! I thought there was some good news in the way your husband looked so brisk. Pox take me but I was in hopes you were dead yourself; but 'tis pretty well as it is; I have saved by it and I should have got nothing by you.'

At one of his dinners the beef was overdone and he sent for the cook, ordering her to take it down and do it less. The cook implied that she could not work miracles. 'Why, what sort of creature are you to commit a fault that cannot be amended!' cried the Dean, who then told Letitia that as the cook was a woman of genius he might by talking so be able in about a year's time to convince her that she had better send up the meat too little than too well done. Turning to the male servants, he said: 'Whenever you imagine the meat is ready, take it, spit and all, and bring it up by force, and I will aid you if the cook resists.' He liked simple fare but liked it good. A woman who had heard he was not easily pleased took a month to prepare a dinner for him, obtaining every delicacy she could purchase and loading the table to profusion. Even then she felt it necessary to apologise for not giving him a tolerable dinner, saying that she feared there was nothing fit for him to eat. 'Pox take you for a bitch!' the Dean burst out; 'why did you not get a better? Sure you had time enough! But since you say it is so bad, I'll e'en go home and eat a herring', which he did.

He was always at ease with his female guests, and Letitia records how he flattered a number of ladies who were supping with him, including herself. The Dean was giving an account of

E

some woman whom he characterised as the nastiest, filthiest, most stinking old bitch that ever was yet seen. Glancing round the table, he gallantly added: 'Except the company, ladies, except the company! for that you know is but civil.' They gracefully bowed their appreciation of the compliment.

At divine service in St Patrick's Letitia observed the pious manner in which the Dean administered Holy Communion, his reverent carriage throughout, and how he bowed to the altar, an action some regarded as papistical. After the service the Dean was surrounded by poor folk at the porch and he bestowed charity upon them. His housekeeper, Mrs Brent, told Letitia that he gave away half his income to poor people, denying himself many luxuries in order to help the distressed; and there is no doubt that he was a practical Christian, not one who fussed about doctrine. He did good by stealth, hiding his benefactions and rather incurring the suspicion of evil than inviting approbation, which drew upon him Dr Johnson's reproach that 'hypocrisy is less mischievous than open impiety', a maxim that would appeal to humbugs throughout the ages. Swift distrusted show and pretension. 'I hate Lent', he said; 'I hate different diets, and furmety and butter and herb porridge, and the sour, devout, starving faces of people who only put on religion for seven weeks.' He had no use for outward display in any shape or form, and the reformation of behaviour late in life did not impose upon him: 'When men grow virtuous in their old age, they only make sacrifice to God of the Devil's leavings.' His view of the average clergyman was succinctly disclosed in an octet headed 'Sylvia':

> Cries Sylvia to a Rev'rend Dean,
>   What reason can be given,
> Since Marriage is a holy thing,
>   That there are none in Heaven?
> There are no women, he replied:
>   She quick returns the jest –
> Women are there, but I'm afraid
>   They cannot find a Priest.

He had no illusions about human beings and defined the main difference between good and evil in a manner that would have hurt his fellow-Christians: 'The motives to the best actions will not bear too strict an inquiry. It is allowed that the cause of all actions, good or bad, may be resolved into the love of ourselves; but the self-love of some men inclines them to please others, and the self-love of others is wholly employed in pleasing themselves: this makes the great distinction between virtue and vice. Religion is the best motive of all action; yet religion is allowed to be the highest instance of self-love.'

Many of his remarks horrified conventional Christians, but no exceptionally intelligent man can embrace a cause or belief without making the rank and file uncomfortable, which explains why no genius can possibly reach the topmost rung of the ladder in any of the recognised professions unless forced thereon by a crisis with which ordinary men cannot deal, as in the cases of Oliver Cromwell and Wellington. As Swift said: 'When a true genius appears in the world, you may know him by this sign: the dunces are all in confederacy against him.' Himself was a genius of a very peculiar kind. His writing has no imaginative or fanciful tricks. His object being to hurt or discomfort people, he wrote in a manner that for sheer precision and clarity has never been matched in English, wherein genius usually takes more flowery forms. Even his handwriting was remarkably legible, every word as readable as print, and his conversation was so much to the point that people who could not face the truth were frightened of him. 'Superstition is the spleen of the soul,' he said, and the superstitious shuddered. He pierced a counterfeit with a deadly shaft: 'As blushing will sometimes make a whore pass for a virtuous woman, so modesty may make a fool seem a man of sense.' But he sympathised deeply with poverty, distress and true humility, treating his servants with generosity, tempered on occasion with severity. When one of them attempted a deception, he exploded: '*You* pretend to tell *me* lies! *I*, you rascal, who have been acquainted with all the great liars of the age!' and he reeled off the names of a dozen leading statesmen and noblemen, concluding: 'Get along, you rascal! How dare *you* tell lies?' He never troubled to invent excuses for his unwillingness to fall in with other people's wishes, refusing the Duchess of Queensberry's invitation to stay with her at Amesbury in these terms: 'Valetudinarians must live where they can command and scold. I must have horses to ride, I must go to bed and rise when I please, and live where all mortals are subservient to me. I must talk nonsense when I please, and all who are present must commend it.'

But indeed his growing deafness made polite company insupportable, and he put 'My Present Case' in verse:

> Deaf, giddy, helpless, left alone,
> To all my friends a burden grown;
> No more I hear my church's bell,
> Than if it rang out my own knell.
> At thunder now, no more I start,
> Than at the rumbling of a cart;
> And what's more wonderful, alack!
> I hardly hear the women's clack.

His ailments did not abate his physical exercise, and when the weather kept him indoors he paced the empty rooms of the deanery or ran up and downstairs for hours on end. Refusing to use spectacles, he read hardly at all. More than anything else he feared insanity and decrepitude. He saw no dignity in senescence. 'There is no such thing as a fine old gentleman', he said sharply to someone who thought there was: 'If the man had a mind or body worth a farthing, they would have worn him out long ago.' At the age of fifty he had gazed at the withered topmost branches of an elm, saying to the poet Edward Young: 'I shall be like that tree; I shall die at the top.'

His birthdays were celebrated by the mob with bonfires, dancing, singing and general rejoicing, but ' 'Tis all folly', he once said, 'better let it all alone.' On such occasions he turned to The Book of *Job*, as so often in the past, and read: 'Let the day perish wherein I was born, and the night in which it was said,

There is a man child conceived.' He echoed Job's question: 'Wherefore is light given to him that is in misery, and life unto the bitter in soul?' In July 1740, though he still had above five years to live, he scribbled to a friend: 'I hardly understand one word I write. I am sure my days will be very few: few and miserable they must be.' A year later his memory began to fail, and he constantly repeated the Lord's Prayer, which was all he could remember of the service he had once known by heart. He walked up and down monotonously for ten hours a day, took his meals alone, and often left them untouched. He looked like a skeleton of his former self, and would see no one. It seemed that his brain was affected, and guardians were appointed to take charge of his affairs. The sight of a face sometimes drove him to fury, and when suffering from an inflammation which extended over the body he was forcibly held down to prevent self-damage.

We cannot be certain of his condition at the end owing to conflicting hearsay evidence, but it is probable that he suffered from violent eruptions of insensate rage, followed by periods of aphasia. According to the latest diagnosis, he was not certifiably mad, but the medical terms used to vindicate his relative sanity are enough to drive a layman mad. Letitia Pilkington tells us that his last intelligible words were uttered when the composer Handel called to take leave of him: 'Oh! a German, and a genius! a prodigy! Admit him.'

The moment for which he had longed came on 19 October 1745, and on the 22nd he was buried at midnight in St Patrick's Cathedral.

He left rather more than £10,000 for the purpose of founding a Hospital for Idiots and Lunatics. Some twenty-four years earlier he had written a set of verses on his own death, wherein he had bidden farewell to Ireland in these lines:

> He gave the little wealth he had
> To build a house for fools and mad,
> And shew'd by one satiric touch,
> No nation wanted it so much.

2

Samuel Johnson

People are nearly always intolerant of qualities they cannot appreciate. Boswell tells us that Johnson had 'an unaccountable prejudice against Swift' and never missed an opportunity of attacking him. But the prejudice is not unaccountable. Johnson, a puritan, hated coarseness of language and loose conversation with women, and Swift could be very coarse both with men and women. Another source of irritation was Swift's 'affectation of familiarity with the great', Johnson being secretly envious of Swift's assertion of superiority over the lordlings and politicians with whom he condescended to be familiar. Then, too, Johnson's semi-sceptical, semi-superstitious nature was horrified by a clergyman's mental licentiousness, revolted by his worldliness, and scared by his profanity. 'This merriment of parsons is mighty offensive', he once said when a group of the clergy were enjoying one another's jokes, and Swift's merriment sometimes seemed to verge on blasphemy. The strength of intellect and character in men of dissimilar temperaments increased the feeling of hostility, and Johnson's Life of Swift is the least sympathetic among his studies of the greater poets.

Like the man who aroused his antagonism, Samuel Johnson started life with many disabilities. Born at Lichfield on 7 September 1709, he contracted scrofula as a baby, and this made him blind in an eye and deaf in an ear. His parents were middle-aged at the time of his birth, and produced another son when Sam was about three. The father, Michael Johnson, was at first a prosperous bookseller who became a magistrate, but owing to an inability to keep accounts gradually lost his business and sank into melancholy. The mother, Sarah, was good-natured, prudent as a housekeeper, and devoted to her children. The domestic atmosphere was inharmonious, partly because Sarah did not let Michael forget that her family were socially superior to his. All Sam's early lessons were learnt from her, and she tended to spoil him, the result being that he loved her and only tolerated his father, who liked to exhibit the child's precocity to neighbours and succeeded in evoking Sam's animosity.

After some preliminary instruction at a dame's institution, Sam went to Lichfield Grammar School at the age of seven. He disliked being taught what he did not wish to learn, though an exceptional memory enabled him to do easily what others contrived with intense application. The headmaster, John Hunter, took pleasure in thrashing boys, and was the only man who ever managed to terrify Sam, whose later fear of God may have been fortified by an early fear of the rod. Having prolonged an agreeable holiday with a cousin for six months, he was rejected by Hunter when he found it convenient to continue his education; and, as his father could not afford to send him to one of the universities, he remained at home for about two years, helping to sell books, annoying some of their wealthy customers by neglect, and refusing, as he put it, 'to supersede the pleasures of reading by the attentions of traffic'. Having given himself a thorough grounding in all sorts of literature, he managed somehow to enter Pembroke College, Oxford, at the age of nineteen as a commoner, and to remain there for a little more than a year, possibly supported by a small legacy of his mother's.

His poverty among so many wealthy contemporaries made him by turns rebellious, contemptuous and indifferent, and he gained a reputation for being sportive and light-hearted, but 'I was rude and violent', he afterwards declared: 'it was bitterness which they mistook for frolic.' He read the books that appealed to him, both Greek and Latin, but avoided the lectures and treated his tutor with disdain. On being asked why he had not attended one of the lectures, he replied casually that he had been sliding. 'I had no notion that I was wrong or irreverent to my tutor', he once remarked; and, when a companion observed that such behaviour displayed great fortitude of mind, he came out promptly with: 'No, sir; stark insensibility.' His money soon ran out, and after thirteen months of contumacious misery disguised as gaiety he returned home.

From the age of twenty, when he left Oxford, he suffered from continual ill-health and a melancholia that sometimes bordered on insanity, and like Swift he tried to alleviate his condition by walking great distances. His father's business was now rapidly declining, and his prospects were dreary. He tried to obtain work as a schoolmaster, but one successful application made him more wretched than usual and only lasted for four months. His father died in 1731 and he made some attempt to keep the business going, but his gloom did not attract clients. Nor did it please women, though he formed a friendship with a religious female at Ashbourne, and lost his heart to another, of whom he later said: 'I wonder when anybody ever experiences measureless delight. *I* never did, I'm sure, except the first evening I spent *tête à tête* with Molly Aston.' He passed six months with an old school-friend named Edmund Hector, now a surgeon at Birmingham, where he met a mercer, Henry Porter, and his wife Elizabeth, whose daughter Lucy had attracted Sam at Lichfield. Hector got him a little journalistic work, but a combination of indolence and discontent drove him home again, his outlook at the age of twenty-five being as bleak as ever. He had fallen in love with Elizabeth Porter, twenty years older than himself, and when her husband died Johnson proposed marriage. She was a lively woman, plump and blonde, her cheerfulness and common sense appealing to him, while his youth and conversational ability attracted her so much that she accepted him. His mother was against 'so preposterous a union' on account of the disparity in age and his inability to earn money. He retorted: 'Mother, I have not deceived Mrs Porter; I have told her the worst of me: that I am of mean extraction; that I have no money; and that I have had an uncle hanged. She replied

that she valued no one more or less for his descent; that she had
no more money than myself; and that, though she had not had a
relation hanged, she had fifty who deserved hanging.'

In fact she had about £600, and having failed to get a job as
assistant master Johnson decided to use part of that money
in starting a school of his own at Edial, near Lichfield. While
a house was being prepared for the purpose their marriage took
place at Derby, presumably in order to escape ridicule at Lichfield,
and in the autumn of 1735 Sam and Tetty (as he called her)
settled down at Edial, where the boarders did not number above
five, among them being the future actor David Garrick, who in
the years to come amused parties with imitations of Johnson's
elephantine love-making and odd mannerisms. The school could
not flourish with so scanty a roll-call of scholars, and after
eighteen months of teaching the nonsensical rules of Greek and
Latin grammar, during which he managed to write the greater
part of a blank-verse tragedy, *Irene*, produced by Garrick twelve
years later, Johnson shut the place down and went to look for
work in London. He was accompanied by David Garrick, then
training for the bar, and they arrived practically penniless in the
metropolis.

In a manner known only to poverty-stricken poets, Johnson
managed to keep himself alive amid the stinks and perils of
London for about four months, at the end of which the proprietor
of *The Gentleman's Magazine*, Edward Cave, offered him some
sort of job, and he returned to Lichfield to put his affairs in order
and collect Tetty. Having persuaded his step-daughter Lucy
Porter to help his mother in the bookshop, he left Lichfield for
London with his wife, and was soon engaged in hack-work for
Cave, translating, sub-editing, writing articles, deciding on the
contributions to be printed in the magazine, and reporting
Parliamentary debates, the reports being on a higher literary
level than the debates. He took whatever job came his way, even
cataloguing a library, though he found it necessary to knock
the owner down for insolence. His first poem, *London* (1738),
was sold for ten guineas, and it tells us clearly that he had

borne much from the rudeness of his intellectual inferiors:

> Of all the griefs that harass the distress'd,
> Sure the most bitter is a scornful jest;
> Fate never wounds more deep the gen'rous heart,
> Than when a blockhead's insult points the dart.

During these years of indigence he formed a friendship with a poet named Richard Savage, whose nature seemed to be entirely at variance with his own. Savage may have been a self-pitying braggart and parasite, but he convinced Johnson that he was the illegitimate son of an Earl and a Countess, the last of whom had pursued him with vindictive malignity. The high spirits, mystery and flamboyance of Savage strongly appealed to Johnson, and they spent many hours either starving or drinking together. When Savage died Johnson wrote his Life (1744), the first indisputably great and truthful biography to appear in the English language. While admitting all his friend's faults, he wrote that 'those are no proper judges of his conduct who have slumbered away their time on the down of plenty'.

Johnson's own destitution worried him much less than his inability to support Tetty, who sometimes depended on the charity of a friend and had to sell whatever bits of property they possessed to support herself. But by degrees their circumstances improved, as Johnson wrote more and more of Cave's magazine and obtained additional journalistic work. At last, in 1746, he accepted an offer from a group of publishers to compile an English dictionary, undertaking to finish it in three years for the sum of £1,575. When informed that forty members of the French Academy had taken forty years to produce a dictionary, he remained undismayed: 'Sir, thus it is. This is the proportion. Let me see: forty times forty is sixteen hundred. As three to sixteen hundred, so is the proportion of an Englishman to a Frenchman.' He took a house in Gough Square, Fleet Street, engaged half-a-dozen helpers, and issued a 'Plan', which a publisher suggested he should address to the Earl of Chesterfield, a politician and patron of letters. But the peer's encouragement was inconsiderable, possibly because Johnson's personality grated on his gentility. Chesterfield considered that 'there is nothing so illiberal and so ill-bred as audible laughter', while Johnson thought that 'the size of a man's understanding might always be justly measured by his mirth', and the Earl was otherwise engaged when the etymologist's guffaws could be heard in his anteroom.

While working on the dictionary Johnson wrote his most notable poem, *The Vanity of Human Wishes* (1749), Garrick produced his tragedy *Irene* at Drury Lane Theatre a month later, and in 1750 he started a bi-weekly periodical called *The Rambler*, nearly all of which he wrote himself, maintaining it for two years, until the death of his wife in March 1752 deprived him of the zest to keep it going. He never ceased to miss her, and three years after their parting he described himself as 'a gloomy gazer on a world to which I have little relation'. But he struggled on with the dictionary, which took seven years to complete, and when it became known that he had finished it Chesterfield made efforts to have the work dedicated to him by writing articles complimenting Johnson and sending a baronet to solicit the favour. Johnson felt that the time had come to put Chesterfield in his place and wrote him a celebrated letter, wherein he asked: 'Is not a Patron, my Lord, one who looks with unconcern on a man struggling for life in the water, and, when he has reached ground, encumbers him with help?' To give his dictionary the proper flavour of scholarship, he approached an Oxford friend, with whose help he managed to obtain the degree of M.A., which suitably adorned the title-page of the great work on its appearance in April 1755.

Johnson hated solitude, and after the death of Tetty he took a number of poor people into his house, among them a sour-faced but good-hearted doctor named Robert Levett, and a blind but cheerful woman named Anna Williams. They, with others, became his permanent dependants, appealing to his sense of humour no less than his benevolence and patriarchal love of power. His never-failing tenderness to those in need was extended to the animal world, and he used to buy oysters for his cat because he was afraid that if he asked servants to do so they would not be kind to puss in his absence. Gradually he gathered round him a circle of friends who loved and admired him with a curious combination of devotion and awe. In 1764 a few of them founded a club, soon to be famous as The Literary Club, the early members including Oliver Goldsmith, Joshua Reynolds and Edmund Burke, as well as two less celebrated figures, Bennet Langton and Topham Beauclerk. A later addition was David Garrick, and towards the close of the century the club achieved international renown. Before its formation Johnson's mother had died, and to pay for her funeral and discharge her debts he had written a tale, *Rasselas* (1759), in the evenings of a single week, receiving £125 for it. His melancholic nature is displayed throughout the story and compressed in a phrase : 'Human life is everywhere a state in which much is to be endured and little to be enjoyed.' A more considerable labour which then engaged his attention was an edition of Shakespeare's works, which might have been completed at an earlier date if his natural indolence had not been encouraged in 1762 by the grant of a Government pension of £300 a year. He had described a pension in his dictionary as 'generally understood to mean pay given to a state hireling for treason to his country', but on receiving the assurance of several friends that his pension was solely a reward for literary merit he decided that his definition had been incomplete and breathed a sigh of relief.

He lingered long over his work on Shakespeare, having collected subscriptions for it from 1756 onwards. Seven years after the idea was launched and much of the cash collected, a young bookseller called on him with the request that a new subscriber's name should appear on the printed list. 'I shall print no list of subscribers,' said Johnson. The caller could not believe his ears. 'Sir', explained Johnson, 'I have two very cogent reasons for not printing any list of subscribers : one that I have lost all the names, the other that I have spent all the money.' Two more years passed before the edition was issued in October 1765, and those who claimed to have subscribed received their copies. By then Johnson was sick of the job and pleased to think he could cease writing for a living. 'No man but a blockhead ever wrote except for money', he once said, but, as he also announced that 'the chief glory of every people arises from its authors', we may assume that he made the first remark for effect. He cannot have given much thought to money-making while writing his Preface to Shakespeare's plays, perhaps the greatest critical essay in the language, because it ruffled more people than it soothed.

Having determined to stop writing for cash, he began writing to oblige friends, composing prologues, prefaces, dedications and what-not for other people's plays, books and poems, and later, as we shall see, writing to please himself. He perceived that life must be filled up, and 'what so easy *to a narrow mind*' as making money? But having a spacious mind he had widely distributed interests. He studied medicine, law, chemistry and theology. Though a Tory in sentiment, he showed little curiosity in politics. 'I would not give half a guinea to live under one form of government rather than another', he said. 'It is of no moment to the happiness of an individual.' And he added some lines to Goldsmith's poem *The Traveller*:

> How small, of all that human hearts endure,
> That part which laws or kings can cause or cure!

His view of communism would not make a good election slogan today: 'It is better that some should be unhappy than that none should be happy, which would be the case in a general state of equality.'

As he was somewhat deaf and shortsighted, his appreciation of painting and music was restricted. 'Surely life, if it be not long, is tedious, since we are forced to call in the assistance of so many trifles to rid us of our time', he remarked of a picture-exhibition; and, when an expert described the performance of a celebrated violinist as difficult, he rejoined: 'Difficult, do you call it, sir? I wish it were impossible.' He had imbibed a fairly large dose of Calvinism from his mother, and this, conjoined to his inherited

melancholia and bad health, made him believe in permanent unhappiness on earth and eternal punishment after death, his
condition being rendered more uncomfortable by a rational mind
at war with irrational beliefs. The creeds and opinions of people
are gravely influenced by the state of their digestions, and
Johnson's religious intolerance, uncertain temper and con-
tradictoriness were the outcome of a diseased constitution.

With his constant sense of sin and its corollary, suffering,
nothing annoyed him more than the assertion that a human being
felt blissful, and when a friend described his wife's sister as really
happy, calling upon her to confirm the fact, which she did, Johnson bellowed: 'If your sister-in-law is really the contented being
she professes herself, her life gives the lie to every research of
humanity, for she is happy without health, without beauty,
without money, and without understanding.' Silence descended;
and some days later he reported what he had said to another
woman, who displayed consternation. But he was impenitent,
saying: 'The same stupidity which prompted her to extol felicity
she never felt, hindered her from feeling what shocks you on
repetition. I tell you the woman is ugly and sickly and foolish and
poor, and would it not make a man hang himself to hear such a
creature say it was happy?' He hated any form of insincerity, and
a young fellow, who hoped to gain his approval by laughing
heartily at whatever he said, received an unexpected thrust:
'What provokes your risibility, sir? Have I said anything that
you understand? Then I ask pardon of the rest of the company.'
Another youngster was foolish enough to ask whether Johnson
would advise him to marry, his future being swiftly determined:
'I would advise no man to marry, sir, who is not likely to propagate understanding.'

A further occupation that made life endurable was eating,
which Johnson did with voracity and complete absorption. 'I look
upon it that he who does not mind his belly will hardly mind
anything else', he pronounced, and no one who sat at table with
him would have questioned the personal feeling behind his theory.
But, when the meal was over and he sat back replete, the

conversation, which had lapsed during his immersion in the viands, became animated, his laughter rang out, anecdotes and witticisms poured from him, and the company sat entranced by his eloquence. He could forget himself in conversation and make his fellow-diners forget everything except him. One of their number has very nearly succeeded in making the world forget that the eighteenth century contained any great characters except Johnson.

On the evening of 16 May 1763 Johnson was introduced to a young Scot named James Boswell at a bookshop in Russell Street, Covent Garden. It was well known that Johnson had an antipathy to the Scots because the Earl of Bute, the King's chief adviser, gave so many jobs to his fellow-countrymen; and on hearing a Scot praise the splendid scenery, the noble prospects, to be seen in his native land, Johnson said that 'the noblest prospect which a Scotchman ever sees is the high road that leads him to England'. As Boswell had a very high opinion of Johnson, he did not wish his nationality to be known, but the bookseller Tom Davies maliciously let it out. Boswell tried to soften the effect by saying, 'I do indeed come from Scotland, but I cannot help it,' and was promptly floored by Johnson: 'That, sir, I find is what a great many of your countrymen cannot help.' However, the young man managed to survive the stroke, and within a few weeks his vivacity had won Johnson's friendship. Boswell's open, cheerful, companionable nature made friends wherever he went, and even those who laughed at him could not help liking him. An excessive interest in himself was balanced by a persistent interest in other people. He loved life in all its aspects, and indulged all his tastes. He drank deeply, fornicated widely, and took equal pleasure in the society of rakes and philosophers. He was as weak as water in the face of temptation, and as strong as the spirits he drank in the assiduity with which he pursued an object. Whether drunk or sober, lost in lechery or abstracted by ambition, he attended to his private journal, from which he was able eventually to compose that unique work *The Life of Samuel Johnson*. The friendship of this singularly contrasted pair was interrupted by Boswell's tour of Europe. Although he loved London and was never happy out of it, Johnson accompanied Boswell to Harwich and saw him off.

While Boswell was viewing Holland, Germany, Italy and Corsica, and incidentally making the acquaintance of Rousseau and Voltaire, two new friends entered Johnson's life and added greatly to his comfort, a brewer Henry Thrale and his wife Hester, whose houses in Southwark and Streatham became second homes for Johnson. Thrale was a large, ponderous person, reserved, self-possessed and apathetic, a stupendous eater, a scanty talker. Johnson liked the man's detachment almost as much as his dinners, and copied his wife in calling him 'my master'. Hester Thrale was the opposite of her husband, whom she obeyed but did not love. She was small, affectionate, lively, enthusiastic, admiring Johnson's conversation so much that she would sit up to all hours making him tea, of which he never seemed to have enough. His friendship meant much to her because it brought all his famous friends to her house, where Goldsmith, Reynolds, Garrick, Burke and the rest were frequent visitors. Hester Thrale, like Boswell, kept a journal, into which many anecdotes of Johnson found their way, and it is from her that we hear of his deep sympathy with the poor. Asked why he constantly gave money to beggars, he replied: 'Madam, to enable them to beg on.' He tended a starving prostitute found in the street, gave two-thirds of his pension to people in need, slipped pennies into the hands of ragged children sleeping in the open so that they could buy breakfast when they woke up, and reprimanded some person who questioned the advisability of giving money to vagrants because they would only spend it on gin and tobacco: 'And why should they be denied such sweeteners of their existence? It is surely very savage to refuse them every possible avenue to pleasure reckoned too coarse for our own acceptance. Life is a pill which none of us can bear to swallow without gilding; yet for the poor we delight in stripping it still barer, and are not ashamed to show even visible displeasure if ever the bitter taste is taken from their mouths.'

On returning from the Continent Boswell married and

Richard Brinsley Sheridan: *from a portrait*
(*school of Reynolds*)

Sydney Smith: *from a portrait by Henry Briggs*

practised as a barrister in Edinburgh, but this did not prevent
him from visiting London, and it appears from a brief duologue in
1772 that Johnson was getting a little tired of his future biographer's attentions. Having stated that strong liquor was
excusable in one anxious to drown care and forget what was disagreeable, Boswell asked: 'Would you not allow a man to drink
for that reason?' and received a disconcerting reply: 'Yes, sir, if
he sat next *you*.' Already hardened against such blows, Boswell
went on praising wine. 'I know no good it does', said Johnson.
'Yes, it makes a man eloquent.' 'Sir, it makes him noisy and
absurd.' 'But this you will allow – it makes a man speak truth.'
'Sir, I see no good there is in that neither, unless he is a liar when
he is sober.' At a later date Boswell sustained a shock that would
have prostrated anyone else: 'Sir, you have but two topics,
yourself and me. I am sick of both.' Fortunately for us Boswell
had the skin of a rhinoceros.

In the autumn of 1773 Johnson toured Scotland with Boswell,
on the whole an enjoyable trip interspersed with awkward
moments, as when Boswell laughed too heartily at something
Johnson said and at something said to Johnson, receiving
punishment proportionate to the crime. Johnson thought little of
Scotland's boasted scenery: 'Seeing Scotland is only seeing a
worse England.' They went from Edinburgh up the east coast,
and Johnson received the freedom of Aberdeen. At Cawdor they
spend a night with the minister Kenneth Macaulay, who got on
Johnson's nerves to such an extent that he described the man of
God as 'the most ignorant booby and the grossest bastard',
words which Boswell thought it prudent to omit from his printed
version of the tour. Incidentally Johnson could always give as
good as he got in language appropriate to the occasion, and once a
foul-mouthed Thames waterman drew this from him: 'Sir, your
wife, under pretence of keeping a bawdy-house, is a receiver of
stolen goods.'

The travellers crossed Scotland on horseback from Inverness
to Glenelg, meeting such a mean reception in the island of Skye
from Sir Alexander Macdonald that Boswell's description, though

F.

much toned down in the published narrative, drew a challenge to a duel from their host. But their reception at Dunvegan Castle by the laird MacLeod more than made up for this, and, though Johnson sometimes broke out with complaints, the remainder of their stay in the island was relatively pleasant. Back on the mainland they visited the Duke of Argyll at Inverary Castle, and Boswell's father at Auchinleck, where the Whiggism of the laird and the Toryism of Johnson upset the harmony of the meeting; for, when Johnson angrily asked what good Cromwell had ever done for his country, the other answered that he had taught kings they had a joint in their necks, a retort that produced a sultry atmosphere.

Johnson wrote a description of their journey and caused something of a rumpus by his denial of the authenticity of Ossian's *Fingal*, supposedly translated from the original Erse by James Macpherson, whose efforts were characterised by Johnson as a gross imposition. What Goethe, Schiller, Byron and Napoleon Bonaparte regarded as an epic of Homeric proportions, Johnson thought a fake, and his remarks caused Macpherson to send him a letter full of threats and invective, to which he replied: 'I received your foolish and impudent note. Whatever insult is offered me I will do my best to repel, and what I cannot do for myself the law will do for me. I will not desist from detecting what I think a cheat from any fear of the menaces of a Ruffian . . . Your rage I defy, your abilities . . . are not so formidable, and what I have heard of your morals disposes me to pay regard not to what you shall say, but to what you can prove.' As Macpherson could not raise a regiment of Highlanders to deal with Johnson, he calmed down on hearing that his antagonist had bought a large oak stick for self-defence.

Although Johnson continued to crack jokes at the expense of the Scots, the habit becoming a sort of game, he approved the Irish, calling them 'a fair people, they never speak well of one another', and reserved his comments on the Welsh, possibly out of deference to Hester Thrale, with whom her husband, their daughter Queeney and Johnson visited her native country

the year following the Scottish trip. His attitude to Wales was
negative: 'I am glad I have seen it, though I have seen nothing,
because I now know that there is nothing to be seen.' His lack
of enthusiasm amounted to boorishness. 'Why is it that whatever
you see, you are to be so indiscriminately lavish of praise?'
he asked Hester. 'Why, I'll tell you, sir. When I am with you
and Mr Thrale and Queeney, I am obliged to be civil for four!'

His incivility reached a climax during the American War of
Independence, his denunciations of the colonists who wished to
govern themselves being of a nature to check conversation, and
his expedition to France with the Thrales in 1775 was diversified
by sudden outbursts of patriotism, which he had once described
as 'the last refuge of a scoundrel'. He disliked French habits,
which he thought were 'gross, incommodious and disgusting',
and formed no high opinion of their towns, noting that Paris,
Versailles and Fontainebleau were 'mean'. Although his health
improved during the visit, and at Versailles he 'ran a race in the
rain' and beat his competitor, he concluded: 'I have seen nothing
that much delighted or surprised me.'

That same year Oxford University conferred on him the
degree of LL.D and thenceforth he was called 'Doctor Johnson'
by his friends, though never by himself. He had recently moved
to a new house in Bolt Court, Fleet Street, and since receiving
his pension had made a point of visiting Oxford, Birmingham,
Lichfield and Ashbourne every year. In 1776 Boswell accompanied him on one of these jaunts, and was introduced to all
Johnson's friends. On their return Boswell arranged a meeting
between one of his own friends and Johnson. This was the
celebrated John Wilkes, whose person and politics were anathema
to Johnson. Some cunning was needed to bring it about, and
Boswell successfully played on the Doctor's vanity. Wilkes
followed this up by ministering to Johnson's greed at dinner,
and Boswell could congratulate himself on having for once
triumphed over the great man's prejudices, which were due to
an intense desire for stability, especially in religion, and a terror
of the uncertainty bred by scepticism.

His exceptional charity to the unfortunate was balanced by his uncharitable behaviour to those who annoyed him by disagreement; and, while he could be ruthlessly brutal to a girl who had left the Church of England to become a Quaker, he could save the life of a hare destined for the pot, explaining to his irritated host that the animal had been caught in the garden, 'and savage indeed must be that man who does not make his hearth an asylum for the confiding stranger'. He endured the jealous quarrels among the inmates of his house with complacency not unmixed with amusement. His negro servant Francis Barber, to whom he left the greater part of his money, was now married, and the household consisted of those two, of Robert Levett and Anna Williams, of Mrs Desmoulins and her daughter, and of a female named Poll Carmichael. 'Poll is a stupid slut', he told a friend; 'I had some hopes of her at first, but when I talked to her tightly and closely, I could make nothing of her; she was wiggle-waggle, and I could never persuade her to be categorical.' The domestic atmosphere at Bolt Court was caught in letters to Hester Thrale: 'Williams hates everybody. Levett hates Desmoulins and does not love Williams. Desmoulins hates them both. Poll loves none of them . . . Discord and discontent reign in my humble habitation as in the palaces of Monarchs . . . There is as much malignity amongst us as can well subsist without any thought of daggers or poisons.' But the same man who could open his heart and purse to misfortune, and smile at the venom of wrangling women, was capable of bellowing his fury at the American colonists. After one such outburst Boswell expressed his sorrow at such intemperate language. The spectacle of a magnanimous Boswell looking grieved must have provoked Johnson, who held himself in check for a while. But the unsuspecting Scot soon gave him an opening by mentioning a man who, unable to resist the temptations of London, was losing his fortune. 'We must get him out of it', suggested Boswell: 'all his friends must quarrel with him, and that will soon drive him away.' Johnson snatched the opportunity: 'Nay, sir, we'll send *you* to him. If your company does not drive a man out of his house, nothing will.'

But Boswell's company was very much to Johnson's liking, as he was the first to admit when not in a rage. He could not stand bores, one of whom was constantly complaining of his digestion. 'Do not be like the spider, man, and spin conversation thus incessantly out of thy bowels', advised Johnson. Another bore, who felt that the company were desirous of knowledge about fleas, received his quietus: 'It is a pity, sir, that you have not seen a lion, for a flea has taken you such a time that a lion must have served you a twelvemonth.' But even a bore was better than solitude, and Johnson depended more than most people upon the company of his friends, the loss of whom by death affected him profoundly. Goldsmith was the first to go in 1774, being followed five years later by Garrick, of whom Johnson wrote that his death had 'eclipsed the gaiety of nations, and impoverished the public stock of harmless pleasure'.

In 1780 the Doctor began to write his best work, the *Lives of the Poets*, including among them his early study of Savage. They contain a good deal of slapdash work owing to his innate laziness, but what is best in them has not been excelled in the art of biography. Most of them were written in Thrale's house at Streatham, where he was now recognised as an autocrat, and where the brewer was steadily eating himself to death. Apoplexy struck Thrale down in April 1781, and Johnson was an executor of his estate, enjoying his dominion at the Southwark brewery and referring to its disposal in a phrase that will last as long as beer is brewed: 'We are not here to sell a parcel of boilers and vats, but the potentiality of growing rich beyond the dreams of avarice.'

Johnson may or may not have fancied himself as the hymeneal comforter of the brewer's widow, but he certainly regarded himself as her counsellor and guardian; and, when it became clear that her affection for him was cooling, and that her interests were centred on someone who did not distantly remind her of Thrale or Johnson, the domestic air at Streatham was charged with emotional storm. She had fallen in love with her daughter's teacher of music, an amiable Italian named Gabriel Piozzi,

possessed of an alluring singing voice. Johnson dared not admit
to himself that his reign was over and tried hard to believe that
Piozzi would merely be an agreeable addition to the Streatham
circle. While in this state of perturbation his old housemate
Robert Levett died, and his tenderness and truth combined to
produce the most moving and sincere elegy we possess, closing
with the simple and touching verse:

> His virtues walked their narrow round,
>   Nor made a pause, nor left a void;
> And sure the Eternal Master found
>   His single talent well employed.

The Doctor still visited Streatham, and in the autumn of 1782
made one more sojourn at Hester Thrale's Brighton house, where
his deepening melancholy and rising indignation made life
uncomfortable for the other visitors. Boswell's presence in
London early in 1783 brightened him up a little, but his mental
agitation occasionally lowered the spirits of Boswell. Asked
whether he had been out for a walk one day, he snapped back:
'Don't talk so childishly. You may as well ask if I hanged myself
today.' Boswell tried another tack, and brought up politics,
but was not encouraged to proceed: 'Sir, I'd as soon have a
man break my bones as talk to me of public affairs, internal or
external.' The death of Anna Williams that August increased
his loneliness and boredom, while the addition of asthma, dropsy
and gout made his insomnia more than usually burdensome.

He wrote letters to Hester Thrale appealing for her sympathy
in his distress, but at last he received the mortifying intelligence
that she intended to marry Piozzi. His rage extinguished his
common sense, and he wrote to accuse her of abandoning her
religion, her fame, her children and her country. Hester naturally
replied that their correspondence must now cease. His fury
abated and he wrote one more letter in which, asking the blessing
of God on her happiness, he thanked her 'for that kindness which
soothed twenty years of a life radically wretched'. But he never
forgave her, and five months after she had placed her own

comfort before his convenience he told Fanny Burney: 'I drive her quite out of my mind. If I meet with one of her letters, I burn it instantly. I have burnt all I can find. I never speak of her, and I desire never to hear of her more. I drive her, as I said, wholly from my mind.' Such emphasis proved that she was constantly on his mind, and her action no doubt hastened his end.

In July 1784 he made the annual round of visits to friends at Oxford, Lichfield, Ashbourne and Birmingham, returning to London in November. Illness was gaining upon him, and the death which he dreaded was a constant spectre. People heard him murmuring to himself Claudio's speech in *Measure for Measure*: 'Ay, but to die, and go we know not where . . .' He was in the awful state of one who could not quite believe and dared not disbelieve in the religion he avowed. Friends called to see him, two of whom sat for many hours in his room. Like most men who have loved to exercise power in action or words, a condition of impotence maddened him. 'I am now like Macbeth – question enrages me', he burst out. At a calmer moment, someone having arranged his pillow, he said: 'That will do – all that a pillow can do.' The thought of extinction terrified him, and he cried out to the surgeon who was gently lancing him: 'Deeper, deeper! I want length of life and you fear giving me pain.' He forced Francis Barber to give him the lancet, and even drove a pair of scissors into his flesh in a last effort to ease pain and prolong life; but in the evening of 13 December 1784 he ceased to breathe, and Westminster Abbey received his body.

3

Richard Brinsley Sheridan

It was generally agreed that Richard Brinsley Sheridan, whose grandfather had been dismissed as a fool by Swift and whose father had been described as a bore by Johnson, was the wittiest and most fascinating character of his age. He inherited his grandfather's light-heartedness, companionableness and carelessness, as well as that ability to produce light verses and smart sallies which had helped to lift the darkness of Swift's mind; but he had nothing in common with his father, Thomas Sheridan, who at one time was as friendly with Johnson as the grandfather had been with Swift.

Thomas was an actor who thought himself Garrick's equal, but he was in a minority. Pedantic and affected on the stage, he managed to run a theatre successfully in Dublin, where he tried to raise the whole tone of audiences and actors; but the strain was too much, a lower tone prevailed, and his theatre was wrecked in a riot. Arriving in London, his pride made him refuse engagements unless on a profit-sharing basis. He was a solemn, earnest man, who believed that if people were taught how to speak they would become civilised, and the rest of his life was devoted to the writing of books and the delivery of lectures on education, elocution and oratory. He gave poetry recitals all over the country, and compiled a dictionary for the purpose of teaching people how to pronounce words correctly. His efforts received a caustic comment from Johnson: 'What influence can Mr Sheridan have upon the language of this great country by

his narrow exertions? Sir, it is burning a farthing candle at
Dover to shew light at Calais.' But by that time the two men
were not on speaking terms. Sheridan had been given a pension
for his labours in the cause of oratory, and when he heard of it
Johnson exclaimed: 'What! have they given *him* a pension?
Then it is time for me to give up mine.' This ill-considered joke
was reported to Sheridan by a man who carefully omitted to
add Johnson's next remark: 'However, I am glad that Sheridan
has a pension, for he is a very good man.' The result was that
Sheridan, who had helped to get a pension for Johnson, never
forgave the gibe, and would not have been appeased by another
of Johnson's references to him: 'Why, sir, Sherry is dull,
naturally dull; but it must have taken him a great deal of pains to
become what we now see him. Such an excess of stupidity, sir,
is not in Nature.'

Apart from being tedious, like most people with a panacea for
human improvement, Thomas Sheridan was vain enough to
think he could grant certificates of merit to others. He actually
presented a gold medal to John Home to signify his admiration
of that author's tragedy *Douglas*, which, though admired at
the time, Johnson called a 'foolish play'. Indeed Thomas thought
so highly of his endeavours to educate the public that when the
public showed no disposition to be educated he announced his
intention of going to America, upon which Johnson expressed
a hope that he would carry out the plan. Boswell objected:
'The Americans don't want oratory.' Johnson replied: 'But
we can want Sheridan.' All the same the quarrel upset Johnson,
who very much liked Thomas's wife, Frances Sheridan, a most
agreeable, intelligent and unpretentious woman, who wrote a
successful novel *Sidney Biddulph* and a comedy *The Discovery*,
with which Garrick made a hit. Of the former Johnson said to
her: 'I know not, madam, that you have a right upon moral
principles to make your readers suffer so much.' Present-day
readers might suffer, too, if not in Johnson's sense of the word.
Partly on account of early hospitality and partly because he
hated enmity, though his nature precipitated quarrels, Johnson

asked Boswell to tell Sheridan that he would like to shake hands with him. But Thomas's vanity had been irretrievably hurt, and they went to their graves unreconciled.

The orator and his wife were in Dublin when their third son Richard Brinsley was born at 12 Dorset Street in September or October 1751. The actual date is uncertain, though he was christened on 4 November. The first son of the Sheridans died young, the second, Charles Francis, preceded the third by more than a year, Richard being followed by two sisters who survived childhood and another brother who died the year he was born. The destruction of the theatre which drove their father to London occurred when Richard was three years old. The two boys were left in Dublin when their mother and father departed, and received some school instruction, but when Richard was six they joined their parents at a house in Bedford Street, at the corner of Henrietta Street, Covent Garden, where their father took them in hand.

At the age of eleven Richard was sent to school at Harrow, where he remained for seven years and where he was extremely unhappy. In after days he confessed that he had been a very low-spirited boy at Harrow, much given to crying when alone. His father neglected him; he had no money; his clothes were frequently shabby; his holidays were often spent at school; and the other boys mocked him for being a player's son. In spite of Thomas Sheridan's attempts and David Garrick's triumphs, actors could not aspire to gentlehood, and the sense of social inferiority had a great effect on Richard's future career. Under such conditions he made no mark as a scholar. He was perhaps too intelligent to be industrious at anything he did not wish to learn, though his remarkable memory enabled him to retain bits of Latin and Greek that had been drilled into him by constant repetition. His solitude and the feeling he had of being deserted were intensified when his father, owing to the disagreeable attention of certain creditors, took the rest of the family to France, where they settled down and lived cheaply at Blois, at which place Mrs Sheridan died in 1766. On receiving the sad news Richard, aged fourteen, wrote to his maternal uncle about mourning clothes, specifying a black suit, a new hat with crepe, and black stockings with buckles, closing his demands with: 'You will excuse the shortness of my letter, as the subject is disagreeable.' In his last years at school he seems to have become livelier, writing lampoons and leading raids on neighbouring orchards, from which apples were collected, and however much he may have bewailed his lot in secret his natural vivacity made a pleasant effect on those contemporaries who could forget that he was a mummer's boy.

In 1769 the family, safe from creditors, settled down in Frith Street, Soho, and Richard joined them, becoming at once the hero of his sister Alicia, who admired and adored him: 'I would most willingly have sacrificed my life for him.' But his father's favourite child was the elder boy, Charles, who appeared steady, prudent and docile, with every quality possessed by boys who gain the approval of their seniors, including a good portion of sanctimoniousness; in short, he had all the makings of the self-seeking, self-righteous humbug he eventually became, and certainly contributed to the portrait of 'Joseph Surface' in his brother's most famous play. The family spent about two years in Soho, where Richard read a lot, studied under a master, received lessons in fencing, and started to write, sketching out a play on Goldsmith's *The Vicar of Wakefield* and making notes on the poetry of Pope. Life at home was rigid, discipline being severe. Thomas Sheridan liked to have his own way in everything, and loved the sound of his own voice. Every morning the family joined in prayers, and on Sunday evenings he preached to them. The girls read aloud and had their pronunciation corrected; the boys were instructed in elocution; and both sexes were forced to realise that life was not frolicsome; in spite of which Richard recalled with pleasure in after life a picture of the family sitting round the table and his father proposing a favourite toast: 'Healths, hearts and homes.' But Richard was something of a sentimentalist, his nature being so amiable that his memory retained only what was pleasant.

The year 1771 found the family in Bath, where Thomas opened an academy, appointing Richard as 'rhetorical usher'. But it came to nothing, and for a while Thomas returned to the Dublin stage, leaving his children at Bath, where they made friends with the Linley family, 'a nest of nightingales', all of whom sang or played musical instruments, the father Thomas Linley being a teacher and composer of music, their 'star' performer being Elizabeth, a girl of seventeen, whose voice had a melting quality unique in that age. Sheridan senior disapproved of his family's friendship with the Linleys. Not only did he regard them as socially beneath him, but he entertained a poor view of music, which, said he, 'often draws persons to mix with such company as they would otherwise avoid'. But his family took advantage of his absence and continued to mix with such company as he would have avoided. Dick, as everyone called Richard (and we shall follow their example), occupied himself in various ways. With an old schoolfellow named Nathaniel Halhed, he wrote a farce and a metrical version of Greek prose, as well as sonnets and lampoons unaided. One of his efforts, 'Clio's Protest', contains a couplet that has gone into the language:

> You write with ease to show your breeding,
> But easy writing's vile hard reading.

In due time he showed that the converse was equally true: that easy reading's vile hard writing.

Apart from these juvenilia, he spent his time dancing, making love, and practising his gift for facetiae on the visitors to what was then the most popular health-resort in Great Britain, where the fashionable world of London congregated at set seasons and the would-be fashionable world went to gaze at their betters.

Everybody in Bath admired Elizabeth Linley's singing, and the male population fell in love with her beauty, which Reynolds and Gainsborough were to reproduce on canvas, Reynolds regarding his portrait of Elizabeth as 'the best picture I ever painted'. Among many others Dick's friend Halhed was enslaved by her charms, Dick's brother Charles fell under her spell, though being a good and dutiful son he nursed his passion in a farmhouse at some distance from the enchantress, and an elderly gentleman named Walter Long was also captivated, though on learning that the prospect of marriage with him upset her he gallantly gave her £3,000. But the most persistent of her wooers was a married man, Captain Mathews, who began by engaging her affection and ended by embarrassing her with his attentions. The violence of his passion frightened her, and, when she began to avoid him, threats of suicide, scandal and abduction were added to his protestations of passion. Afraid of disclosing the facts to her mother and father, she abandoned herself to despair, determined to kill herself, and was about to take laudanum when Dick Sheridan called, prevented the act, received her confidences, promised that she should no longer be pestered, and went off to see Mathews, whose position as a married man made him vulnerable to Dick's commands.

But her experiences had left Elizabeth in a state of panic. She wished to leave Bath at once, and if possible enter a French convent. Dick's sister Alicia mentioned some friends of hers with whom Elizabeth could stay at St Quentin while looking for a convent, and it was agreed between them that Dick should accompany her to France. Beyond doubt he was already in love with her, though she was too much under the influence of the conflicting emotions aroused by another man to be in love with him, and it seems almost certain that at this moment he wrote a poem which later appeared in his opera *The Duenna*:

> Had I a heart for falsehood framed,
>   I ne'er could injure you:
> For tho' your heart no promise claimed,
>   Your charms would make me true.
> To you no soul shall bear deceit,
>   No stranger offer wrong:
> But friends in all the ag'd you'll meet,
>   And lovers in the young.

But when they learn that you have blest
Another with your heart,
They'll bid aspiring passion rest,
And act a brother's part.
Then, lady, dread not here deceit,
Nor fear to suffer wrong:
For friends in all the ag'd you'll meet,
And brothers in the young.

On the evening of 18 March 1772 Elizabeth's family were performing at a concert, her own absence being excused on account of illness. Dick had engaged a waiting-woman to accompany her, and she was carried from home to the post-chaise in a sedan-chair. On the way Dick encountered Mathews, who was about to call on him. Dick said he had an affair of honour to settle, and asked Mathews to wait at the Sheridans' house until he returned. Arriving in London next morning, they called on some of Dick's relations, to whom he introduced Elizabeth as an heiress he hoped to wed in France. But the relations could not or would not assist the elopement, and that night they went on to an acquaintance named Field, who being in the brandy business was able to place them on a vessel just about to sail from London to Dunkirk. Field was Charles Lamb's godfather, and Sheridan rewarded him in the years to come with a free pass to Drury Lane Theatre, which enabled the godson to see *The School for Scandal* and write a celebrated essay thereon.

The runaways had a rough passage to Dunkirk, and Elizabeth was extremely ill. So much did Dick love her that 'had she died, as I once thought she would in the passage', he wrote many years later, 'I should assuredly have plunged with her body to the grave'. From Dunkirk they went to Calais, where two French officers could not take their eyes off Elizabeth at the theatre. Dick glared at them and they glared back, but neither side could speak the other's lingo and they had to be content with glaring. In order to place himself in a position to defend her from all misunderstandings, Dick persuaded Elizabeth to marry him. A year later she wrote to him: 'When I left Bath I had not an idea of you but as a friend. It was not your person that gained my affection. No, Sheridan, it was that delicacy, that tender compassion, etc., that were the motives which induced me to love you.' Already his delicacy and tenderness had inspired her love, and she agreed to his proposal. They were married by a Roman Catholic priest in the neighbourhood of Calais, but as they were both minors they could not be legally bound without the consent of their parents, and on their return to England their union remained a close secret between themselves. Moreover it did not involve sexual intimacy, for some six months afterwards she was pining for a time when her dear Dick would be able 'to make me his own in every sense of the word'. They journeyed from Calais to Lille, where they boarded with an English family before she entered a convent, at which her health was so poorly that a Yorkshire physician named Dr Dolman took her into his house in order to have her directly under his eye, Dick staying at the Hôtel Bourbon on the Grande Place. Dolman had been told of their marriage, and just before Elizabeth went to stay with him and his wife he wrote to Dick sending 'compliments and wishes of health to your lady'. Her letters to her parents explaining her action brought Thomas Linley post-haste to Lille, where he found her staying with the Dolmans.

Meanwhile Bath, a hotbed of scandal, had been seething with rumours. Mathews was denounced as a villain, Sheridan as a seducer, and the gossipers had the time of their lives. Mathews felt that he had been cheated, and stung by the odium he had incurred he tried to shift the whole blame of the episode on to the shoulders of his supplanter by inserting a paragraph in the *Bath Chronicle* branding Sheridan as 'a liar and a treacherous scoundrel' and threatening those who had spoken ill of himself with public castigation. No doubt Thomas Linley carried this information to Lille, for Sheridan at once wrote to Mathews that the moment he returned to England he would not sleep 'till he had thanked him as he deserved'. Linley cannot have been in a friendly mood when he arrived in France, but Sheridan had no difficulty in reconciling him to Elizabeth; and, as the father was chiefly concerned that his daughter should fulfil her singing engagements, which filled his pocket, he promised that she should return to Lille afterwards if she willingly went back to complete her contract. All three arrived in London at 9 o'clock on the night of Wednesday, 29 April.

The first thing Sheridan did was to locate Mathews, who was lodging in Crutched Friars. Obtaining pistols, he called there shortly after midnight. On being told that he must come again in the morning he continued to batter at the door and bawl at the windows for about two hours. At last he got in and found the shivering Mathews in a conciliatory mood, which became almost abject when he caught sight of his visitor's pistols. It soon appeared that Sheridan had not actually seen the defamatory paragraph, and Mathews was able to convince him that he had been misinformed, that no quarrel was intended, and that his brother Charles was the real culprit. Sheridan calmed down, and Mathews promised to send an explanation to the Bath newspaper withdrawing any expressions that might have been misinterpreted. The following Saturday Dick reached Bath with Elizabeth and her father, and immediately called at the office of the *Bath Chronicle*, where he was shown the libellous paragraph. Furious, he next saw brother Charles, who denied all complicity. That same night Dick and Charles started for London, leaving their sisters and Elizabeth ignorant of their intention but in a state of alarm and occasional fainting-fits. A young friend named Ewart agreed to act as Dick's second, and Charles took the challenge to Mathews, who argued for two hours in order to avoid an unqualified apology and recantation. But Dick was adamantine, and a duel was arranged for six o'clock the following evening, Monday, 4 May, in Hyde Park.

They foregathered at the Ring,[1] swords their weapons. Dick made a final appeal that Mathews should retract. It was refused, and Dick took up his position; but Mathews objected to the unevenness of the ground. They moved to another spot, but the

1. Roughly where Rotten Row now is.

presence of an observer necessitated another remove. Again Mathews noted onlookers, and they went to the Hercules Pillars at Hyde Park Corner to wait for privacy in the park. Returning, Dick drew his sword on even ground; but Mathews complained of a watchful officer near-by. Though assured by Ewart that no one would stop the waiting four-horse chaise if the victor were compelled to fly, Mathews would not be comforted and suggested postponing the duel to the early morning. Dick was tired of this trifling and requested the observant officer to leave, which he did; but during their colloquy Mathews also left. Another visit to the Hercules Pillars resulted in a different arrangement, and they all met in a room at the Castle Tavern, at the junction of Henrietta and Bedford Streets. Once more Mathews tried to propitiate Sheridan, who continued to demand nothing less than an open and absolute apology, and the disputants set to by candlelight.

'I struck Mr Mathews' point so much out of the line', recorded Sheridan, 'that I stepped up and caught hold of his wrist, or the hilt of his sword, while the point of mine was at his breast.' Whereat the surgeon in attendance seized Sheridan's arm and cried, 'Don't kill him!' Sheridan tried to disengage his arm, saying that his opponent's sword was in his power. Mathews called out two or three times, 'I beg my life.' The combatants were parted and the surgeon said: 'There, he has begged his life, and now there is an end of it.' Ewart declared that the surgeon should not have interfered in the first instance, and the surgeon admitted he had been wrong but that he had acted hastily to prevent mischief. On a hint from Mathews that Sheridan had benefited from the interference, the surgeon stated that both the swords were in Sheridan's power before he had interposed. Mathews objected that he had never quitted his sword, upon which Sheridan swore that his opponent should either allow his sword to be broken or go on guard again. Mathews at first refused, but the sight of Sheridan breathing fire made him think better of it, and he threw his sword down. Sheridan picked it up, broke it, and flung the hilt to the far end of the room. Mathews.

G

complained that he could never show his face again if it were
known that his sword had been broken. It was agreed that the
duel and its termination should never be mentioned by any of
them so long as Mathews himself never misrepresented the
affair. Sheridan insisted that Mathews still owed him a public
apology, and after much argument a statement was extracted
from the defeated and reluctant man, his words duly appearing
in the Bath newspaper: 'Being convinced that the expressions
I made use of to Mr Sheridan's disadvantage were the effects of
passion and misrepresentation, I retract what I have said to his
disadvantage, and particularly beg his pardon for my advertise-
ment in the *Bath Chronicle*.'

When the two warriors reappeared in Bath, one became a
figure of romance, the other a melodramatic villain. Sheridan's
father was unsympathetic, especially as he had to foot the bill
of his son's expenses, and the two lovers, who had not dared to
tell their parents of the marriage, were not allowed to meet; but
secret interviews took place and they wrote letters and poems
to one another. From some of her hastily-penned notes it is
clear that he had entirely won her heart: 'I love you to distraction,
and . . . would prefer you and beggary before any man with a
throne . . . Oh, my dearest love, I am never happy but when I
am with you. I cannot speak or think of anything else.' Each
was jealous if the other seemed friendly with a member of the
opposite sex, and while taunting Dick with flirting Elizabeth
assured him of her own feelings: 'If I thought it possible for
me to change my present sentiments for you, I should despise
myself. Never shall you have the least reason to suspect my
constancy or my love.' She told him where she would be on a
particular day, and they met, seemingly by accident, at the
homes of friends. Sometimes she complained because he did not
write: 'Upon my knees, half-naked, once more I am going to
tire you with my nonsense . . . I do insist that you write to me,
you lazy wretch, can't you take so much trouble? I can receive
your letter by the same method. My sister is very impatient
that I don't come to bed, but I feel more happiness in this

situation, though I am half froze, than in the warmest bed in England.' Repeatedly she said that 'while I live I can never cease to be your own Eliza'.

Throughout these endearments the villain of the piece, Mathews, shunned in Bath, was brooding on his wrongs in Wales. At last, unable to bear the affront to his pride any longer, he despatched an emissary with a paper giving an account of the duel more favourable to himself, which he requested Sheridan to sign. Instead of doing so, Sheridan wrote a full description of the actual occurrence, which he sent to the man who had acted as second to Mathews. At that moment Dick's father was in London arranging the departure of his son Charles to Sweden, where a job at the Embassy awaited him, while Elizabeth was fulfilling singing engagements at Oxford, Cambridge and Chester, after writing to her lover: 'With what rapture shall we meet when we may do so without constraint, when I may live in your arms without fear of parents or the ill-natured world.'

A challenge to another duel instantly followed Sheridan's refusal to sign the paper witnessing to the honour of Mathews, and after composing letters to Eliza, his father and sisters, Dick met his enraged antagonist on Kingsdown Hill at 3 o'clock in the morning of 1 July. Mathews asked for pistols, but Dick insisted on rapiers, though with such weapons his opponent was far more skilled than he. After several passes they closed. Dick, hoping to repeat an earlier manoeuvre, charged, but Mathews received him on the point of his rapier, which snapped. Mathews then gripped Sheridan's sword-arm, tripped him up, and they both fell, Mathews eventually uppermost. From a duel it now became a stabbing-match, Mathews striking Sheridan's face with the hilt and hacking at his neck with what was left of the rapier. Having lost control of his weapon, Sheridan was at the man's mercy. Told to beg his life, he refused, dragged his rapier from the other's grasp and gave him a wound in the belly. Then his rapier broke, possibly against a piece of armour worn by Mathews, and in self-defence he lifted his hand, which was badly cut. Mathews now had a part of his own rapier as well as what was left of Sheridan's, and improved the occasion by stabbing at the unarmed man repeatedly. Sheridan succeeded in deflecting most of the strokes with his hand, but received several in the neck. One of the thrusts broke the frame of a miniature of Elizabeth which hung round his neck. At last it dawned on the seconds in the affray that it was time to act. Both implored Sheridan to beg for his life, to which he replied, 'No, by God I won't.' But Mathews had satisfied himself, rose from the ground, gave up his rapier, exclaimed with a curse, 'I have done for him', and departed for London *en route* for the Continent. Sheridan was helped into a near-by cottage, where a peasant gave him water. He believed that he was dying, but after some time he was driven in the waiting chaise to the White Hart Inn at Bath. His wounds were dressed and he was taken home, where he amused himself during convalescence by reading all the lies about the encounter in the local Press. On one point the scandal-mongers agreed: that Sheridan was a hero and Mathews an assassin. Crowds visited the place where the duel had occurred, and the kindly peasant there placed a stone on the spot where he had found the broken rapiers, a sleeve-button, and the setting of Elizabeth's miniature in a pool of blood, thriving on their exhibition.

Elizabeth was at Oxford when the newspapers arrived containing full accounts of the duel and a statement that Dick was at the point of death. Convinced that she would not sing if she knew what had happened, her father withheld the information, and she was the only person at the concert ignorant of the affair. The family left Oxford immediately after the performance, and a few miles from Bath they were met by a friendly parson named Panton, who asked Elizabeth to join him for the rest of the journey. She did so, and on the way he tactfully broke the news. In great agitation she declared that she must see Dick at once, for she was his wife. But Dick's father had now returned from London, was excessively angry over the incident, refused to see his erring son, and absolutely forbade his family to have anything further to do with the Linleys. Somehow Dick's sister Alicia managed to arrange messages between the lovers, and after a while Thomas Sheridan, influenced by the public emotion in Dick's favour, interviewed his son.

But Elizabeth's impulsive announcement of their marriage caused both fathers to prohibit further intercourse between the two, Linley because his daughter was a source of income to him, old Sheridan on account of his pride, and the young people were bullied into acquiescence with the will of their parents. Alicia reported that 'many traps were laid for both parties, but they contrived to evade them, attributing what she had uttered before Mr Panton and others to mere agitation of mind'. As already stated, their marriage in France was not legally binding, and their parents had no intention of recognising its validity. But their promises not to enter a formal union were extracted by threats, and they rightly regarded themselves as already married, witness this message from Elizabeth to Dick: 'Oh! my dearest love, when shall I see you? . . . I did not know till now how much I loved you. Believe me, had you died, I should certainly have dressed myself as a man and challenged Mathews. He should have killed me, or I would have revenged you and myself . . . God in Heaven bless you . . . and restore you once more to health, to happiness, and the arms of your Eliza.'

Soon they met in public, and he wrote to complain that her manner had been reserved. 'If I was prudent, it was my father's conversation that made me so', she replied. 'He declared he would sooner follow me to the grave than see me married to you, as you would ruin me and yourself in a short time by your extravagance. I know he watched us last night; 'twas that which made me cautious.' In spite of their promises of obedience they were kept apart, spied upon, lectured and restricted in their movements; but they occasionally managed to evade observation, and while his father was busy obtaining sworn evidence to prove Mathews a would-be assassin Dick was seizing every opportunity to meet Elizabeth by stealth. Each of the lovers was compelled to give an undertaking not to see or correspond with the other,

as well as a solemn oath never to marry, but in Dick's opinion
'Conscience has no more to do with gallantry than it has with
politics', a view he emphasised in a verse:

> The faith which to my friend I swore
>   As a civil oath I view;
> But to the charms which I adore,
>   'Tis religion to be true.

No doubt his father felt that he could not be trusted, and when an
engagement took Thomas Sheridan to Dublin his son was
banished to Farm Hill, Waltham Abbey, Essex, where he was
ordered to study for the Bar. 'I feel I love you every day more
tenderly', Elizabeth had just written to him; 'I cannot support
the idea of a separation.'

Dick's punitive residence at Waltham lasted from August
1772 until the following April. He wrote long letters to a friend,
Thomas Grenville, tried to drug his emotions by studying
mathematics, mensuration, astronomy, geography, history,
Latin and the law, occasionally relieved his solitude with a visit
to London, yet had to admit that 'my love is almost the only
feeling I have alive . . . I *love*, therefore I *am*'. He wrote an
account of his romance, but it has not survived. 'Tell me she is
happy', he begged Grenville; 'if she is otherwise, tell her to be
so. O upon my soul it were the part of an angel to come down
from Heaven to watch over her and reconcile her mind to peace. I
wish dying could assure me of the power to come from Heaven
to her with that happiness which I fear she will never know here.
It is impious to say it, but I believe I should exchange a Robe
of Glory for *her* livery.'

A letter to his father, who had paid all his debts, closes 'Your
truly affectionate and dutiful son', but their definitions of duty
would not have harmonised. He discovered, or thought he had,
that ambition was a more satisfactory object than love, largely
because it depended on oneself, but the man whose passion is
thwarted usually does his best to find solace in a substitute.

Comfort may also be sought in the love of another woman, and Dick was not the man to neglect that form of consolation. Apparently one was not enough for him, and Elizabeth heard from reliable sources that two women, one married, one single, had received his attentions, which may have been pressed further than flirtation in the second case. Elizabeth was deeply distressed. She wrote to say that he had made her suffer so much that she could not consent to risk her future life and happiness with him, and she begged for the return of her letters. He tried to excuse his behaviour and said that he would not return her letters unless he were assured that she loved another man; to which she replied, 'Believe me I am incapable of loving any other man', and again declared her decision that all was over between them, adding that, after refusing certain 'gentlemen of fortune' on Dick's account, she had vowed on her knees to her parents 'that I never would be yours'. Her father had then pressed another suitor upon her; and, though she assured the fellow that it was not possible for her to love him, he persisted in his suit. Such was the position, and she concluded: 'Be assured I will not open any letter of yours nor will I write again. If you wish me to think my happiness is dear to you, return my letters . . . For God's sake write no more.'

But she reckoned without his persuasive powers. In the early spring of 1773 she fulfilled certain engagements in London, and by some stratagem they met. Neither man nor woman could resist Dick when he laid himself out to fascinate, and on 13 April, a week after he was entered at the Middle Temple, Elizabeth Linley married Richard Sheridan at Marylebone Church in the presence of the bride's father, who no doubt had been favourably influenced by the bridegroom's financial sacrifice as well as his fascination, for the greater part of the £3,000 which had been settled on Elizabeth by a previous wooer was now made over to her father. The young man's charm did not operate on his own father, at least from a distance. On hearing the news in Ireland Thomas Sheridan went mad. He cursed Dick, swore that henceforth he would have but one son, Charles, and ordered his daughters to eliminate the young renegade and his low-born wife from their visiting-list, thus fully earning Johnson's attribution: 'Such an excess of stupidity is not in Nature.'

Just before their marriage Elizabeth had captivated London with her singing, receiving ovations such as Garrick had been given in his prime. She had sung before the King and Queen at Buckingham House, had been handsomely complimented, majestically ogled and royally compensated by George III, and offers by impresarios came pouring in. The combination of exquisite beauty and an enchanting voice bewitched people, and she could certainly have made a fortune if Dick had not put his foot down, scorning the thousands of pounds she could have earned within six months. There was considerable vanity in his refusal to let his wife sing for money: he did not wish to be known solely as 'Mrs Sheridan's husband', and he refused to be dependent on her. This attitude laid him open to criticism, but Dr Johnson defended him when the subject came up in conversation: 'He resolved wisely and nobly to be sure. He is a brave man. Would not a gentleman be disgraced by having his wife singing publicly for hire? No, sir, there can be no doubt here. I know not if I should not *prepare* myself for a public singer, as readily as let my wife be one.' His preparation would have been striking, if unmelodious. But Sheridan had suffered at Harrow from being a player's son, and had no wish for a child of his to be teased as a songster's son. As we shall find, his vanity urged him to dissociate himself from the stage except as a means of making money; and when George III asked him to become director of oratorios, almost certainly as a bribe to make his wife sing, he declined the job. During their honeymoon, which was spent in a cottage at East Burnham, near Slough, Dick turned down the lucrative offers for her services while wondering where the next meal was coming from. 'I feel myself absolutely and perfectly happy', he wrote to Grenville, adding that he was planting carrots and cabbages in the garden, and that whatever effect his wife's voice 'might have upon the sheep on the Common, the mutton still obstinately continued stationary at the butcher's.'

But they had a gig and a horse, and a man to look after Dick, gig and horse.

They were both supremely happy, and often in the days to come looked back upon these idyllic months as Paradise Won. But Dick perceived, as one of his stage-characters was to declare, that, 'if we would make love our household god, we had best secure him a comfortable roof', and he trusted his pen to provide it. He wrote articles and commentaries, but soon realised that they would not provide food and drink. Clearly they could not remain in their Eden and live on vegetables; so in the autumn of that year they stayed with friends in London and soon took a house in Orchard Street, where Elizabeth's singing drew the fashionable world to their parties and Joshua Reynolds painted her as 'St Cecilia'. In this way his wife's gift benefited Dick, who gained the entrée to an aristocratic world ravished by her voice. But he was not content with reflected glory, and continued to write, among other things a defence of the Americans against Johnson's pamphlet *Taxation no Tyranny*, containing a trenchant sentence: 'If America is ours by conquest, it is the conquerors who settle there that are to claim these powers.' Fortunately for Sheridan, who accused Johnson of rashness and ignorance, this was never published. Had it been, Johnson might have said something displeasing about 'the dullard's whelp', duly reported to the victim by Boswell.

Sheridan also wrote a 'Lyric Ode' and other ephemera, but by the autumn of 1774 he was busy with a play which appeared anonymously at Covent Garden Theatre on 17 January of the following year. He called it *The Rivals*, and it contains a few of his own experiences as a lover at Bath, the angry father being in part a portrayal of his own. It was much too wordy; the audience were restive; a section hissed; and after two performances it was withdrawn. When he broke the news to his wife, she exclaimed: 'My dear Dick, I am delighted. I always knew it was impossible you could make anything of writing plays, so now there is nothing for it but my beginning to sing publicly again, and we shall have as much money as we like.' 'No', he replied, 'that shall never be. I see where the fault was; the play was too long and the parts were badly cast.' He went through it carefully, cut every scrap of dialogue that seemed to drag or was repetitive, insisted on having another actor in the part of 'Sir Lucius O'Trigger', and on 28 January the play reappeared on the stage. Its success was immediate, sixteen performances being given that season to immense applause. There is a general belief that no amount of tinkering will save a play which has been damned by the first-night audience. *The Rivals* is the classic example to the contrary and may be described as, excepting only Goldsmith's *She Stoops to Conquer*, the best comedy of characters produced on the English stage between the plays of Shakespeare and Shaw.

An actor named Clinch stepped into the part of 'Sir Lucius O'Trigger', making a success of it, and for his benefit Sheridan knocked off a short farce called *St Patrick's Day*, which was done with Clinch in the leading part on 2 May of the same year. It contains a piece of dialogue which was a familiar quotation before the compilation of familiar quotations:

Justice Credulous: I don't like death.
Mrs Bridget Credulous: Psha! there is nothing in it: a moment, and it is over.
Justice Credulous: Ay, but it leaves a numbness behind that lasts a plaguy long time.

Scarcely pausing between his labours, Sheridan next wrote an opera, *The Duenna*, the songs being set to music by his father-in-law Thomas Linley. Produced at Covent Garden Theatre on 21 November 1775, four days after the birth of the author's only son Tom, it became more successful than any opera written in English up to that period, even than *The Beggar's Opera*, which had been performed sixty-three times in 1728, while Sheridan's piece scored seventy-five performances during the first season and countless more in the ensuing years. It was the wittiest and most popular opera in the language until the arrival of W. S. Gilbert. The scene is set in Seville, the characters are Spanish, and a remark by one of them shows that Sheridan was already gaining acquaintance with the nobility: 'In England they were formerly as nice, as to birth and family, as we are; but they have long discovered what a wonderful purifier gold is, and now no one there regards pedigree in anything but a horse.'

On 10 June 1776 David Garrick bade farewell to the stage, and Sheridan became manager and part-proprietor of Drury Lane Theatre. We need not attempt to understand the curious financial arrangements which were to occupy Sheridan at intervals for the rest of his life, for he made little attempt to understand them himself. There were mortgages, sub-mortgages, transfers, bills, loans, underwritings, interest on annuities, and all the other adjustments with which an immense business was then carried on. It is enough to say that between 1776 and 1812, a period that included the rebuilding of the theatre twice, the first owing to a collapsing structure, the second owing to destruction by fire, Sheridan was wholly responsible for it, earned a large salary from it, and managed to raise whatever capital was necessary during crises by that mesmeric charm he exercised even over financiers and money-lenders. His love of affairs led him to obtain an interest in the Haymarket Opera House and the Pantheon in Oxford Street, and his ability to turn an awkward corner was proved when, to the amazement of his wife, he saved the credit of a Drury Lane partner by raising £18,000 at a moment's notice. More remarkable still, he persuaded his father to act as stage-manager at Drury Lane, but the older man's fussy and dictatorial methods soon got on the nerves of the actors and after two years his contract was not renewed. Thomas Sheridan admitted at the end of his life that he had thwarted Dick's schemes and wishes throughout that time, and felt no surprise that his son had got rid of him; but he was furious when it happened, especially on hearing that Thomas Linley had taken his place, and again refused to see Dick for several years, a rupture that grieved the young man, who, strange though it may seem, longed for his father's affection. It must have added to the father's embitterment when Dr Johnson proposed Dick for The Club of which Gibbon, Reynolds, Burke, Garrick and Charles James Fox were members. 'He who has written the two best comedies of his age is surely a considerable man', said the Doctor, referring to *The Rivals* and *The Duenna*, and Sheridan was elected on 14 March 1777, eight weeks before the production of his very best comedy.

Sheridan began his control of Drury Lane Theatre with a production of Dryden's version of Shakespeare's *The Tempest*, for which he wrote songs set to music by Linley, and this feeble inception of his enterprise gives the key to his management. He was solely concerned with making money, and fortunately *The Rivals*, reproduced at his own theatre, was played 153 times in the course of the season. He then adapted Vanbrugh's comedy *The Relapse* to the genteel taste of his time, entitled it *A Trip to Scarborough*, and 99 performances repaid his labour, the first being on 24 February 1777. But all this time, in addition to his managerial duties and financial operations, he had been busily polishing his next original comedy, which he completed at No. 55 Great Queen Street, where he and his wife had moved from Orchard Street in order to be near Drury Lane Theatre. For once he worked really hard on a play, refining and correcting *The School for Scandal* to such a degree that he was unable to convince himself it had reached the acme of elegance, and he never passed a final version for the press. Having put the last touches to the acting version, he wrote: 'Finished, thank God!' to which the prompter added 'Amen'. But he died without finishing it to his complete satisfaction. David Garrick was not so fastidious, expressed his keen admiration of the original manuscript, and attended many rehearsals.

This politically innocuous play was almost suppressed by political influence. There was an election in the City for the office of Chamberlain, the contestants being the notorious demagogue John Wilkes and the Ministerial nominee Hopkins, who had been charged with lending money to young men under age. As 'Moses', the usurer in the play, is guilty of similar practices, the piece was reported to authority as an attack on the

Government candidate in the interest of Wilkes, and the Lord Chamberlain refused a licence the day before the first performance. Sheridan at once called on Lord Hertford, who then held the office, laughed him out of opposition, obtained the licence, and *The School for Scandal* was performed for the first time on 8 May 1777, before a house that sparkled with social celebrities. Probably no comedy since the time of Shakespeare had been received with equal delight, and at the fall of the screen there was such a roar of laughter and applause that a passing pedestrian believed the theatre was collapsing and flew for safety. As usual the critics earned their money by finding fault, and at a later performance a rival dramatist, Richard Cumberland, refused to laugh at the comedy; on hearing which, Sheridan seemed hurt, complaining of the other's ingratitude, since Dick himself had witnessed Cumberland's recent tragedy at Covent Garden and had laughed heartily at it from beginning to end. *The School for Scandal* was an unparalleled success in the author's lifetime, both in Great Britain and in America, where it became George Washington's favourite play, and after nearly two hundred years it remains fresh and entertaining, the one perfect comedy of manners in the language.

Sheridan was very much liked by the actors at Drury Lane. He was on easy, friendly terms with them, and at rehearsals his patience and courtesy were so much to their taste that they did not complain when their salaries were in arrears. He invented nicknames for several members of the staff, but not all of them were aware of this, and it is doubtful if a conceited scene-painter named Capon knew that Sheridan called him 'Pompous Billy'. The policy of the theatre under his direction was the policy of practically every theatre under any direction: to stage plays for the sake of dividends. At this period blank-verse dramas were very popular, especially Shakespeare's when carefully disembowelled and sentimentalised, and audiences would sit listening to pretentious poppycock by the hour if they felt it was praiseworthy to do so, as indeed they will to this day. But, being an intelligent man, Sheridan laughed at the rubbish which playgoers took seriously, and as a man of genius he could not be depended upon to act as a man of business. He therefore took the risk of ridiculing the pseudo-Shakespearean stuff that passed for good drama and received the respectful homage of unintelligent audiences, and the last play of consequence that he produced was partly a satire and partly a parody, the sort of thing that Max Beerbohm was to write for readers, not playgoers, 140 years later.

The Critic, or *A Tragedy Rehearsed*, was first seen on 30 October 1779, and at once became a stock piece. As the author had not finished the last scene two days before the opening performance, his associates inveigled him into a room where pens, ink, paper, a good fire and a comfortable armchair were provided, together with two bottles of claret and a dish of anchovy sandwiches. The moment he entered he was locked in, and a voice from the other side of the door informed him that he would not be let out until the job was done. Sandwiches, claret and scene were soon despatched.

Again Richard Cumberland did not laugh at a play by Sheridan, this time because he was caricatured as 'Sir Fretful Plagiary', whose outburst over the journalists who criticised his works was not peculiar to himself: 'The newspapers! Sir, they are the most villainous – licentious – abominable – infernal – Not that I ever read them – no – I make it a rule never to look into a newspaper.' As for abuse, 'why, one is always sure to hear of it from one damned good-natured friend or other!' Since the burlesque had been preceded by *Hamlet* the previous evening, Sheridan's joke about the clock striking was oddly apposite. Says 'Mr Puff,' the author whose tragedy is being rehearsed: 'I open with a clock striking, to beget an awful attention in the audience: it also marks the time, which is four o'clock in the morning, and saves a description of the rising sun, and a great deal about gilding the eastern hemisphere.' Later in the play the heroine,

Ophelia, goes mad, and Mr Puff justifies her costume: 'When a heroine goes mad, she always goes into white satin, she is the Governor's daughter 'Tilburina', and at one moment indulges in 'poetical second-sight', describing the condition of the approaching Spanish Armada, but her father checks the rhapsody:

> Hold, daughter! peace! . . .
> The Spanish fleet thou canst not see – because
> It is not yet in sight.

Tilburina loves the Spanish prisoner 'Don Whiskerandos', who, when assured of her love, cries:

> Art thou then true? Begone cares, doubts and fears,
> I make you all a present to the winds;
> And if the winds reject you – try the waves.

When Mr Puff is reminded that one of his lines perilously resembles something in Shakespeare, he is unconcerned: 'That's of no consequence; all that can be said is that two people happened to hit upon the same thought – and Shakespeare made use of it first, that's all.' One of the characters, 'Lord Burleigh', makes an entrance, shakes his head, does not utter a word, and goes off. Mr Puff explains his action in a manner familiar to many modern producers: 'By that shake of the head, he gave you to understand that even though they had more justice in their cause, and wisdom in their measures – yet, if there was not a greater spirit shown on the part of the people, the country would at last fall a sacrifice to the hostile ambition of the Spanish monarchy.' 'The devil!' exclaims a critical onlooker, 'did he mean all that by shaking his head?' 'Every word of it', replies Mr Puff, 'if he shook his head as I taught him.' Don Whiskerandos fights with a beefeater and receives a mortal wound, crying:

> O cursed parry! – that last thrust in tierce
> Was fatal. – Captain, thou hast fenced well!
> And Whiskerandos quits this bustling scene
> For all etern –
> *Beefeater:* Nity, he would have added, but stern death
> Cut short his being and the noun at once.

Obviously Sheridan could not take the fashionable drama very seriously; and, although his expressed dislike of Shakespeare was largely owing to the period's emasculated versions of the poet, his real interests lay elsewhere. He had never forgotten the inferior social position from which he had suffered at school, and he longed to win a place for himself in the great world. Proprietorship of a theatre might keep the wolf, if not the bailiffs, from the door, but did not help to remove the stigma of his birth as an actor's son, which could only be done by entering Parliament. He was aware of his chief failing, an overmastering vanity, and once revealed the knowledge: 'They talk of avarice, lust, ambition, as great passions. It is a mistake; they are little passions. Vanity is the great commanding passion of all. It is this that produces the most grand and heroic deeds, or impels to the most dreadful crimes. Save me but from this passion, and I can defy the others. They are mere urchins, but this is a giant.' He was, and remained through life, an actor, but he pined for a stage where he could exhibit his genius as a 'star' performer without the assistance of a cast of players, and he yearned for pre-eminence in aristocratic circles. Thomas Creevey recognised the vital importance of being a politician in those days: 'I became a member of the House of Commons in 1802, and the moment a man became such then, if he attached himself to one of the great parties in the House – Whigs or Tories – he became at once a public man, and had a position in society which nothing else could give him. I advert particularly to such persons as myself, who came from the ranks, without either opulence or connections to procure for them admission into the company of their betters.'

With the assistance of the friends won for him by his wife's singing and his own plays, Sheridan stood for Parliament as a Whig, and with the further assistance of bribes for the votes and beer for the voices he became M.P. for Stafford in 1780, representing that city at Westminster during the next twenty-six years. Long afterwards he told Creevey that the happiest moment of his life occurred after the dinner celebrating his election, 'when he stole away by himself to speculate upon the prospects of distinguishing himself which had been opened to him'. The chief friends who helped him to the seat were the Duchess of Devonshire, her sister Lady Duncannon (later Countess of Bessborough), and Mrs (afterwards Lady) Crewe, all of them famous figures in the social world and each notable for beauty.

By this time Sheridan had made so great a reputation as a playwright and conversational wit that everyone wanted to know him, and he was the 'star' guest at receptions given by leading hostesses. With a tall, upright, well-proportioned figure, he carried himself with grace and dignity. His manners were courtly, polite, engaging, and serene. The upper part of his face was handsome, likened by Byron to that of a god, with an expansive forehead and brilliant eyes; but the lower part was loose and uncomely, reminding Byron of a satyr. He had powerful but thin arms, small and delicate hands, described by someone as:

> Good at a Fight, but better at a Play,
> Godlike in giving, but the Devil to pay!

In public speaking he had a singularly clear and mellifluous voice, though in private his speech was slovenly. He was, as his face implied, excessively good-natured and tragically weak. He always meant well but could not implement his good intentions. 'I have so many daily instances of his engaging for what he is wholly unable to perform', wrote his sister, 'that where one's support is at stake it cannot be looked on as a bright prospect.' He was unfailingly kind-hearted, going out of his way to be polite and pleasant to people who were ill-treated or ignored by others, but forgetfulness made him inconsiderate. He had the catlike quality of being distracted from his course by incidents on the way; so that however definitely he set out to do something, the object would be banished from his mind if something else aroused his interest *en route*. Whatever the circumstances he never knew despondency until the close of his life, and even though exhausted by fatigue his mere presence would cheer people up.

H

But the most remarkable aspect of his nature was his faculty for making others act in a manner contrary to their wishes, for getting his own way against apparently insuperable odds, coupled with a miraculous inability to offend people. 'Everybody in the world speaks well of him', says 'Sir Peter Teazle' in *The School for Scandal*. 'I am sorry to hear it', replies 'Sir Oliver Surface'; 'he has too good a character to be an honest fellow. Everybody speaks well of him! Psha! then he has bowed as low to knaves and fools as to the honest dignity of genius and virtue.' Everybody did not speak well of Sheridan; he owed too much money and was a little too honest for that; but he was quite incapable of arousing hostility. 'He *could not* make enemies', wrote Hazlitt. 'If anyone came to request the repayment of a loan from him, he borrowed more. A cordial shake of his hand was a receipt in full for all demands. He could "coin his *smile* for drachmas", cancelled bonds with *bon mots*, and gave jokes in discharge of a bill. A friend of his said, "If I pull off my hat to him in the street, it costs me fifty pounds, and if he speaks to me it's a hundred!" ' Even his wife was astounded at the seemingly impossible things he accomplished. She was fully cognisant of all his difficulties at the theatre. She kept the accounts at Drury Lane, read the plays, helped with the songs and music, and settled quarrels. Sheridan had a habit of helping himself when he needed money, and the salaries of the actors were sometimes in abeyance. He had the rare ability of making money and the less rare ability of spending it faster than it was made, being persistently in debt to someone or other and habitually paying his debts twice over to unscrupulous creditors. But situations that would have turned another man's hair grey were to him but momentary and easily surmounted embarrassments. When Mrs Siddons declared that she would not appear as Lady Macbeth unless her salary were paid, Sheridan ignored her threat until fully persuaded that she meant it, when he called at her house, got her into a good humour, and took her in his carriage to the theatre, where she played the part without pressing her claim. She had made her name under his management and he admired her so much that Sam Rogers wanted to know whether he had ever made love to her. 'To that magnificent and appalling creature!' he exclaimed: 'I should as soon have thought of making love to the Archbishop of Canterbury.' Her brother John Philip Kemble was also indignant with Sheridan over something and stated his intention of dressing the manager down before the company. Sheridan arrived, Kemble scowled, but within two minutes the latter had been soothed and was soon brimming over with cordiality.

Again and again the miracle worked. Sheridan was irresistible, exercising some hypnotic power with the aid of his tongue and a pair of eyes that thrilled women and disarmed men. Michael Kelly, who directed the Italian Opera in which Sheridan had an interest, was arrested for £350 which had been spent on upholstery for the Opera House. On hearing this Sheridan sent for the upholsterer, taxed him with inconsiderateness, talked him over, gave him a valueless bond and borrowed £200 from him before they parted. Once a sum of about £3,000 was owed to the singers, who declined to perform until paid. Kelly tried the bankers, but they assured him that Sheridan had let them down too often and they refused to advance the money. Kelly rushed in a panic to Sheridan's house and related what had happened. 'Three thousand pounds?' said Sheridan; 'there is no such sum in nature.' But he went to the bankers, and emerged with the entire amount within a quarter of an hour. Handing it over, Sheridan told Kelly to keep enough out of it to buy a barrel of native oysters which they could deal with that evening.

Such was the man who entered Parliament in 1780 to make a typically spectacular reputation there. He was soon on friendly terms with the great Whig leaders, Edmund Burke and Charles James Fox, and a member of Brooks's, the notable Whig club. Though he remained in many respects a loyal Whig, he was too intelligent and independent to toe the party line on certain matters, and his intellectual superiority no less than his volatility laid him open to the suspicion of the dull and uniform types that make up the majority of every party, many of whom regarded his cleverness as trickiness, his independence as perversity. As honest as a man can be who lives in a world of wire-pulling, he was not open to bribery; he never acted in an underhand way to the detriment of others; and he never used his position to make money. He fought at all times, with or without the support of his party, for Catholic emancipation, the suppression of the slave trade, the mitigation of the Game Laws, political freedom in Ireland, the reform of the Scottish boroughs (which he achieved), universal suffrage, and the liberty of the Press. In home affairs he was always on the side of freedom and democratic progress, while championing America's fight for independence and the right of Frenchmen to make their own constitution following the Revolution. But in foreign affairs he was primarily a patriot, and when Napoleon threatened England he not only joined the volunteers for home defence but supported the Tories in their efforts to avert the danger. A naval mutiny at the Nore in 1797 was stamped out as a result of his advice to the Tory Government, and he received the unstinted praise of his political opponents, William Pitt and Henry Dundas, neither of whom had cause to love him, for he had called Pitt 'the Angry Boy', a name that had stuck, and had said of Dundas: 'The Right Honourable Gentleman is indebted to his memory for his jests and to his imagination for his facts.' He had also genially pulled Dundas's leg in the House by remarking: 'If, as has been stated, gentlemen serve the country without at the same time serving themselves, we have at present a most gentlemanly administration, and one gentleman, Mr Secretary Dundas, is three times as much a gentleman as any of them, for he has three places.' Dundas, who had recently married an attractive woman, replied that he was not to be envied, as his task in the various offices was almost too great for human powers, at which point Sheridan interrupted that he would be happy to relieve Dundas from the fatigue of the *Home* department.

As a debater Sheridan was unrivalled for his gaiety and good-temper. He never showed the least sign of irritation; his manner was consistently imperturbable; and his humour took the sting out of his attacks. For example, the support given to the Whigs during the passage of Pitt's India Bill was steadily weakening, and Sheridan said he was not surprised, since a person was specially employed to corrupt members in order to obtain votes. The Secretary to the Treasury at that time was John Robinson, and when Sheridan's statement was received with cries of 'Who is it? Name him! Name him!' he rose to address the Speaker: 'Sir, I shall not name the person. It is an unpleasant and invidious thing to do. But don't suppose that I abstain because there is any difficulty in naming him. I could do that, sir, as easily as you could say "Jack Robinson".' Some of his passages in the House have become familiar quotations, such as his comment on a Ministerial speech: 'It contained a great deal both of what was new and what was true, but unfortunately what was new was not true and what was true was not new.' He was just as ready on the hustings at election time. An opposing Tory candidate lost his temper and exclaimed that he would like to knock Sheridan's brains out. When it was the latter's turn to speak, he began: 'You have heard my opponent's amiable desire. I have but one suggestion to make. Let him be very careful when he performs the operation. Let him pick up my brains, for he needs them sadly.' Other people grievously lacked his manner of telling stories; and when Lord Lauderdale stated his intention of repeating one of the wit's repartees, Sheridan warned him: 'A joke on your lips is no laughing matter.'

The odd thing is that a man who could not manage his private affairs seems to have been a capable man in public affairs. For the greater part of Sheridan's political life the Tories were in power, but during the brief interregnums of Whig or coalition government he occupied the posts of Under-Secretary for Foreign Affairs and Secretary to the Treasury, discharging his duties competently. He indulged in a certain amount of nepotism, getting his brother Charles various Irish posts, culminating with the appointment of 'Joseph Surface' as Irish Secretary of War. Dick himself seems to have been remarkably free of spoilsmanship, complaining at the close of his life that it was easy for the Earl of

This and the Marquis of That, with large fortunes from inheritance or public money, to boast of their patriotism, of not yielding to temptation, but that no one knew the temptations of those with equal pride and talents and passions who never had a shilling of their own; in saying which he wept, possibly at the thought of what he had missed. But no man is wholly free from corruption on his weakest side, and Sheridan's weakness was not a love of money but vanity. He longed to astonish the world, to achieve something that would give him a reputation unique among his fellows, and the chance came when a party in the House of Commons decided to impeach the Governor-General of India, Warren Hastings, for high crimes and misdemeanours.

An embittered and vindictive man, Philip Francis, had supplied Edmund Burke with a lot of information about Hastings, who without enriching himself had acted in an arbitrary way when ordered by his employers, the East India Company, to enrich the shareholders. Burke's personal interests made him anxious to believe Francis, and he worked himself into a pathological state of moral indignation, imparting some of his resentment to Sheridan. When the subject came up in the House of Commons, it fell to Sheridan to attack Hastings on his treatment of the Begums of Oude, and the member for Stafford seized the opportunity for a display of oratory unique in the history of the British Parliament. His speech on 7 February 1787 lasted for five and a half hours, and bowled everyone over. The three most famous orators of the age witnessed to its effect. Edmund Burke called it 'the most astonishing effort of eloquence, argument and wit united, of which there is any record or tradition.' Charles James Fox said: 'All that I have ever heard or read, when compared with it, dwindles into nothing and vanishes like vapour before the sun.' And William Pitt declared that 'it surpassed all the eloquence of ancient and modern times, and possessed everything that genius or art could furnish to agitate and control the human mind.' At the conclusion of the speech the House, for the first time on record, not only echoed with shouts and applause but adjourned for the purpose of recovering from the emotional state into which members had been thrown. They were, said Pitt, 'under the wand of the enchanter' and incapable of balanced judgment. Sheridan's friends hugged him, and for some weeks the rest of the world would have liked to do the same. It was the chief topic of conversation until he repeated the performance at the trial of Warren Hastings in Westminster Hall during the first week of June 1788. Fifty pounds were paid for a seat on this impressive occasion, and Society flocked to hear the great performer, who did not disappoint them. In the course of his speech the strain told upon him and at one point he could not go on. The High Court of Parliament adjourned for several days so that he could recuperate. He closed the immense oration with the words, 'My Lords, I have done', and fell back into the arms of Burke, an effective *coup de théâtre*.

Most famous political speeches are fustian in print, and Sheridan did not authorise versions of his Hastings performances. The reports that have survived suggest that his success was largely owing to the personality of a first-class actor. Here for example is a piece of pure melodrama: 'Is there anything in Machiavel, any treachery upon record, any perfidy among individuals or nations, any cold Italian fraud you have ever known or heard of, comparable in any degree to a management thus black and perfidious?' Hastings must have smiled while listening to this: 'The serpent may as well abandon the characteristic obliquity of his motion for the direct flight of an arrow, as he can excuse his purposes with honesty and fairness.' And the smile must have broadened to a grin when he heard this: 'His crimes are the only great thing about him, and these are contrasted by the littleness of his motives.' Perhaps the best passage in the speeches because substantially true is that in which Sheridan referred to the purely commercial aims of the British administration: 'It was in this manner that nations have been extirpated for a sum of money, whole tracts of country laid waste by fire and sword to furnish investments; revolutions occasioned by an affidavit, an army employed in executing an arrest, towns besieged on a note of hand, a prince expelled for the balance of an account, statesmen occupied in doing the business of a tipstaff, generals made auctioneers, a truncheon contrasted with the implements of a counting-house; and the British Government in every part of Hindustan holding a bloody sceptre in one hand and picking pockets with the other.'

Sheridan had gained his heart's desire; he had become the talk of the kingdom; and his vanity was glutted. Whether in solitude he believed a word of his indictment may be questioned. 'The counsel,' he once wrote, 'is not only not bound to ask his conscience, but he is bound *not* to do it. He has a duty and a trust which ought to receive no aid from conviction.' But as an actor he had flung himself into the part for which he had been cast, and believed every word of it at the instant of utterance. Soon afterwards his sense of humour came uppermost, and, when someone asked why he had complimented the historian Gibbon with the epithet 'luminous', he answered 'I meant *vo*luminous.' Before the end of 1788 he was heartily sick of the whole affair, telling the Duchess of Devonshire that he wished Warren Hastings would run away and Burke after him. But the trial dragged on for seven years, at the conclusion of which Hastings was acquitted on every charge. Many years later Sheridan was introduced to Hastings by the Prince of Wales at the Pavilion, Brighton, and made a sort of apology for the violence of his words at the trial, which he asserted were due to political necessity. No one, he averred, had a greater respect for Hastings than himself. With the utmost gravity Hastings replied that it would be a great consolation to him in his declining days if Mr Sheridan would make that sentence more public. But vanity, like other vices, has to be paid for at one time or another, and the great orator looked, and no doubt felt, extremely foolish as he mumbled some sort of excuse.

Several writers of genius, for instance Dickens and Kipling, could not escape from their childhood and remained emotionally immature to the end of their days; but Sheridan was always in search of a childhood he had somehow missed, reaching maturity at a bound, and spent much of his future life trying to capture his lost youth by acting as a child. His pranks and practical jokes, his delight in shocking or astonishing people, his love of mystery, his pleasure in disarming opposition and getting his own way, his high spirits and his vanity, are all those of a child. Above all he displayed a boy's adoration of high rank, and his friendship with the Prince of Wales resembled that of a clever lower-form youth with the imposing captain of a football team. It gave him enormous pleasure to place his intelligence at the service of the Prince, to advise him on policy, to amuse him, to feel his own influence over such a man, and to know that his future monarch regarded him with affection. Such was his loyalty that eventually he lost the confidence of his fellow-Whigs, who were envious of his ascendancy in the Prince's councils. Though shrewd enough to perceive that 'in religion, as in friendship, they who profess most are the least sincere', Sheridan could never understand why his early friends, Burke and Fox, ceased to trust him.

The Prince of Wales was an attractive man of many accomplishments, popular with the aristocracy as well as the mob, exercising his charm over both sexes. He could talk easily and wittily about scandal, politics, literature, music and prize-fighting; he could drink most men under the table, and entice such women as took his fancy into bed. He spent money like water and was always in debt, a condition that impelled him to support the Whigs against his father's Tory administration, the Whigs having promised that if they came to power he would benefit financially. Sheridan became his chief adviser, wrote or supervised his letters when the question of the Regency came up on account of George III's insanity, and quite early in their relationship did him a service of inestimable benefit. The Prince was hysterically in love with a Roman Catholic, Mrs Fitzherbert, who would not grant him the final intimacy unless they were married. He was willing to sacrifice the throne for her sake, and on 15 December 1785 the marriage took place in dead secrecy, which meant that it would soon become the subject of general conversation. By the Act of Settlement a prince could not succeed to the throne if he married a Papist, and by the Royal Marriage Act any marital union was invalid without parental consent if the sovereign's son were under the age of twenty-five. Legally therefore the Prince was not married to Mrs Fitzherbert. The subject came up in the House of Commons when the Prince's debts were discussed some sixteen months after the secret ceremony, and Fox went so far as to speak of 'the utter falsehood' of the assertion that the Prince was married, a calumny which he denied *in toto* 'in point of fact as well as of law'. As the Prince was an unblushing liar, and as the legal aspect of the matter enabled him on this occasion to lie with conviction, he had certainly primed Fox, who declared that he was speaking 'from direct authority'. Knowing that Mrs Fitzherbert would feel herself disgraced by this public avowal, the Prince tried to laugh it off: 'Only conceive, Maria, what Fox did yesterday! He went down to the House and denied that you and I were man and wife. Did you ever hear of such a thing?' She was furious, and the Prince begged Sheridan to appease her without alienating Fox. It was a tricky situation, and no one but Sheridan could have handled it. With extraordinary tact and skill he managed to calm the House, save the face of Fox, vindicate the Prince, and please Mrs Fitzherbert.

There was a considerable likelihood that the Prince would become Regent at the end of 1788, and the leading Whigs were excitedly appointing themselves to various governmental offices in that event. According to the Duchess of Devonshire, who was privy to all their intrigues, Sheridan might have been nominated Chancellor of the Exchequer had he chosen the office, but he preferred 'reaching it by degrees and when he had proved his capability to the public'. Unlike the other famous Whigs, he was strangely self-effacing where office and emoluments were concerned, and he refused to accept a seat in the House of Commons unless he were given complete freedom to speak and vote as he wished. His financial incorruptibility and mental independence were sufficient to make him unpopular with other politicians, who in self-defence accused him of dishonesty, disloyalty and trickery. His wife was constantly begging him to make use of his friendship with the Prince of Wales and other grandees: 'Do, my dear Dick, sacrifice a little of your *false delicacy* (which nobody has towards you) to our future happiness, and manage this matter.' But he would not ask favours of anyone, or use his position to better his situation, such behaviour shocking all the time-servers and place-seekers of the age. Public applause and fame were his temptations, and his pride also demanded success with women.

Some men adore their wives and yet cannot help being sexually unfaithful to them, partly from vanity, partly from sensuality. Sheridan was one of them, and many opportunities for infidelity were offered him. After his entry into politics he and his wife lived in the social world that revolved round the Prince of Wales at Carlton House and the Duchess of Devonshire at her Piccadilly mansion. They stayed at places like Chatsworth, Woburn, Crewe Hall, Wynnstay and Delapré Abbey, and while Elizabeth lost money at whist Dick drank with the male and flirted with the female guests. We do not know whether he had an affair with the Duchess of Devonshire, though the man who could melt the heart of an attorney would have little difficulty in seducing a susceptible duchess. But we do know that he went beyond flirtation with the Duchess's sister, Lady Duncannon, because her husband threatened an action for divorce, the scandal being averted by the intervention of the Duke of Devonshire. Another beauty, Mrs Crewe, was early on the scene, Sheridan having eulogised her in a number of dedicatory lines to *The School for Scandal*, the last of which runs: 'Thee my inspirer and my model – Crewe!' Elizabeth, fully aware of what was happening, wrote to a friend: 'Sheridan is in town, and so is Mrs Crewe; *I* am in the country, and so is *Mr Crewe*; a very convenient arrangement, is it not?' It must have been an open secret, for Dick's sister passed the information on to another sister: 'You know that Mrs Crewe among other lovers (favoured ones I mean) has had our brother in her train.' But with the growth of Sheridan's fame and the decline of Mrs Crewe's beauty his passion ebbed and she became jealous even of his wife, displaying spleen while they were staying with her. There is no such bore as a cast-off mistress, and Sheridan vented his pique by making love to a member of her household. Elizabeth had forgiven his lapses again and again, but this was the limit, and she wrote to her great friend Mrs Canning: 'At the moment in which he (Dick) was swearing and imprecating all sorts of curses on himself, on me, and his child, if ever he was led by any motive to be false to me again, he threw the whole family of Crewe into confusion and distress by playing the fool with Miss Fd (little Emma's governess) and contriving so awkwardly too, as to be discovered by the whole house, locked up with her in a bedchamber in an unfrequented part of the house.' Hell knows no fury like a woman scorned, and Mrs Crewe had revenged herself by making him ridiculous before her guests.

Previous to this incident Elizabeth had begged him many times to abandon a social circle in which deep drinking and indiscriminate copulation were the chief hobbies, assuring him that 'I love thee better than all the world besides and ever will', that he was wasting his genius on frivolity, that 'I think of nothing all day long but how to do good, somehow or other, for you', and that she would prefer solitude and poverty with him to anything the world could offer. From 1784 to 1790 they were living near Dorking at a house known as Deepdene lent them by the Duke of Norfolk, their London residence being in Bruton Street, Berkeley Square. They saw little of one another because Sheridan's intimacy with the Prince of Wales frequently took him to Brighton, and politics occupied much of his time. Elizabeth, too, was excessively busy, attending to theatrical matters, looking after a dead sister's children, living in the social whirl, and generally overworking herself. Naturally she had admirers, one of them being the Duke of Clarence (afterwards William IV), who did his utmost to seduce her, but she fought them all off, telling her frantically jealous husband that he alone possessed her whole-hearted devotion. Her love for him was too deep for jealousy, but it was not impervious to ridicule, and after the absurd episode of the governess she 'lost confidence in his professions and promises', even permitting the advances of a madly passionate lover, Lord Edward Fitzgerald, some of whose warm feeling she reciprocated. There can be very little doubt that the daughter she bore on 30 March 1792 was also Fitzgerald's.

In his play *A Trip to Scarborough* Sheridan had tried to excuse his own lapses by leaving in a line by Vanbrugh, from whose play it was adapted: 'No man worth having is ever true to his wife, or ever was, or ever will be so.' But a wife's behaviour should be rigid:

> That wife alone unsullied credit wins,
> Whose virtues can atone her husband's sins;
> Thus, while the man has other nymphs in view,
> It suits the woman to be doubly true.

A comforting reflection for an erring husband, especially as he meant well: 'I am determined to reform, though not yet.' But Sheridan's true feeling for his wife came uppermost in the present crisis, and he realised that he alone was responsible for what had occurred. Like so many of her family, Elizabeth was the victim of consumption. The birth of her child, though momentarily favourable to her health, in effect hastened the disease, and Dick decided to take her to the Hot Wells at Bristol. She was much upset when her chief friend Mrs Stratford Canning had taken exception to her affair with Fitzgerald and had ceased to call on her. Dick wrote to implore Mrs Canning not to harbour ill thoughts of his wife: 'Convinced as I am that there is *no chance of saving her life* but by tranquillizing her mind, and knowing as I do, and as I did hope you knew, that God never formed a better heart, and that she has no errors but what are the Faults of those whose conduct has created them in her against her nature, I feel it impossible for me not to own that the idea of unkindness or coldness towards her *from you* smote me most sensibly, as I see it does her to the soul.' He went to see Mrs Canning, who made some allusion to Fitzgerald, upon which he broke out passionately: 'Oh, not a word of that kind! She is an angel if ever there was one. It is all my fault. It is I, I that was the guilty fiend', and he wept piteously. Mrs Canning's heart was softened, and leaving her own children she accompanied them to Bristol. On 6 May 1792 they passed over Kingsdown, and Dick visited the spot where he had fought that duel so many years before. 'What an interval has passed since', he wrote to the Duchess of Devonshire, 'and scarce one promise that I then made to my own soul have I attempted to fulfil. . . . My nerves are shook to pieces. The irregularity of all my life and pursuits, the restless, contriving temper with which I have persevered in wrong Pursuits and Passions makes . . . reflection worse to me than even to those who have acted worse.'

They took lodgings in a white bow-windowed house looking over Strawberry Garden, and twice a day Elizabeth was taken in a sedan-chair on Clifton Downs, Dick walking by her side. 'I am confident if she can recover', he wrote to the Duchess, 'there never was on earth anything more perfect than she will be; and to be different, she says, to me for ever from what she has been, makes her so seriously eager to live.' He was with her all day long, and Mrs Canning remarked his gentle attentions and unremitting efforts to keep her in good spirits: 'He bore her in his arms to the spring, he was never absent from her, he watched by her bedside, read the Scriptures to her, joined in her devotions, and rendered her every office of tenderness and duty.' One night she asked to be placed at the piano, and Dick described the scene: 'Looking like a shadow of her own Picture' (the one by Reynolds of St Cecilia) 'she played some notes with the tears dropping on her thin arms. Her mind is become heavenly, but her mortal form is fading from my sight, and I look in vain into my own mind for assent to her apparent conviction that all will not perish.' On 27 June she knew her end was near and took leave of her family. One of her last acts was to give the sole guardianship of her daughter to Mrs Canning, making Dick swear he would never on any account interfere 'in the education or in any other way of my poor child'. For the first time in his life Dick knew real misery. Up to then success had been so easy; he had been able to charm away all opposition in the commerce of life; but he could not charm away the spectre of death. 'I cannot describe to you how sunk I am and how horrid the solitude of the night is to me', he confessed. Mrs Canning described the last scene to Alicia Sheridan: 'Your brother behaved most wonderfully, though his heart was breaking; and at times his feelings were so violent that I feared he would have been quite ungovernable at the last. Yet he summoned up courage to kneel at the bedside till he felt the last pulse . . . and then withdrew.' She died in the early morning of 28 June, and was buried in Wells Cathedral. Dick could hardly bear to leave the vault that shut her from his sight, and afterwards wrote: 'The victory of the grave is sharper than the sting of death.'

The previous year he had taken a house at Isleworth, to which he now returned. He could not bear to be without his wife's little daughter, and Mrs Canning allowed the child to remain with him. He appeared to have recovered his normal good spirits, though one of his guests who occupied an adjoining bedroom heard him sobbing for many hours in the night; and we learn from himself that 'I exert myself in every way and avoid remembering or reflecting as much as possible, but there are thoughts and forms and sounds that haunt my heart and will not be put away.' In the autumn of 1792 he left Isleworth for a house near Mrs Canning's at Wanstead, and there, a year later, Elizabeth's daughter died. Again Sheridan was grief-stricken; but he was not the man to yield to any mood for long, and he plunged into business concerning the theatre, made rash bets at Brooks's, purchased houses he did not need and sold them, bought horses he never used, orated in the House of Commons, and drank heavily. The surveyors reported that Drury Lane Theatre was unsafe. A much larger house rose on its site at a huge cost, Sheridan becoming more and more entangled in the finances and not perceiving that he was being cheated by the backers. The new Drury Lane opened in the spring of 1794 with *Macbeth*, Mrs Siddons and her brother John Philip Kemble in the leading parts. As the theatre was burnt down fifteen years later, this may have started the strange superstition that *Macbeth* is an unlucky play, quotation from which brings tribulation.

Sheridan had an extremely generous and affectionate nature. No one applied to him for financial help in vain, if within his power to give, and he helped his brother and sisters on countless occasions. He never resented his father's ill-nature and stupidity, longed for a reconciliation, was delighted when Thomas handsomely forgave him for having done nothing to forgive, and fondly attended to the needs of the old man on his deathbed in 1788. But Dick's nature was at the mercy of the obverse of these virtues. He was a spendthrift and a sensualist. He could not keep money, could not stop drinking, and could not remain chaste. Perpetually hard-up, he was forced to send urgent appeals to the treasurer at Drury Lane Theatre for small sums to get him out of difficulties, especially when he found himself 'money-bound', as he called it, at an inn. The treasurer was conjured 'by the love of God' to send £15 'by tomorrow's coach', or he heard that the writer was 'undone for the want of £35', or that £20 must be sent 'be the consequences ever so', or that £10 must be begged, borrowed or stolen for immediate needs, or that '*without fail* and immediately' the bearer must be given 'five guineas to buy hay and corn for my coach horses – they have not had a morsel of either since last night.' So heedless was Sheridan's disposition that his letters were unopened for weeks together, some of them containing money, and he took them about in a bag, intending to deal with them at the first opportunity; but other things distracted him and they went on accumulating, often being destroyed unread. A visitor noticed that not a few neglected letters had coronets on their seals, but to gain his attention they would have had to be wrapped up in bank notes. Sometimes he had not the money for the hackney-coach in which he paid visits, and on one occasion he was wondering how to settle the bill when he caught sight of his intimate and disputatious friend Joseph Richardson walking along the street, stopped to give him a lift, began a heated argument, allowed Joseph to get the better of it, alighted while the other was chortling over his victory, and left him to settle the day's fare at his destination.

Dick's amorous engagements were of an equally extemporaneous nature. Less than two months after the death of his wife he fell in love with Pamela Seymour, aged eighteen, reputed to be the natural daughter of the Duke of Orleans and Madame de Genlis. There was a strong resemblance between Pamela and Elizabeth Sheridan. The mother and daughter stayed with him at Isleworth, and when he suddenly proposed marriage Pamela accepted him. But her resemblance to Elizabeth had a similar effect on Lord Edward Fitzgerald, who fell passionately in love with her, a passion she returned, and Dick was soon mourning their marriage.

By this time his drinking habits had begun to destroy his good looks, and Romeo was degenerating into Bardolph. But his fascination remained, and when he met Esther Ogle at Devonshire House, though she started by calling him a 'terrible creature' and a 'fright', she soon came under his spell. Her early antagonism put him on his mettle, and he determined to win her, though he was more than twice her age. She capitulated, but her father, the Dean of Winchester, tried to prevent the marriage by insisting that Sheridan should settle £15,000 on her. To the astonishment of everyone Sheridan found the money by that abstruse process of mortgaging shares in Drury Lane Theatre, and the marriage took place on 27 April 1795. With part of her money he bought an estate, Polesden in Surrey, and became a country gentleman, in which capacity he was popular with the poor, fighting against the enclosure of their common lands, letting his farm tenants pay little or no rent in a bad year, helping the needy, and refusing to punish poachers or thieves, saying that they wanted what they stole more than he did. At moments he took a keen interest in the estate, at other moments no interest at all. He had little taste for rural scenery, and though he liked to blaze away at birds and rabbits he seldom hit one.

It is perhaps needless to say that his second marriage ran on uneven lines. Esther was wayward and uneconomical, like himself, and they were not interested in the same things. His letters to her were full of affectionate terms and sensual endearments. He called her 'Hecca', praised her emerald eyes, said she was his 'only delight in life', his 'only real pleasure on earth'. When she failed to write he was in despair, but she comforted him with: 'How much better you are than anything on earth, and how well I love you.' A son, Charles Brinsley, was born to them in January 1796, and this appeared to seal their attachment, but a few years later her indifference to his interests coupled with his drinking habits caused a cleavage, and she talked of a separation. At length he persuaded her to make the best of him. He could not endure domestic friction, and one of his last letters to her contains this sentence: 'Never again let one harsh word pass between us during the period, which may not perhaps be long, that we are in this world together. . . .'

He had far more in common with Tom, the son of his first wife, than he had with his second wife, and did everything in his power to further the lad's interest, even borrowing money from the Prince of Wales to get Tom into Parliament, a thing he would never have done for himself. Tom inherited some of his father's gift for witty repartee, and they had many friendly spars together. Having expressed a wish to enter Parliament, Tom said: 'I think, father, that many men who are called great patriots in the House of Commons are great humbugs. For my part, if I get into Parliament, I will pledge myself to no party, but write upon my forehead in legible characters "To be let".' Upon which his father suggested: 'And under that, Tom, write "Unfurnished".' The father was solicitous for the boy's health, fearful that he would fall a victim to his mother's disease, as indeed he did; and once, when Tom was in a highly nervous condition, a servant dropped a lot of plates with an immense clatter. Their host rebuked the fellow, saying: 'I suppose you've broken all of them.' 'No, sir, not one.' 'Then, damn it!' exclaimed Dick, 'you have made all that noise for nothing.' In his miraculous manner Sheridan raised £1,500 when his son became co-respondent in a divorce suit, for Tom also inherited his father's weakness for married women; and, on the young man's announcement that he intended to marry, Sheridan thought he was acting too rashly: 'Tom, if you marry Caroline Callander, I'll cut you off with a shilling.' 'Then, sir, you must borrow it', said Tom, who eloped with the said Caroline, a lovely Scottish heiress. They were married in June 1805 and their three daughters were renowned for beauty in the years ahead, becoming the Hon. Mrs Norton, Lady Dufferin and the Duchess of Somerset. The manner in which Sheridan cut his son off with a shilling was not common with parents who issued the threat. First he influenced the directors to appoint Tom manager of Drury Lane Theatre; then he helped the young man to become joint-proprietor of the Lyceum; and when the Prince of Wales bestowed upon Sheridan the Receivership of the Duchy of Cornwall, the recipient implored his benefactor with tears in his eyes to transfer the appointment to Tom. But the Prince refused, saying that it was not only justifiable but honourable to himself to select his old friend for the office.

This sinecure brought Sheridan about £900 a year, with occasional pickings. In 1810 he and his wife were staying the night with the Creeveys at Richmond, and the two men were left alone after dinner. 'A damned odd thing happened to me this morning', Sheridan confided in Creevey, 'and Hester and I have agreed in coming down here today that no human being shall ever know of it as long as we live; so that nothing but my firm conviction that Hester is at this moment telling it to Mrs Creevey could induce me to tell it to you.' He had called at Cox's bank, where he had frequently cajoled a clerk to advance him more than his due from the auditorship of the Duchy. The clerk was in cheerful mood and on being asked for £10 wanted to know whether Sheridan had received his letter. But Sheridan refused to accept two-penny post letters because he never had the money to pay for them, the recipient being responsible for the cost. The clerk said that £1,300 had been placed to the Receiver's credit, as a large fine had been paid for one of the estates in the Duchy, and this sum was Sheridan's percentage as auditor.

Creevey informs us that Sheridan promptly took a house at Barnes Terrace and spent the lot in two months, giving dinners and driving about in a large job coach on which his family arms were painted.

Creevey saw a good deal of Sheridan at the Pavilion, Brighton, during the first decade of the nineteenth century, and vouches for the fact that 'I never saw Sheridan . . . take the least more liberty in the Prince's presence than if it had been the first day he had ever seen him. . . . The Prince always showed by his manner that he thought Sheridan a man any prince might be proud of as his friend.' But Sheridan once took a liberty with the Prince. At Boodle's Club in June 1789 His Royal Highness drank so many bumpers to his brother the Duke of York, who had just survived a duel unscathed, that the members asked Sheridan to get him off the premises before he had to be carried. Persuasion proving unsuccessful, Dick pushed the bottle away with the words, 'You *shall not* drink any more.' The Prince was angry, saying 'Sheridan, I love you better than anyone, but *shall not* is what I can't put up with.' However, he left on his legs.

In those days heavy drinking was regarded as a sport, and men admitted their drunkenness without shame, though Sheridan was not always willing to ascribe his unsteady gait to liquor. 'Pray let me caution you', he wrote to Creevey, 'not to expose yourself to the *air* after dinner, as I find malicious people disposed to attribute to wine what was clearly the mere effect of the atmosphere.' The quantity of wine drunk nearly every evening at the Pavilion, Brighton, would have been notable in any company of inebriates; and the royal host's horror of tea-drinking would have surprised temperance reformers. Lady Harrington and her family came under his observation and provoked this comment: 'Whether it be taste or insanity I cannot say . . . I have seen them drink tea just before dinner, I have even seen them drink tea after supper, and the whole family, young and old, were possessed with this slipslop propensity.' From which we may surmise that if any tea-drinking took place at the Pavilion it was done conspiratorially behind locked doors.

RICHARD BRINSLEY SHERIDAN   115

Sheridan was the licensed buffoon at many of these gatherings, and he often played pranks like a high-spirited boy when well past the age of fifty. Once he entered the drawing-room disguised as a police officer with the object of arresting the Dowager Lady Sefton for taking part in some illegal sport. Another time the company were playing a game in the dark, and he sat on the lap of a haughty Russian dame, who kicked up a shindy. He often slept at the Pavilion, and one evening in 1805, having drunk too much, he asked Creevey to tell the Prince that he had gone to bed. But the Prince refused to believe that he was unwell, handed Creevey a bottle of claret, and said: 'I'll drink a glass of wine with him, and if he refuses I admit he must be damned bad indeed.' Sheridan could not oblige and remained in bed till after supper, when he suddenly appeared in the ball-room among the dancers at 2 a.m. 'powdered as white as snow, as smartly dressed as ever he could be from top to toe.' He asked Creevey to accompany him to the kitchen for a bite of supper, and in a very short while all the servants were attending to his wants. He ate his fill, drank a bottle of claret, and was happily dancing between 3 and 4 in the morning.

It happened that at the beginning of November that year he and Creevey travelled to London together. Sheridan insisted that they should spend a night on the road at the Cock in Sutton, where he was well known and would be able to arrange a nice little dinner. They set off in Sheridan's hired chaise, with the box-keeper of Drury Lane in the dicky, a man named Edwards, who at that time acted as Sheridan's valet when away from London. They arrived at the Cock, where Sheridan was obviously unknown, and as his letter had not arrived no dinner had been prepared. He seemed mystified and kept going in and out of the room with a bothered and preoccupied air. At last a meal was set before them: soup, fish, woodcock and other courses, including claret, sherry and port. It soon became clear that Sheridan had brought it all with him, having had it prepared by a cook at the Pavilion.

Creevey noticed at some dinner in 1806 that a certain lady was ignored by the rest of the party, 'but old Sherry with his usual good taste was very attentive to her'. The Creeveys dined with the Sheridans and were waited on by theatre box-keepers, scene-shifters, thief-takers and sheriff's officers, who acted as un-liveried servants. Even in dismal mood Sheridan could be very funny, though according to Mrs Creevey his jests were some-times a little obscure after an evening's drinking. 'At 2 o'clock in the morning', she wrote to her daughter in July 1806, 'that terrible Sheridan seduced Mr Creevey into Brooks's, where they stayed till 4, when Sherry *affectionately* came home with him, and upstairs to see me. They were both so very merry, and so much pleased with each other's jokes, that, though they could not repeat them to me very distinctly, I was too much amused to scold them as they deserved.'

Creevey, a Whig, always felt a trifle anxious over Sheridan's independence, though greatly admiring 'such extraordinary talents'. As we have seen, Sheridan kept his head over the French Revolution while Whigs and Tories were losing theirs, and later, recognising the danger of Whiggish fraternisation with Napoleon, he sided with the Tories, though he did not agree that everything depended on Pitt, telling the House: 'No single man can save the country. If a nation depends only upon one man, it cannot, and, I will add, does not deserve to, be saved. It can only be done by the Parliament and the people.' Pitt died in 1806, his Government being followed by 'All the Talents', headed by Fox. Incidentally Sheridan christened them by that name, just as the Bank of England became known as 'The Old Lady of Threadneedle Street' from a passage in one of his speeches. Fox had promised him a seat in the Cabinet, but the leading Whigs distrusted his freedom of mind and he became the Treasurer of the Navy, with apartments in Somerset House, where he celebrated his appointment with a sumptuous enter-tainment, attended by the Prince of Wales and half the nobility. A dinner, a ball, a supper, music and songs, must have compelled him to borrow a substantial advance on his salary. He made it clear that the Cabinet could never expect him to sacrifice his independence of opinion to any consideration of office, 'at least, if ever they should so expect, they would be disappointed.' Which explains why he remained out of the Cabinet. But the combination of talent did not last. Fox died in September 1806; Sheridan replaced him as member for Westminster after a furious election, his supporters at Stafford never forgiving him for deserting them; and, when the King demanded an assurance from his new Ministers that they would bring in no measure of relief for the Roman Catholics, the Cabinet resigned; upon which Sheridan, who knew that such an assurance could not be binding, declared: 'I have known many men knock their heads against a wall, but I have never before heard of a man collecting bricks and building a wall for the express purpose of knocking out his own brains against it.' At the General Election which followed the dissolution of Parliament in 1807 the Whiggish nobility ganged up to prevent Sheridan's re-election for Westminster, and with the assistance of the Prince of Wales he was returned for Ilchester.

Meanwhile he was making a steady income out of Drury Lane Theatre, though he had made one grave mistake. In 1796 a youngster of nineteen named William Ireland managed to convince not only Sheridan but a leading Shakespearean actor, J. P. Kemble, and a leading Shakespearean scholar, Edmund Malone, that the manuscript of a play called *Vortigern and Rowena* was written by Shakespeare. It was played for one night because the audience decided it was not by Shakespeare, and Sheridan had to foot the bill. But a play by 'Monk' Lewis, *Castle Spectre*, was a huge success; so much so that when the author, who had not received his fees, offered to bet Sheridan all the money his play had earned, Sheridan said: 'No, I can't afford to do that, but I'll bet you all it is worth.' He frequently helped to furbish the works of others, and an actor who had a lot of singing to do and a great many words to learn begged him to make a certain speech as short as possible. Sheridan obliged with a single line: 'There stands my Louisa's cottage; she must be either in it or out of it', which got the laugh of the evening.

Sheridan also adapted certain plays, one of them, from the German of Kotzebue, being called *Pizarro* and produced with acclamation in May 1799. It is a turgid and tedious work, and its sole interest for us is that it illustrates the declension of the playwright into the politician. Much of its patriotic piffle was used by him in the House of Commons, a suitable place for it, and the author was so proud of the stuff that he authorised its publication, although in the days of his genius he had already laughed such absurdity off the boards in *The Critic*. What contributed to its success was a spectacular production and the fact that the nation had recently been thrilled by Nelson's victory at the Battle of the Nile. There was a lot of music in the show, and though Sheridan had no ear for it he was able by making rumbling noises to get exactly what he wanted from Michael Kelly the composer. Incredible though it may seem, the author was polishing off the concluding scenes of the play during the last rehearsal on the day of the first performance. In an agony of apprehension, Mrs Siddons, Charles Kemble and William Barrymore must have been among the world's finest memorisers in order to learn the remainder of their parts before the curtain went up that evening.

The performances of Sarah Siddons were of course the outstanding events of Sheridan's management of Drury Lane Theatre, but one other episode is worth mentioning. A boy actor named William Betty drove playgoers off their heads, or further off their heads than usual. He was one of those freaks, like a performing sea-lion, that occur at intervals and induce convulsions in the half-baked. This 'Young Roscius', as he was called, having made a sensation in Ireland and Scotland, was thirteen years old when he appeared in London. So great were the crowds fighting to enter the theatre that the military had to deal with them, and the House of Commons adjourned to see him as Hamlet. At the age of seventeen he went to Christ's College, Cambridge, and the rest of his stage career was on a less elevated level.

On 24 February 1809 a tragedy befell Sheridan. The House of Commons were debating on the Peninsular War when the

windows were irradiated by a red glare and the news spread
that Drury Lane Theatre was on fire. A member suggested that
the debate should be adjourned owing to a calamity suffered by
'a respectable individual, a member of that House'. But Sheridan
rose to say that 'whatever might be the extent of the private
calamity, I hope it will not interfere with the public business
of the country', and then drove to the theatre. Having viewed
the scene he entered the Piazza Coffee-House and calmly watched
the conflagration through the window, helped by a bottle or two
of his favourite sustenance. A friend expressed astonishment at
the tranquillity of his demeanour. 'A man may surely be allowed
to take a glass of wine at his own fireside,' he replied.

When everything else failed, his wit always came to the
rescue. As he took immense labour and trouble over his works
and speeches, writing many passages over and over again, he
was accused by envious dullards of carefully preparing his witty
sallies and waiting for occasions to deliver them; but, as his life
was about as active as that of a dozen other men, the charge is
clearly ridiculous. No doubt some of his sayings had been evolved
before publication, but no man can obtain a genuine reputation
for wit whose genius is not constantly displayed on the spur of
the moment, and most of Sheridan's repartees were obviously
impromptu. A few examples will suffice. General Tarleton had
boasted of having butchered more men and lain with more women
than anybody else. Sheridan heard of the boast and instantly commented: '*Lain with.* What a weak expression! He should have
said *ravished.* Rapes are the relaxation of murder.' On being
warned that heavy drinking would destroy the coat of his stomach,
he remarked: 'Then my stomach must digest in its waistcoat.'
The company thought he was cornered when the Duchess of
Argyll asked: 'Why do our young men of birth persist in
dressing, looking and talking like boxers, grooms and coachmen?' Sheridan could throw some light on the problem: 'My
dear madam, I never had a turn for family secrets, but I suspect
birth to be the general cause.' Much of his humour arose from
his financial predicaments. Wearing a pair of brand-new boots,

he asked his friends to guess how he came by them. All their shots were wide of the mark, and 'No, you've not hit it, nor ever will', he declared: 'I bought and paid for them.' A creditor insisted that he should name a date for the settlement of a long overdue account, and he was agreeable: 'Certainly, the Day of Judgment – but no, stay, that is a busy day – make it the day after.' Many of his creditors dunned him for sums he had already paid. A young man at one of his dinner-parties noticed that he was most attentive to a particular guest, flattering him and filling him up with drink. In time the guest fell drunk on the floor and Sheridan told his servant: 'Jack, take his hat and give him to the watch.' The young man, amazed at such an inhospitable proceeding, asked for an explanation, which Sheridan gave him: 'Oh, he's only the bailiff of a man who says falsely that I owe him money.'

The burning of Drury Lane Theatre ruined Sheridan, inasmuch as he could no longer derive a regular income from it, though when a committee was formed under Samuel Whitbread to rebuild it Sheridan's share in the property was estimated at about £28,000. Whitbread, a brewer and politician, was excessively cautious and Sheridan had great difficulty in getting his due except in driblets. He was allowed 'no concern or connection of any kind whatever with the new undertaking', and on this point Whitbread remained firm. But Sheridan experienced one more moment of glory before the shadows fell. He went to Oxford for the purpose of receiving an honorary degree, but at the last moment encountered some professorial opposition and his name was withdrawn at his own request. Invited to attend the ceremony in the Sheldonian, he entered before the official procession, was tumultuously received by the assembly, and when he was seen to take an ordinary seat the theatre echoed with cries: 'Sheridan among the Doctors!' So he was conducted to the chairs occupied by the Doctors and enjoyed the unique distinction of sitting among them unrobed.

The fates were now conspiring against the man who had once been a popular hero. In 1811 the Prince was finally installed as

Regent of the realm, and to Sheridan's disgust he maintained the Tories in power, treating his old allies as Prince Hal had treated Falstaff and Company on becoming Henry V; but then the Whigs annoyed him by thinking they could control him as easily as Falstaff thought he could run the country the moment Hal was King. Sheridan felt that as the seat at Ilchester had been obtained for him by the Prince he could not hold it while continually voting against the Regent's Tory Ministers, and at the next election again stood for Stafford. But the townsmen of that place had not forgiven him for deserting them in favour of Westminster, and he was defeated, the result being partly owing to the fact that he could not get the money out of Whitbread with which to bribe the voters.

When Drury Lane Theatre was reopened in 1812 the prologue was written by a young poet named Lord Byron, who soon met Sheridan and was enchanted by him, recording that '*he* talked and *we* listened without one yawn from six till one in the morning.' At some gathering Byron declared that whatever Sheridan had done was the best of its kind, having written the best comedy (*The School for Scandal*), the best opera (*The Duenna*), the best farce (*The Critic*), and made the best oration (on Warren Hastings), ever conceived or heard in his country. This statement was repeated to Sheridan next day and he burst into tears, on hearing which Byron wrote in his diary: 'Poor Brinsley! If they were tears of pleasure, I would rather have said those few, but sincere, words than have written the Iliad . . .' But Sheridan's tears were a mixture of pleasure and pain. No longer having a seat in the House of Commons, he was subject to arrest for debt, and in August 1813 he was taken to a sponging-house in Tooke's Court, Cursitor Street, for a debt of £600. From there he wrote an agonised appeal to Whitbread, whose action in withholding money had placed him in such a position. Either Whitbread or the Regent delivered him in three days, and when he reached home he burst into a long passionate fit of weeping.

At the request of his friend the Earl of Essex, he paid one visit to the new Drury Lane Theatre to see Edmund Kean, and during an interval he was found in the Green-room surrounded by the actors, who drank a bumper to his health. Some of his old friends sent him money and one of them lent him a house in Savile Row, which was soon besieged with creditors. The Prince Regent later asserted that he had placed £3,000 to Sheridan's credit, so that he could get back into Parliament, but that the solicitor who received the money had used it to pay debts. This may have been true, though the Prince had difficulty in distinguishing between fact and fiction. Sheridan himself suffered from mental confusion owing to alcohol, though when picked up drunk in the street he was witty enough to hiccup his identity: 'Gentlemen . . . my name is Wil-ber-force.' (William Wilberforce was noted for his efforts to suppress the slave trade and for exceptional sobriety.)

The vultures were gathering, and Sheridan took to his bed, unable to digest food and suffering from ulcers. On 15 May 1816, he wrote from Savile Row to beg Samuel Rogers for £150: 'I am absolutely undone and broken-hearted . . . They are going to put the carpets out of window, and break into Mrs Sheridan's room and *take me* – for God's sake let me see you.' Rogers sent the money by Thomas Moore, who found Sheridan cheerful and even hopeful that the sale of his works would settle his affairs if only he could get up. Mrs Sheridan was also ill with cancer, and disorder reigned in the house. In the hall, bare of furniture but full of creditors, Sheridan had caused a notice to be posted: 'I know your necessities before you ask them, and your ignorance in asking.' The Regent got to hear of his condition and sent money, but Mrs Sheridan declined it, knowing that her husband did not wish for help in that quarter. At length, a sheriff's officer arrested Sheridan and would have carried him off in his blankets if Dr Bain had not said that his patient would die and the man would be prosecuted for murder. Bain contemplated an operation and asked Sheridan if he had ever sustained one. 'Yes, when sitting for my portrait or having my hair cut' was the reply.

The threatened sale of his first wife's portrait by Reynolds affected him more than anything else and increased the agitation which exacerbated his internal condition. After periods of great pain and semi-consciousness, peace came to him on 7 July 1816. His body was taken to the house of a friend in Westminster, whence the funeral procession passed to the Abbey. The pall-bearers and mourners included dukes, marquises, earls, viscounts, bishops, barons, right honourables, and the Lord Mayor of London. He was buried in Poet's Corner next to Garrick, and perhaps the worst thing that can be said against him is that he would much rather have been placed among the politicians.

4

Sydney Smith

A Christmas house-party at Sheridan's Polesden residence in 1808 included a professional comedian Charles Mathews, a journalistic joker Henry Brougham, and a humorous clergyman Sydney Smith, the last of whom reported that the details of his two-days stay were 'not uncomical'. The guests were entertained with a lavish dinner, superb wines, and excellent music. Afterwards there was a concert, but the fiddlers stopped playing because a blind fiddler suddenly arrived and insisted on sharing in the performance. He turned out to be Mathews, who was excessively funny in his self-cast part. The time came for the well-satisfied guests to retire; but not a candle could be found in the house, and the party had to stumble upstairs in the dark and feel their way to bed. Next morning's breakfast supplied all that the stomach of man could desire, except butter. 'This is not a butter county', Sheridan explained. But no one bothered about candles, butter or anything else, declared Sydney Smith, when under the spell of Sheridan's wit and conversation. It may not have been apparent at the time, but a greater wit and more richly endowed personality than Sheridan, Mathews and Brougham put together was a member of that house-party, the Church of England parson who supplied these details.

Sydney Smith was born at Woodford in Essex on 3 June 1771. His father, whose money had been inherited from commercial forebears, was of a nomadic nature and when not engaged in travelling about the world spent his time buying houses in various parts of England, spoiling them in his attempts to improve them, and selling them at a loss. Four sons and a daughter were born at different residences, two of the boys being sent to Eton, two to Winchester, where Sydney was educated and introduced to all the horrors of public-school life in those days. In after years he wrote passionately against the iniquities and absurdities of such a system, and even had the hardihood to attack the so-called manliness of games, 'in which the greatest blockheads commonly excel the most'. As for learning the classics, he derided the whole business, boys being taught to 'love the instrument better than the end . . . not what may be read in Greek, but Greek itself'. In spite of the prevailing brutality and stupidity he did well, ending up as Prefect of Hall. In 1789 he became a scholar of New College, Oxford, where he worked hard and lived simply while most of his contemporaries drank too much and took life easily. At the end of two years he was made a Fellow of his College, receiving £100 a year, and thereafter he had no financial help from his father. Somehow he paid £30 out of his first year's pittance to settle the debts of a brother. 'I did it with my heart's blood', he confessed. It meant solitude and rigorous living for him, and he looked back on his years at Oxford with almost as much distaste as Winchester had aroused.

In 1792 Sydney took his degree and had to decide on a profession. With some inclination to be a doctor, he had a strong predilection for the Bar, but his father refused to help him, and the only respectable alternative then was to be a parson. He was ambitious and knew that 'in the church a man is thrown into life with his hands tied, and bid to swim; he does well if he keeps his head above water'. But lacking private means and parental assistance he had no choice, and took orders in 1794. Had the episcopal hierarchy known what would happen as a result of his ordination, they would have clubbed together and made him a barrister.

For three years he ministered to the poor on Salisbury Plain, having received the curacy of Netheravon, near Amesbury, from the squire, Michael Hicks-Beach, M.P. for Cirencester. At first it was impossible to persuade the farmers and labourers to attend church, but he gradually overcame their resistance, and his charitable work, especially for the children, gained their approval. The dullness of the place was profound, the arrival of the butcher's cart from Salisbury once a week being the chief event. He felt as if he were dead and buried, but he had hopes of 'a joyful resurrection' when Hicks-Beach asked if he would act as friend and tutor to Michael, the squire's eldest son, at a German university preparatory to Oxford. Sydney did not take long to answer in the affirmative, and left Netheravon in the spring of 1797. Weimar was their chosen destination, where Goethe and Schiller resided, but the unforeseen activities of Napoleon made a scholarly existence insecure on the Continent, and they decided in favour of Edinburgh, where the leading professors, Dugald Stewart, John Playfair, James Gregory and Joseph Black, were increasing the fame of the University. Visiting the industrial districts of the north and climbing Skiddaw on the way, they reached Edinburgh in June 1798 and took lodgings in South Hanover Street. Sydney remained in the city for five years, during which he created an epoch in the literary and political history of Great Britain.

He attended the University lectures, did a little preaching, looked after Michael, made several lifelong friends, and enjoyed social life, though he found that 'it requires a surgical operation to get a joke well into a Scotch understanding'. When Michael was ready for Oxford his younger brother took his place at Edinburgh; and as Sydney already had another pupil and was earning about £800 a year he resolved to get married. For some years he had been engaged to his sister's friend Catherine Pybus, and in July 1800 they were united. He obeyed one of his marriage vows at once by endowing his wife with all his worldly goods, consisting of 'six small silver teaspoons, which from much wear had become the ghosts of their former selves'. But Catherine had a small dowry, Hicks-Beach sent a cheque for £750, and they were able to take a house, No. 46 George Street. Their forty-five years of married life were wholly happy and entirely

free from friction, and in case this sounds dull it should be added
that Sydney never failed to create an atmosphere of laughter,
good humour and high spirits.

Although they were opposed in politics, Walter Scott became
very fond of Sydney, and they met at the weekly dinners of the
Friday Club, which Scott started as a northern counterpart of
Johnson's Club. Three of its members call for notice because
they helped to make a success of *The Edinburgh Review*: Francis
Jeffrey, Henry Brougham and Francis Horner. The 'bold and
sagacious idea' of founding this periodical arose in the mind of
Sydney, who persuaded the others to join him in the venture.
Jeffrey, who soon became the *Review's* most famous editor, was
at first opposed to the project, but he could not resist Sydney's
infectious enthusiasm and at last gave way. It was an extremely
dangerous experiment because their intention was to make the
policy of reform articulate at a time when any criticism of
Toryism was regarded as treachery to the country, when a man
who held progressive opinions was considered seditious, and
when success in any profession could only be attained by time-
serving. Henry Dundas was at that time the chief power in
Scotland, the instrument of William Pitt's policy, and criticism
of his acts was tantamount to blasphemy. If discovered, the
founders of *The Edinburgh Review* would therefore be marked
men, and its contributors faced with professional ruin. Nevertheless, under Sydney's persuasion, the risk was taken, and the first
number appeared in October 1802. It was an instantaneous
success. Sydney saw the first two issues through the press, after
which Jeffrey became the regular salaried editor, but since wit
and humour are the sole preservatives of polemics the only
articles by the early contributors that can still be read with delight
are the irreverent, frivolous and satirical effusions from the pen
of Sydney Smith, who attacked with ridicule every oppressive
law and obsolete convention of the time. All the evils exposed
by the *Review* were eventually rectified by the reform party
when it came to power a generation later, and it would be
impossible to over-estimate the influence on the public mind

K

and on Parliament of this, the first great critical quarterly, in which Macaulay's essays began to appear more than twenty years after its establishment.

Having exploded his bomb, Sydney took his wife and a recently born daughter to London, settling down at No. 8 Doughty Street, where a son Douglas was added to the family. He quickly made friends, and soon the pair were guests at the great home of Whiggery, Holland House, Sydney even daring to make jokes at the expense of its dictatorial mistress, Lady Holland. He did a certain amount of preaching, but was too honest in the expression of his opinions to please those who might have helped him, and a sermon he gave in Temple Church favouring Catholic emancipation caused great offence. He needed money badly, but a year passed before he could improve his position. Towards the close of 1804 he was asked to deliver a series of lectures on Moral Philosophy at the Royal Institution in Albemarle Street. They became the talk of the town, and the place was soon besieged with people begging for seats. Describing the sensation he had created as 'the most successful swindle of the season', he said that the lectures had caused 'such an uproar as I never remember to have been excited by any other literary imposture.' In one of them he originated the phrase 'a square peg in a round hole', which was roughly how he saw himself during this sudden burst of fame. More lectures were demanded and he was asked to name his terms, which enabled him to take and furnish a house in Orchard Street. His reputation brought him many invitations to the homes of the nobility, and he was much too fond of good dinners to refuse them, telling Jeffrey: 'In this pleasing and detestable place I neglect every duty and have no more virtue left in me than hath an antient harlot.'

But his virtue was about to be restored. In the middle of 1807 he spent some months with his family in a cottage at Sonning, near Reading, and composed a series of 'Letters', supposedly written by one 'Peter Plymley' to his brother 'Abraham', a country clergyman. They contained a scathing indictment of the average Protestant's attitude to Catholic emancipation, but

were so entertaining that no new novel could be more eagerly
devoured. Their effect was likened to that of a spark on a heap
of gunpowder. For the first time the barbaric absurdity of
Protestant opinion was exposed to the world, and nothing kills
like ridicule. The anti-emancipationists were no longer regarded
as pillars of religious integrity and upholders of the national
faith, but as intolerant ignoramuses and objects of fun. The
ground was at last cleared for rational discussion, and Sydney's
raillery ultimately benefited the Catholics far more than all the
serious arguments of those who appealed solely to reason. The
authorities did their utmost to identify the author, but the
secret was well kept and, apart from intelligent folk like Sheridan,
Byron and the Hollands, no one knew for certain the real writer's
name until the 'Letters' were included in Sydney's collected
works thirty years after.

The Whiggish Government known as 'All the Talents' was
useful in one respect. Through the influence of Lady Holland the
living of Foston-le-Clay, some twelve miles from York, was
given to Sydney Smith in 1806. In those days the clergy frequently
did not reside in their parishes but paid some neighbouring
curate to perform the necessary duties; and Sydney might have
remained permanently in London if a new Archbishop of York
had not called his attention to an Act of 1803 enforcing rectors
to live in their rectories. Though hating the country, where
in his opinion the squires were idiots and he always had the feeling
that creation would expire before tea-time, he was not a man to
complain but always and instantly made the best of a bad job. Also
he loved his wife and children and his main object in life was to
make everyone round him as happy and cheerful as possible.
Modest as well as merry, he was completely unreserved, saying
that he lived with open windows and doors and could be seen
by those who wished to look at him as clearly in five minutes as
in five years. When alone he suffered from depression, when in
company he felt exhilarated, and his gaiety affected everyone
else. His conversation combined sense and nonsense in equal
measure, and he was certainly the most entertaining talker on

record. Nor did he reserve his wit and humour for special
occasions, but kept his family in fits of mirth for hours together,
and sometimes sent the servants running from the room in peals
of laughter. His conversation and writing were spontaneous,
welling out of him without the least straining for effect, and
his actions had the same air of unpremeditation. He kept himself
constantly employed on all sorts of objects, and the interest he
took in people and things was as instinctive as his joviality.

This remarkably uninhibited parson flung himself into
parochial work in 1809, having reached the age of thirty-eight.
With £200 which he got for the publication of his sermons, he
took his family to Heslington, close to York, where he lived for
five years, there being no rectory at Foston, which had been
without a resident clergyman since the time of Charles II.
'Fresh from London, not knowing a turnip from a carrot, I was
compelled to farm three hundred acres, and without capital to build
a parsonage house.' Very soon he felt 'an ungovernable interest
about my horses or my pigs or my plants', and became absorbed
in the mysteries of ploughing, baking, brewing, churning,
drilling beans and fattening poultry. He taught his eldest child,
doctored his family as well as the poor of the parish, became a
Justice of the Peace and annoyed his fellow-magistrates by
always favouring poachers against the squires, started allotments
for the poor, tried to make candles and stop chimneys from
smoking, and fed the hungry with broth, rice and porridge. He
made up his mind to take no part in the sports of the gentry,
and thought that the clergy who did were endangering their
faith: 'Ten thousand good shots dispersed over the country do
more harm to the cause of religion than the arguments of
Voltaire and Rousseau.' At first he hoped that the Hollands
would be able to get him a living in London or near-by, but as
time went on his prospects dimmed and he became reconciled
to his lot: 'I may see as many crosiers in the clouds as I please,
but when I sit down seriously to consider what I shall do upon
important occasions, I must presume myself rector of Foston for
life. God in his mercy grant that this may be pure hypothesis.'

In 1813, finding an architect too expensive, he added that profession to his others, hired a carpenter and mason, and began work on his rectory in June. He bought four oxen for the waggons in which bricks and mortar were transported, but the condition of the roads was such that the beasts stuck in the mud, and he replaced them with a team of horses. That autumn his second son Wyndham was born and the building went on: 'I live trowel in hand . . . my whole soul is filled up by lath and plaster.' An eight-week frost held up the operations, which were redoubled early in 1814, and on 20 March the family, having been bogged in the field leading to the house, slept in the carpetless, chairless, wet-walled rectory. The money he had spent on parsonage, farm-buildings, laying out the grounds and road-making, came to about £4,000, much of which he had to borrow, and for many years £130 out of his annual income of £600 went to the repayment of his debt. He named his house 'The Rector's Head' and claimed that it was 'equal to any inn on the North Road'. Commodious and comfortable, it still stands, the only visible memorial to the ingenuity of England's greatest wit.

Sydney bought 'an ancient green chariot' at York, and in this conveyance the family visited friends and went to church in wet weather. He contrived all sorts of gadgets for use in the house and grounds, such as air-tubes for the fires, a speaking-trumpet for shouting directions to his labourers, a telescope for keeping them under observation, a Universal Scratcher against which animals could rub themselves instead of damaging gates and hedges in that pursuit. His store-room contained an extra-ordinary assortment of medical appliances, including a suit of rheumatic armour, something like a diver's costume, each part of which could be filled with hot water. Everyone in the parish with an illness came to him for treatment, and everyone faced with a problem applied to him for advice. The poor loved him, though he could occasionally be tyrannical. A small girl who was caught eating one of his fallen peaches was made to stand on the lawn all day with a placard bearing the word 'Thief' round her neck; and a lad discovered contemplating his fruit-trees with larcenous intent had his ears pinched with such vigour that they tingled at the remembrance in old age. But such episodes were rare, and a certain incident in the Garden of Eden may have caused the clergy to be sensitive about fruit. He made up for such episodes by keeping a stock of sweets for children who demanded them.

In the midst of all his activities he found time to educate both his boys, write articles for *The Edinburgh Review*, and keep up a correspondence with his friends, from which we may extract a few passages:

'Let me beg of you to take more care of those beautiful geraniums, and not let the pigs in upon them. Geranium-fed bacon is of a beautiful colour; but it takes so many plants to fatten one pig that such a system can never answer.'

'I will write to Mr Bailey on the very interesting subject of venison – a subject which is deemed amongst the clergy a professional one.'

'Lord Tankerville has sent me a whole buck; this necessarily takes up a good deal of my time.'

'What is real piety? What is true attachment to the Church? How are these fine feelings best evinced? The answer is plain: by sending strawberries to a clergyman. Many thanks.'

'Nothing can be more disgusting than an Oratorio. How absurd to see 500 people fiddling like madmen about the Israelites in the Red Sea!'

'You have met, I hear, with an agreeable clergyman. The existence of such a being has been hitherto denied by the naturalists: measure him and put down on paper what he eats.'

On a fellow-wit at Holland House: 'Luttrell, before I taught him better, imagined muffins grew; he was wholly ignorant of all the intermediate processes of sowing, reaping, grinding, kneading and baking.'

Meetings were being held by the clergy all over the country to petition Parliament against the emancipation of the Catholics. In 1825 Sydney turned up at one of them in the Three Tuns, Thirsk,

and at another in the Tiger Inn, Beverley, speaking in the cause
of toleration at both places, but speaking in vain. His friends
visited Foston and he made an annual trip to London. Life
became easier in 1825 when the Earl of Carlisle's influence
obtained another living for him, which could be held along with
Foston, and the following year he went alone to Paris, reporting
his daily doings to his wife. What he saw of the Bourbons made
him prophesy an early revolution, which duly took place, but he
thoroughly enjoyed himself and was introduced by the Hollands
to everyone of note. He admired the profusion of mirrors in
French drawing-rooms, in one of which he saw himself reflected
on every side: 'I took it for a meeting of the clergy, and was
delighted of course.' The only purchase he made for himself was
a huge seal containing the arms of a French peer, which he
decided should henceforth be the arms of his branch of the Smith
family and bought for four francs.

During the three months of Whiggish coalition at the close of
1827 Sydney was made a Canon of Bristol, and next year was
chosen to deliver the Gunpowder Plot anniversary sermon in
the Cathedral. On such occasions, following a banquet and many
Protestant toasts, the sentiments delivered from the pulpit
were violently anti-Catholic, and Sydney's oration urging
emancipation horrified the congregation. The Mayor and
Corporation glared at the preacher. 'Several of them', he said,
'could not keep the turtle on their stomachs.' So greatly were they
vexed that they determined never again to attend that com-
memorative service, and the new Canon was abused in pulpits and
pamphlets. He managed to obtain an exchange of livings, and
in the summer of 1829 moved the family from Foston to Combe
Florey, a pretty Somerset village between Taunton and Mine-
head. The recent death of his eldest child, Douglas, had hurt him
more than he could have believed possible, and he was glad to
leave a place where everything reminded him of his lost boy.

Again he ministered to the physical ailments as well as the
spiritual needs of his new parishioners, leaving as little as
possible to 'the professional and graduated homicides', of whose

curative methods he said that 'The Sixth Commandment is suspended by one medical diploma from the north of England to the south'. He declared that the villagers liked being doctored by him because he never mixed the Thirty-nine Articles with his prescriptions, and his visitors were equally pliable: 'Everybody who comes is expected to take a little something; I consider it a delicate compliment when my guests have a slight illness here'. Despite the beauty of his new surroundings he could not like the country, referring to 'the serious apoplexy of a country life', and after the marriage of his two daughters his longing for London increased. Flowers, green turf and birds were not worth an hour's rational conversation, he said, and 'all lives out of London are mistakes'. He loved to entertain his metropolitan friends, and it pleased him to be able to enlighten them on serious subjects. Henry Luttrell came, and 'was very agreeable, but spoke too lightly, I thought, of veal soup. I took him aside, and reasoned the matter with him, but in vain. To speak the truth, Luttrell is not steady in his judgments on dishes'.

With the arrival of the Whigs in power after the death of George IV, the leading writers for *The Edinburgh Review* were elevated, and Sydney expected a bishopric; but the politicians were frightened of his mental independence and all they dared offer was a Residentiary Canonry of St Paul's Cathedral with an income of £2,000 a year. This meant being in London for three months annually, which delighted him. A future Prime Minister, Lord Melbourne, said that 'Sydney Smith has done more for the Whigs than all the clergy put together, and our not making him a bishop is mere cowardice', but disinterested appreciation of genius is not a quality to be expected of politicians in office. However, their failure in gratitude did not lessen his efforts in the cause of progress, and when the first Reform Bill was rejected by the House of Lords he delivered a speech in the Castle Hall, Taunton, which turned that august assembly into an object of ridicule and added a new character to the common speech:

'I do not mean to be disrespectful, but the attempt of the Lords to stop the progress of reform reminds me very forcibly of the great storm of Sidmouth, and the conduct of the excellent Mrs Partington on that occasion . . . In the midst of this sublime and terrible storm, Dame Partington, who lived upon the beach, was seen at the door of her house with mop and pattens, trundling her mop, squeezing out the sea-water, and vigorously pushing away the Atlantic Ocean. The Atlantic was roused. Mrs Partington's spirit was up. But I need not tell you that the contest was unequal. The Atlantic Ocean beat Mrs Partington. She was excellent at a slop or a puddle, but she should not have meddled with a tempest. Gentlemen, be at your ease – be quiet and steady. You will beat Mrs Partington.'

They did; since when Mrs Partington has been a popular member of the House of Commons, still good at a slop or a puddle but useless in a storm.

Sydney would have been a most efficient bishop, but he could never have been relied upon to behave like one. Although he described the Church of England as a branch of the Civil Service, he could defend his profession better than anyone else. A country squire became abusive in the heat of argument and said: 'If I had a son who was an idiot, by Jove I'd make him a parson!' 'Very probably', returned Sydney, 'but I see that your father was of a different mind.' On the other hand he made many remarks that orthodox Christians did not expect from the lips of a clergyman. For example:

'The Church attempting to be useful is much as if Sheridan were to take to keeping accounts – but it cannot last.'

'I must believe in the Apostolic Succession, there being no other way of accounting for the descent of the Bishop of Exeter from Judas Iscariot.'

'Before I form any opinion on Establishments, I should like to know the effects they produce on vegetables. Many of our clergy suppose that if there was no Church of England, cucumbers and celery would not grow; that mustard and cress could not be raised. If Establishments are connected so much with the great laws of nature, this makes all the difference; but I cannot believe it.'

'When a man is a fool, in England we only trust him with the immortal concerns of human beings.'

Speaking of Milman's *History of Christianity*: 'No man should write on such subjects unless he is prepared to go the whole *lamb*.'

To a fellow-Canon: 'Please take this service for me, as I am so rheumatic in my *professional* joints.'

On a proposal to surround St Paul's Cathedral with a wooden pavement: 'Let the Dean and Canons lay their heads together and the thing will be done.'

In answer to a lady who said she would go on her knees if he would grant her request: 'I like to see you in that attitude, as it brings me in several hundreds a year.'

Replying to a question as to whether he would object to burying Dissenters: 'I should like to be burying them all day long.'

Reproving an unorthodox person: 'It is a vile heresy and you deserve to be burnt for it – with green faggots.'

The entire bench of bishops thought that Sydney deserved to be burnt with green faggots in 1837, when the first of his Letters to Archdeacon Singleton appeared as a pamphlet. The recently established Ecclesiastical Commission, largely composed of bishops, had made several recommendations, most of which benefited the episcopacy at the expense of the deans and chapters. Sydney suggested that the incomes of the wealthier bishops should be reduced, not those of the lesser dignitaries. He said that men took Holy Orders because they were ambitious to obtain good jobs, a shocking theory to those who liked to believe that the clergy had a sacred vocation. He had no illusions about bishops, who were out of touch with the common life of the Church. 'What bishops like best in their clergy is a dropping-down-deadness of manner', he declared, and he followed up his attacks on the hierarchy with a second Letter in 1838 and a third in 1839, emphasising the material aspect of his profession: 'To get a stall, and to be preceded by men with silver rods, is the bait which the ambitious squire is perpetually holding out to his second son.' A leading Whig, Lord John Russell, wrote to say that the arguments in the first Letter had not convinced him, to which Sydney replied in his second that 'the idea of convincing a Russell that he was wrong never came across my mind. Euclid would have had a bad chance with you if you had happened to have formed an opinion that the interior angles of a triangle were not equal to two right angles'. In biblical fashion Sydney smote both politicians and prelates hip and thigh, and his friend Luttrell asked Thomas Moore: 'Could you have conceived any man taking such pains to upset a brilliant position in Society as Sydney has been taking lately?' The bishops of course were extremely cross, and one of them, the Bishop of Gloucester, announced that Sydney owed his position at St Paul's not to his piety but to his levity, on which the Canon commented: 'Is not this rather strong for a Bishop and does it not appear to you, Mr Archdeacon, as rather too close an imitation of that language which is used in the apostolic occupation of trafficking in fish?' (Billingsgate in short.) He then gave a synopsis of his public work for the reform of abuses, and fervently echoed the Bishop's prayer for divine assistance in the betterment of his Lordship's understanding. As a result of these Letters the episcopal recommendations were considerably modified in the Residence and Plurality Bill then before Parliament.

Sydney engaged in a dozen other controversies, throwing the light of common sense wherever it was needed, and got himself into hot water with the leaders of finance, politics, science and religion; but nothing could affect his popularity in Society, where his ample figure and jovial face, his white hair and rubicund complexion, his hearty laughter and inexhaustible merriment brightened up every dinner-party and reception he attended. For us his chief fault was his superabundant sense of fun which convulsed so many people that they were disabled by laughter from recording his conversation. But we have sufficient illustration of his comical outbursts to show that, besides being a serious and acute social critic, he was an incarnate Falstaff, whose improvisation on Bardolph's nose is no funnier than Sydney's reception of the news that a certain Scot was about to marry an Irish widow twice his age and more than twice his size:

'Going to marry her! Impossible! You mean a part of her; he could not marry her all himself. It would be a case, not of bigamy but trigamy; the neighbourhood or the magistrates should interfere. There is enough of her to furnish wives for a whole parish. One man marry her! – it is monstrous. You might people a colony with her; or give an assembly with her; or perhaps take your morning's walk round her, always provided there were frequent resting-places and you were in rude health. I once was rash enough to try walking round her before breakfast, but only got half-way and gave it up exhausted. Or you might read the Riot Act and disperse her; in short, you might do anything with her but marry her.'

In June 1831 Macaulay went to a large party in order to meet Ramohun Roy, a Brahmin distinguished for learning and knowledge, who had become a Unitarian and so a social curiosity. Ramohun Roy did not turn up, but Sydney Smith was so amusing that Macaulay said the Canon's company was some compensation for missing the Indian. 'Compensation!' exclaimed Sydney: 'Do you mean to insult me? A beneficed clergyman, an orthodox clergyman! . . . to be no more than compensation for a Brahmin; and a heretic Brahmin too; a fellow who has lost his own religion and can't find another; a vile heterodox dog, who, as I am credibly informed, eats beefsteaks in private! A man who has lost his caste! who ought to have melted lead poured down his nostrils if the good old Vedas were in force as they ought to be.'

Innumerable spurts of Sydney's wit, often bordering on burlesque, appear in the memoirs of his time. We may select a few:

'How can a bishop marry? How can he flirt? The most he can say is: "I will see you in the vestry after service".'

On catching sight of the Brighton Pavilion: 'It looks as if St Paul's Cathedral had come down and pupped.'

To a man whose favourite theme was the North Pole, and who complained that Jeffrey had shut him up by damning the North Pole: 'Jeffrey respects nothing, absolutely nothing. Why, you will scarcely credit it, but strictly between ourselves it is not more than a week ago that I heard him speak disrespectfully of the Equator!'

To a child who said that she was stroking the shell of a turtle to please it: 'Why, you might as well stroke the dome of St Paul's to please the Dean and Chapter.'

To a doctor who advised him to take a walk on an empty stomach: 'Whose?'

To his brother 'Bobus' who had been very successful in life: 'You and I are exceptions to the laws of nature. You have risen by your gravity, and I have sunk by my levity.'

To a lady who complained of the oppressive heat: 'Heat, madam! It was so dreadful here that I found there was nothing left for it but to take off my flesh and sit in my bones.'

Towards the end of his life Sydney admired the novels of Dickens as much as he had previously loved those of Scott, and heard with pleasure that Dickens had written to a friend: 'I wish you would tell Mr Sydney Smith that of all the men I ever heard of and never saw, I have the greatest curiosity to see and the greatest interest to know him.' They struck up a friendship and often dined with one another. Possibly an unqualified admiration prevented Dickens from putting Sydney into one of his stories, though the only writer capable of doing justice to such a character was Shakespeare, who had partly done it in *Henry IV*.

As Sydney's creed was primarily rational and humane, he taught practical Christianity. People should be happy and do good: it was as simple as that. There were no rhetorical flourishes and no doctrinal theories in his sermons, which were notable for solid sense and basic morality. For him active benevolence was more important than dogmatic belief, and ritual should not be mistaken for religion. Naturally he found the

Tractarian Movement in the Church of England inimical to common sense, and he attacked the Puseyites in a sermon at St Paul's, telling them that they turned the Christian faith into 'a religion of postures and ceremonies, of circumflexions and genuflexions, of garments and vestures, of ostentation and parade; that they took up tithe of mint and cummin, and neglected the weightier matters of the law – justice, mercy, and the duties of life.' Not that Sydney objected to tithes where material comfort was concerned. In the summer of 1839 his brother Courtenay, whose debts he had paid with his 'heart's blood' at Oxford, died without making a will, and Sydney inherited a third of his estate, over £30,000: 'After buying into the Consols and the Reduced, I read Seneca "On the Contempt of Wealth". What intolerable nonsense! . . . I have been very poor the greater part of my life, and have borne it as well, I believe, as most people, but I can safely say that I have been happier every guinea I have gained.'

He was beginning to feel his age: 'I have gout, asthma, and seven other maladies, but am otherwise very well.' He called gout 'the only enemy that I do not wish to have at my feet'. The older he grew the more bearable a rural life became: 'I am afraid this country does look enchantingly beautiful; you know the power truth has over me.' And even his neighbours appeared less obtuse: 'I must do her the justice to say that when my jokes are explained to her, and she has leisure to reflect upon them, she laughs very heartily.' But no one could be thrilled by existence in these conditions: 'I saw a crow yesterday, and had a distant view of a rabbit today.'

The prospect of death did not daunt him, and, though he felt afraid of 'the very disagreeable methods by which we leave this world', he could extract humour out of common ailments: 'Mrs Sydney has eight distinct illnesses and I have nine. We take something every hour and pass the mixture from one to the other.' They were having trouble with their second son Wyndham, who was quite unmanageable and coarse in his tastes, much given to gambling, drinking and lechery. In his will Sydney left

£200 a year to Wyndham on condition that he lived apart from his mother, after whose death he would inherit the bulk of the property. Wyndham was known in London Society as 'the assassin' because he had once fought a savage dog unarmed. He became a deep drinker and the father of many illegitimate children. His two sisters married well, the elder to a famous physician Dr (later Sir Henry) Holland, the younger to a barrister, Nathaniel Hibbert, who inherited an estate and lived at Munden House, Watford.

At the age of seventy-four Sydney wrote to a French critic, who was preparing an article on his works and wished for personal details: 'I dine with the rich in London, and physic the poor in the country, passing from the sauces of Dives to the sores of Lazarus. I am, upon the whole, a happy man; have found the world an entertaining world, and am thankful to Providence for the part allotted to me in it.'

Towards the close of 1844 an attack of giddiness caused him to be severely dieted. He journeyed to London for the ministrations of his son-in-law Dr Holland and the comfort of his house, No. 56 Green Street, Park Lane, where, he said, 'a suite of rooms are perfectly fitted up for illness and death'. The low diet made him feeble and he could not digest food properly, saying to a friend: 'Ah, Charles, I wish I were allowed even the wing of a roasted butterfly', and to another: 'I feel so weak both in body and mind that I verily believe, if the knife were put into my hand, I should not have strength or energy enough to slide it into a Dissenter.'

Although he knew that death was near, he remained cheerful, his hatred of mental stagnation making him study books on music. At last he was too ill to receive friends, though one of them, Monckton Milnes, managed to gain admission and asked what sort of night he had passed. 'Oh, horrid, horrid, my dear fellow!' exclaimed Sydney: 'I dreamt I was chained to a rock and being talked to death by Harriet Martineau and Macaulay.' He became delirious and was heard to cry out the name of his dead son – 'Douglas, Douglas!' At one lucid interval he bestowed a living on a poor and friendless clergyman; at another he said to the nurse, who jokingly pretended she had used a wrong bottle and given him a dose of ink by mistake: 'Then bring me all the blotting paper there is in the house.'

The end came on 22 February 1845, and those who had once cried with laughter at his fun now wept with grief over his loss. But a great peace descended upon the prelacy.

5

Benjamin Disraeli

In the spring of 1844 a novel entitled *Coningsby* made a sensation both in England and America, and the most eminent Canon of St Paul's Cathedral was curious to meet the author. They dined in a large company and 'I sat next to Sydney Smith, who was delightful', recorded Benjamin Disraeli; 'I don't remember a more agreeable party.' Although he was to meet nearly every leading writer, warrior, statesman and monarch of his age, none of them could make a party so agreeable as his neighbour on that occasion.

Benjamin liked to think that his forefathers had once been great landowners in Spain and merchants in Venice, but knew for a fact that his grandfather had arrived in England half-way through the eighteenth century, had changed his name from Israeli to D'Israeli, and had made a small fortune, inherited by his son Isaac. Every attempt to turn Isaac into a business-man failed: he was a born bookman, and is still remembered for his *Curiosities of Literature*. When not reading in the British Museum, he passed the hours in his library. Having married the daughter of an Italian Jew, their union resulting in four sons and a daughter, he spent his life browsing among books. Their second child, Benjamin, entered the world on 21 December 1804, at a house in what came to be known as Theobald's Road, London, but when the lad reached the age of twelve his grandfather died and the family were sufficiently well-off to move to a better quarter, his next twelve years being spent at No. 6 Bloomsbury Square. Isaac, though a Jew by race, was never one by religion, remaining a contented sceptic all his life, but for the sake of his children's chances in the world he allowed them to be baptised as Christians, and Benjamin joined the Church of England in his thirteenth year, when he went to a school near Walthamstow run by a minister of the Unitarian persuasion. Here he was wretched because he could take no pleasure in the games and interests of the other boys: 'School I detested more than ever I abhorred the world in the darkest moments of my experienced manhood.' But being intensely ambitious, with a love of power, he learnt how to box, and the bullies of the school were soon made aware of his prowess. He left at the end of three years and continued his studies of Greek and Latin at home. Longing for fame and a spectacular career in politics, he yet took his father's advice and at the age of seventeen began work with a firm of solicitors in the City, where he spent three years dreaming of greatness and reading about the deeds of famous men.

In 1824 he and his father spent six weeks on the Continent, where his appetite was whetted for architecture, painting, good wine and good cooking. Already he had decided to drop the profession of law along with the apostrophe in his surname: 'The Bar: pooh! law and bad jokes till we are forty; and then, with the most brilliant success, the prospect of gout and a coronet.' He wanted to cut a great figure, which meant in his case the acquisition of cash: 'To enter high society a man must either have blood, a million, or a genius.' Though conscious of genius, his blood was against him, so he staked all on getting money. In partnership with two friends he gambled on the Stock Exchange, and lost about £7,000 in seven months, a debt that took him nearly thirty years to discharge. Next he thought of a scheme, a daily newspaper to compete with *The Times*, which he put up to his father's friend, the publisher John Murray, who believed in his ability, found half the capital, and wanted Sir Walter Scott's son-in-law J. G. Lockhart to be editor. Disraeli went to Scotland and soon infected Lockhart with his enthusiasm.

But Sir Walter jibbed at the word 'Editor', as in those days a gentleman could not be a journalist, and Disraeli rapidly substituted 'Director-General' for the obnoxious title. Even so the two Scots did not feel happy about it; but Disraeli persuaded Lockhart to talk it over with Murray and took him to London for that purpose, where their conference was expedited by the offer of £1,000 a year to Lockhart as editor of *The Quarterly Review*, a more respectable appointment than the other, together with £1,500 a year for articles in the daily paper and his cooperation 'by all other means consistent with his rank in life'. But a financial panic in the City put an end to their project, the competitor of *The Times* lasted for six months, Murray lost £26,000, and the friendship between the publisher and the enthusiastic organiser cooled.

Having decided that gambling as a means of making a fortune was risky, Disraeli next turned his attention to fiction. He wrote a novel for anonymous publication and called it *Vivian Grey*. It was finished by his twenty-first birthday, arrangements for its publication by Henry Colburn being made by Sara Austen, who had acted as the author's amanuensis, and, to maintain his incognito, had copied the manuscript for the printer. Sara was the wife of Benjamin Austen, a solicitor; both were friends of the Disraeli family, and both believed in the genius of the young novelist. Sara longed to be in the literary swim, stimulated Disraeli in his writing, and enjoyed keeping the authorship secret in her dealings with Colburn. Following much advance puffery the novel made a sensation and earned the writer £200, the publisher having been the gambler this time. But when it became known that Disraeli was the author he was violently attacked in all the papers that had not yet reviewed the work, and it took him several years to recover from the smart. All the same he wrote another volume of *Vivian Grey* while touring northern Italy with the Austens in the autumn of 1826. He did this for the sake of £500 which Colburn gave him for it, and the second part of the story is bad enough to prove that he wrote it against the grain. But in the first volume we have a portrait of Disraeli as he saw himself, intelligent, adroit, ambitious and wittily epigrammatic, as these phrases illustrate:

'How those rooks bore! I hate staying with ancient families; you are always cawed to death.'

'No one is petted so much as a political apostate, except, perhaps, a religious one.'

'He who anticipates his century is generally persecuted when living, and is always pilfered when dead.'

'If you wish to win a man's heart, allow him to confute you.'

For about three years after his return home he was ill from what the doctor called 'chronic inflammation of the membranes of the brain'. At moments of relative well-being he made spectacular appearances in London dressed in striking garments; we hear of blue trousers, green velvet trousers, a canary-coloured waistcoat, etc., and it is not surprising that he was stared at: 'The people quite made way for me as I passed. It was like the opening of the Red Sea, which I now perfectly believe from experience.' His family left Bloomsbury in 1829 for Bradenham, near High Wycombe, where they resided at an old manor house. Here he could avoid his creditors, take a rest-cure and write a novel, *The Young Duke*, which came out in 1831 and contained some typical witticisms:

'Let me die eating ortolans to the sound of soft music.'
'A want of tact is worse than a want of virtue.'

With the money he made on the outright sale of the book to Colburn, and a loan from Austen, he travelled in Spain and the Near East with a friend named Meredith, who was engaged to his sister. He boasted of his fame in being 'the first who has passed the Straits with two canes, a morning and an evening cane'. His foppery displeased the officers of the garrison at Malta, where he appeared in the costumes of a Spanish grandee and a Greek pirate. They went to Athens, called on the Grand Vizier of Turkey, 'who was daily decapitating half the province' of Albania, spent four weeks at Constantinople, a week at

Jerusalem and some months in Egypt, where Disraeli climbed the great pyramid and voyaged 700 miles up the Nile. His friend Meredith died of smallpox in Egypt, and he broke the news to his sister in rather flowery language before starting for England, which he reached in October 1831 just after the House of Lords had rejected the Reform Bill.

At once he plunged into politics and social life, being liked by women, partly envied and partly despised by men. He made up his mind to succeed as a speaker first in the House of Commons, then in the House of Lords. From his novel *Contarini Fleming*, published during this period, we are able to perceive the cause of his social success, a mixture of audacity, vanity and self-assurance. He also brought out an exotic story called *Alroy*, a dream-picture of himself as a conqueror, in which prose is made to appear like poetry but only succeeds in being piffle. While trying hard to be another Shakespeare, he did his best to be another Caesar. Starting as a radical, he was twice defeated at High Wycombe; then, following an attempt to compete with Homer as a poet, he wooed High Wycombe for the third time, again without success. He now recognised that to get into Parliament he would have to join one of the chief parties; so he became a Tory, but failed to win an election at Taunton. Meanwhile his financial situation was desperate, and he lived, so to speak, in the shade of the sponging-house. Benjamin Austen came to his rescue and lent him at different times something like £1,500, charging interest at 2½ per cent. These loans were no doubt regarded as an investment in Disraeli's ability, but as time passed and the debtor made excuses for not repaying them Austen began to dun him, their friendship being strained to breaking-point. When Disraeli became a well-known figure in Society it is fairly certain that Sara Austen's embarrassing attentions and her husband's annoying reminders grew troublesome. The combination of boredom and irritation eventually severed the connection, and after Disraeli had paid his debt the time came when they saw no more of one another.

What may have helped to increase his vexation with the

Austens was a passionate affair which absorbed his interest between 1833 and 1836. He fell in love, or more likely in lust, with Henrietta, Lady Sykes, the wife of a baronet, Sir Francis Sykes. Probably Disraeli shared her favours with Lord Lyndhurst, who gave her a good deal of money. The baronet had no objection to these arrangements, as he was enjoying an affair with a doctor's wife, Clara Bolton, with whom Disraeli had also been intimate; but there was a scandal in the county when Lord Lyndhurst and Lady Sykes stayed at Bradenham, because Disraeli was supposed to be responsible for introducing his mistress and her other lover to his parents and sister. Lady Sykes was a haughty, sensual woman with social aspirations, and she must have exhausted Disraeli, whose health was impaired and who made two attempts to break the liaison, but failed to do so until Henrietta was found in bed with Daniel Maclise, when he had a good excuse for a final separation. Apparently Sir Francis Sykes was able to swallow Disraeli and Lyndhurst but choked over Maclise, and a court case ensued; but some sort of agreement must have been patched up because the baronet's own affair made a divorce difficult, and no doubt Mrs Bolton's husband derived financial benefit from the situation. Naturally Disraeli had to describe his marvellous experience, and the novel he wrote, *Henrietta Temple*, was marvellous enough to be utterly unlike life, but it sold well because the society in which he moved was more interested in gossip than in genius.

At this point Disraeli again turned his attention to politics. His defeat at Taunton had been embittered by a libellous speech from the Irish leader Daniel O'Connell, who had implied that Disraeli was descended from 'the blasphemous thief who died upon the Cross'. As O'Connell, having killed a man in a duel, had sworn never to fight another, Disraeli challenged the Irishman's son, who replied that he was not responsible for what his father said but only for what was said against his father; upon which Disraeli published an open letter containing enough material to provoke duels with a covey of O'Connells, but the police were warned and a magistrate bound Disraeli over to keep the peace. He then commenced a series of letters to *The Times*, in which he vilified O'Connell and trounced the leading Whigs, Palmerston, Melbourne and Lord John Russell, which resulted in his recognition by the Tory Party and election to the Carlton Club.

In January 1837 he stayed with Count D'Orsay and wrote a novel, *Venetia*, which contains sympathetic portraits of Byron and Shelley, and a statement, 'Poets are the unacknowledged legislators of the world', which suggests that he still thought of himself as a poet. But at last politics claimed him. With the accession of Queen Victoria a new Parliament was called, and Disraeli chose to stand as a candidate for Maidstone, though he had the choice of seven other constituencies. He was subjected to much heckling and much abuse by the Whiggish townsmen, who amused themselves by yelling 'Shylock!' and 'Old Clothes!' when he stood up to speak, but he was elected, and the wife of his fellow-member Wyndham Lewis predicted that in a few years he would be 'one of the greatest men of his day'. Fate ordained that she would help him to fulfil her prophecy.

The Whigs were returned to power in November 1837, and Disraeli sat with the Tories behind their leader Sir Robert Peel. On 7 December he attempted to make his maiden speech, but O'Connell's followers wished to avenge their leader and every sentence was received with yells, hoots, cat-calls, hyena laughter, and all the other sounds that come so naturally to politicians. His last words were heard above the uproar and long remembered: 'I sit down now, but the time will come when you *will* hear me.' He persevered, and within eight months had won the attention of the House. He had also won something more than attention from Mrs Wyndham Lewis, and they began to correspond on affectionate terms, which were strengthened by the death of her husband. She was twelve years his senior, and there is little doubt that her house in Park Lane and an income of £4,000 a year were more prominent in his consciousness than the softer emotions. Nevertheless he was soon fond enough of her to admit that 'when I first made my advances to you, I was

influenced by no romantic feelings', and he was worldly enough
to know that he could have made a better match from a financial
point of view. 'Dizzy married me for my money', she told a
friend many years later, 'but if he had the chance again he would
marry me for love.' It is more than probable that when their
marriage took place at St George's, Hanover Square, in August
1839 he was as much in love with her as with her money; and it is
certain that within a very short while her character had taken the
place of her income in his affection. Mary Anne, as he always
called her, and Dizzy, as she always called him, were perfectly
matched. Each was to the other the only person in the world who
really mattered, who came before everybody and everything else.
Cheerfulness and courage were her chief attributes, patience
and fortitude were his.

The main question Parliament had to face in the 1840s was
the repeal of the Corn Laws and the popular cry of 'Cheap bread',
which as Disraeli said gave one an appetite at once. In 1841 he
was elected for Shrewsbury, and a Tory Government came to
power with Peel as Prime Minister. Disraeli expected an
appointment and was greatly upset when he did not receive one.
People believed that the scandal caused by the Sykes-Lyndhurst-
Disraeli affair had caused Peel to pass him over. However, he had
now become leader of a small group of M.P.s called 'Young
Englanders' who intended to watch the Government closely and
criticise whatever actions they disapproved. As a sort of textbook for this group, and a pronouncement of its ideals, Disraeli
wrote *Coningsby*, which in the spring of 1844 established him
as an author of repute. But he was an aphorist, not a novelist,
and his stories are chiefly memorable for clever comments on
men and affairs, though Taper and Tadpole in *Coningsby* soon
entered the language as typical time-servers, tuft-hunters,
place-seekers and wire-pullers. From the aristocracy of the south
Disraeli moved to the industrialism of the north for his next
novel, *Sybil*, and gave a picture of the hideous conditions of the
poor, a job that Dickens did better in *Hard Times*, though
Disraeli's achievement, since he was a Tory politician, was the

more courageous and surprising of the two. 'The Youth of a Nation are the trustees of Posterity', he proclaimed, and it became his business in the world to show that the Party usually associated with the reaction of tradition and the ancient aristocracy would henceforth, in the hands of youth, represent the hope of youth.

Disraeli's reputation in the House of Commons was won by his devastating attacks on Sir Robert Peel, under whose administration the Corn Laws were repealed. When in opposition Peel had assailed such a policy, so Dizzy had the pleasant task of quoting the past Peel against the present Peel. For many years Sir Robert had been the leading personality in the Commons, but within a few weeks of Disraeli's onslaught even his own supporters were laughing at him. Moreover Disraeli, from being the leader of a clique, became the representative of the agricultural interest in Parliament, and in time the creator of a new Party representing Tory Democracy. When the Corn Bill was read for the third time and passed, Disraeli likened the ratting Tories who gave it a majority to the conversion of the Saxons by Charlemagne: 'Ranged on the banks of the Rhine, the Saxons determined to resist any further movement on the part of the great Caesar; but when the Emperor appeared, instead of conquering he converted them. How were they converted? In battalions and baptised in platoons.' One of the few people who did not believe that the millennium would arrive with cheap bread, Disraeli foresaw the future with as clear a vision as his contemporaries could see the past. Peel never recovered his pre-eminent position in the House of Commons after Disraeli had made mincemeat of him, and when the Irish Coercion Bill was defeated as a result of his opponent's tactics he resigned.

By the year 1847 Disraeli was an outstanding figure in British politics, and he dropped his sartorial foppery along with his verbal frivolity. At a later date, referring to himself, he wrote in a novel: 'There is a tone of levity about him which is unfortunate. Men destined to the highest places should beware of badinage . . . an insular country subject to fogs, and with a

powerful middle class, requires grave statesmen.' Feeling that
he was destined to the highest place of all, he toned himself
down, though he never quite survived the early impression he
had made and could not radically alter his disposition to flam-
boyant speech and witty comment. Nothing in England could give
so much consequence to a man as the ownership of land, and with
the help of his wife, his father and a wealthy political supporter
he purchased Hughenden Manor, near High Wycombe. He
also managed to be elected to Parliament by the county of
Buckingham, which he represented for the rest of his career in
the Commons. One of the first things he did annoyed his new
constituents, for he supported a Whig motion for the removal
of the civil and political disabilities of the Jews, telling the House
that all the early Christians had been Jews, that 'England would
not be a Christian country if it had not been for a Jew', and that
as a Christian 'I will not take upon me the awful responsibility of
excluding from the legislature those who are of the religion in the
bosom of which my Lord and Saviour was born'. The Tories
were against him, the motion was defeated in the Lords, and the
Jews had to wait until he became leader of his Party before they
could sit in the Commons without taking the Christian oath.
To emphasise his freedom from the prevailing bigotry, his novel
Tancred appeared in 1847. It was an exposure of western
materialism and an attempt to show that, as in the past, the
Holy Land could provide a message to reanimate and spiritualise
a world given over to mundane progress.

In spite of the fact that no one but Disraeli could make the
Whigs look foolish, the Tories still distrusted him, and a great
deal of manoeuvring, trimming and wire-pulling on his part
and that of his friends preluded his appointment as leader of the
Tory Party in the House. Matters were not made easier for him
at the elections, when his opponents dealt in personalities. One
elector shouted out that Disraeli's wife had picked him out of the
gutter. 'My good fellow', retorted Dizzy; 'if you were in the
gutter nobody would pull *you* out.' He told another heckler, who
had complained of his wordiness: 'When I speak I must measure

my words. I have to open your great thick head. What I say is to
enlighten you. If I bawled like you, you would leave this place as
great a fool as you entered it.' He was equal to any interruption,
whether in the House or on the platform, and he seemed to thrive
on hostility; but he was completely at ease only at Hughenden,
where he loved his trees, his books, his peacocks, above all his
wife, at whose odd remarks and behaviour everyone but himself
laughed. Yet he could appreciate her oddity as well as her sterling
qualities, for he said of her: 'She is an excellent creature, but she
never can remember which came first, the Greeks or the Romans.'

With the swing of the political pendulum the Tories had a brief
period of power in 1851, when Disraeli was Chancellor of the
Exchequer under the premiership of Lord Derby, and Queen
Victoria, who had begun by saying, 'I do not approve of Mr
Disraeli', changed her opinion under the influence of his epistolary
style. The Commons however continued to disapprove of him,
showing their distaste when he produced a Budget, on which
the Government was defeated, and his leadership of the House
lasted for ten months. A Coalition Government was formed,
though Disraeli had informed them that 'England does not love
Coalitions', and under its auspices Great Britain soon drifted
into the Crimean War, which was followed by the Indian Mutiny.
In 1858 the Tories returned to Downing Street with Disraeli
again as Chancellor of the Exchequer, one of his first acts being
to convert the Thames from a sewer into a river by a system of
main drainage, whereby the death-rate in the Metropolis was
considerably diminished. He also enraged his opponents by
producing a Reform Bill, his first step towards Tory Democracy.
The Whigs regarded reform as their own prerogative, asserted
that the Bill did not go far enough, defeated it, returned to office,
and shelved the subject.

In opposition once more, Disraeli attacked the Government's
foreign policy and upheld the Established Church, the power of
which was being undermined by Dissenters. Disraeli considered
the Church an essential part of England and English life, the
spiritual symbol of the nation, 'the only Jewish institution that

remains', and he declared that without its guidance people would create altars and idols in their own hearts and imaginations. For this reason he did not wish for alterations in its creed, and when Dean Stanley suggested that the Athanasian Creed be omitted from the Prayer Book he remarked: 'Mr Dean: no dogmas, no deans.' In 1859 Darwin's *The Origin of Species* shook the theologians, and the general public got it into their heads that men were descended from monkeys. But Disraeli preferred the ancient teaching that man was a fallen angel, and, with Bishop Wilberforce in the chair, he clarified his position before an audience at the Sheldonian Theatre, Oxford, in November 1864: 'What is the question now placed before society with a glib assurance the most astounding? The question is this: is man an ape or an angel? My Lord, I am on the side of the angels.' This statement was treated as a huge joke throughout the country, and the shop windows were filled with cartoons of Dizzy sprouting wings. But he was being quite serious in his own way, for he believed that the spirit of man was more significant than the animal in man.

Lord Derby became Prime Minister for the third time in 1866, with Disraeli as his right-hand man in the Commons. A new Reform Bill was drafted, and the politician who now became Disraeli's chief antagonist, W. E. Gladstone, could not conceal his rage over the 'diabolical cleverness' with which Dizzy steered the Bill through the Commons, though his Party were in a minority. Even G. W. E. Russell, a perfervid Gladstonian, recorded that Disraeli showed himself absolute master of the House, a whale among sprats, and when he got a majority at the first reading the Tories could not contain themselves, receiving him at the Carlton Club with an enthusiasm unknown in such institutions. Any other man would have surrendered to their appeal and stayed to supper, but Mary Anne was expecting him and he would not disappoint her. 'I had got him a raised pie from Fortnum and Mason's, and a bottle of champagne', she recorded, 'and he ate half the pie and drank all the champagne, and then he said "Why, my dear, you are more like a mistress than a wife".' She took this as a compliment, and he meant it as one.

The third reading of the Reform Bill was passed without a division, and Disraeli was solely responsible for the achievement. 'We have dished the Whigs', said Derby, who resigned the premiership in 1868, thanked Disraeli for twenty years of cordial and loyal co-operation, and advised the Queen to make him Prime Minister. Victoria was delighted, for by that time she had fallen under the spell of his enigmatic personality. Mary Anne was in ecstasies, for her dream had at last come true. Dizzy himself was too realistic for rapture, replying to someone's congratulations: 'Yes, I have climbed to the top of the greasy pole.' His Party in the House were easily outvoted by a combination of Whigs, Liberals and the Irish, and under the compelling oratory of Gladstone favouring the disestablishment and disendowment of the Irish Church the Tories were defeated.

After ten months of power Disraeli resigned in December 1868, much to the sorrow of Queen Victoria, who at his request created Mary Anne Viscountess Beaconsfield in her own right. At the age of sixty-four he was again forced into a limitless prospect of leading the Opposition, and he seemed to have lost his joy in the fight. Having created a party machine to whip up Toryism in the country, he solaced himself by writing a novel, *Lothair*, which is full of religion and politics and such neat epigrams as:

'My idea of an agreeable person is a person who agrees with me.'

'The pursuit of science leads only to the insoluble.'

'I have always thought that every woman should marry, and no man.'

'The great majority of men exist but do not live.'

'You know who the critics are? The men who have failed in literature and art.'

'The fun of talk is to find out what a man really thinks, and then contrast it with the enormous lies he has been telling all dinner, and perhaps all his life.'

Though inevitably described by the leading critics as a sin against taste, a mass of un-English verbiage and dull as ditchwater, the novel was a big success in England and America, the sales being unaffected by the Franco-German war of 1870, concerning which Disraeli was the only public man in England to perceive that all the old principles of diplomacy had been obliterated and that a new age of unprincipled power had dawned.

Unlike Gladstone, he was not a man who made speeches merely for the pleasure of letting off steam, and when Matthew Arnold wanted to know why he had remained silent while Gladstone and Bright were orating all over the country during a Parliamentary recess in 1872, he answered: 'The Ministers are so busy going about apologising for their failures, that I think it a pity to distract public attention from the proceeding.' There were signs that people were getting tired of oratory that year, because in a public procession he and his wife were received with enthusiasm by the populace all the way from the City to their house at Grosvenor Gate. Mary Anne was now eighty. 'We have been married thirty-three years, and she has never given me a dull moment', said Dizzy, and they hated being separated from one another. 'I have nothing to tell you, except that I love you', he wrote to her from his seat in the Commons. Her death from cancer in December 1872 prostrated him, and for a while he could attend to nothing. But in January 1874 he had to pull himself together, for the Tories won a General Election and had a majority of 50 over the other parties in the House. Now he was Prime Minister in the fullest sense, but when congratulated he said sadly: 'Yes, but it has come too late.' He was in his seventieth year, and Mary Anne was dead.

His period in office was mainly notable for the creation of Queen Victoria as Empress of India, for the purchase of the controlling shares in the Suez Canal, when Disraeli beat all the gamblers and financiers who had tried to defeat him, and for the success of the Berlin Congress. More consoling to him than any of these achievements was his amorous friendship with Lady Bradford, whose husband was one of his colleagues. Though the mother of a family, she was fifteen years younger than Disraeli, who fell in love with her, saw her on every possible occasion, wrote to her two or three times a day, confided in her, and left her in no doubt that she was absolutely necessary to his existence. Indeed he went so far as to propose marriage to her sister, Lady Chesterfield, with the sole object of acquiring her as a sister-in-law; but the other lady did not feel complimented and nothing came of it. Lady Bradford's letters to him were read before he opened the urgent official despatches that came by special messenger, and the hour of a Cabinet meeting would be changed if it clashed with her passage through London.

At first she encouraged him, feeling flattered by the attentions of a Prime Minister; but, when his visits and civilities became too frequent, and his obvious devotion placed her in a slightly invidious position, she cooled. This distressed him, but a kindly letter made the sun shine again. Then began a see-saw of emotions; when she was gracious he was happy, when aloof he felt miserable. His daily visits to her house in Belgrave Square, when interested pedestrians would see the bent man with pallid mask-like face strolling through what he called the 'green glades' of Green Park, his hands behind his back, were cut down to three a week, and even his letters were rationed. He implored her to let him see her regularly if only for a minute, and to let him write daily if only a word. 'I want to see only one person . . . and I want to see her always. Otherwise I would rather be alone,' he told her. Whether in solitude or engaged in the business of his profession he could not help thinking of her, and when she sent her portrait for his gallery at Hughenden he was enraptured – 'I would sooner have it than stars and garters' – and carried it with him to and from London. As the years went by he saw less and less of her, and he wrote sorrowfully: 'I fear our Romance is over, if indeed it ever existed except in my imagination – but still I sometimes dreamed that the dream might last until I slumbered for ever.'

From his correspondence with Lady Bradford and her sister we obtain glimpses of his association with Queen Victoria, who under his influence ceased to be a sad and brooding widow and became a lively responsive sovereign. His mere presence could charm away her sorrows and provoke the happy laughter which had not been heard since her husband died. By making her more sociable and urging her to take a public part in national functions, he popularised the British monarchy, giving it a prestige that has never since been lost. With much adroitness and acute insight, he managed to make her feel responsible for his own thoughts and actions; and when he wrote to her after the successful negotiation of the Suez affair: 'It is just settled: you have it, Madam', she could really believe that the entire business had been conceived and executed by herself. 'Everyone likes flattery', he once said, 'and when you come to Royalty, you should lay it on with a trowel.' But his flattery was not laid on with a trowel solely to gain his purpose: it was part of his natural kindliness, a desire to please others, and Victoria, an extremely shrewd woman and an excellent judge of character, never suspected him of the insincerity with which his opponents charged him. As a romancist he could reverence her, as a realist he could laugh at her, and the combination of these qualities resulted in a deep affection. Her feeling for him was nothing less than love. 'I can only describe my reception by telling you that I really thought she was going to embrace me,' he wrote: 'She was wreathed with smiles, and, as she talked, glided about the room like a bird.' He was suffering from gout, and though etiquette forbade she asked him to sit down. On receiving bouquets of primroses and snowdrops from Osborne, he likened the sender to Queen Titania, and called her 'the Faery' in his letters to Lady Bradford. Everything possible was done for his comfort by Victoria, who mothered him, worried about his health, sent him presents, and gave him the benefit of her inmost thoughts. In return he did as she wished in non-political matters, bringing in Bills to control the 'horrible practice' of vivisection and to stop the slaughter of young seals. But he drew the line at her insistence that England should make war on Russia.

An insurrection in Bulgaria had caused ruthless reprisals by

Benjamin Disraeli

Harry Labouchere (1887)

the Turks, and the humanitarians in England, led by Gladstone, called for the expulsion of the Turks from Europe. Disraeli knew that this would mean the occupation of Constantinople by Russia, and withstood the popular agitation, taking advantage of which the Tsar declared war on Turkey. Meanwhile Disraeli's bad health had compelled him to retire to the Upper House as Earl of Beaconsfield, and Gladstone had it all his own way in the Commons. The belligerence of Russia started a popular outburst of patriotism in England, and everyone whistled or sang a music-hall ditty:

> We don't want to fight, but, by jingo if we do,
> We've got the ships, we've got the men, we've got the
> money too,

which gave currency to the word 'Jingoism'. Stormed at from right and left, either to fight Russia or to eliminate Turkey, Dizzy kept his head and called Russia's bluff by sending a fleet to the Dardanelles, by concentrating troops at Malta, and by influencing Austria to back his policy. Russia climbed down, and a conference of Powers was held at Berlin in 1878 to discuss the situation, Great Britain being represented by the Earl of Beaconsfield, who alone addressed the Congress in English, the rest in French.

Bismarck, President of the Congress, at once recognised Beaconsfield as his match, saying, 'The old Jew, that is the man!' In fact the old Jew was his superior in diplomatic cunning. Beaconsfield's policy was that Russia should be excluded from the Mediterranean Sea, and he made it clear that if his proposals were not accepted he would break up the Congress, even going so far as to order a special train for his departure. Bismarck had his own reasons for making a success of the meeting, and on discovering that Beaconsfield would carry out his threat prevailed on the Tsar to yield. On returning home, his efforts crowned with success, Dizzy was received with acclamation, and made a short speech from the windows of No. 10 Downing Street: 'Lord Salisbury and myself have brought you back peace;

M

but a peace, I hope, with honour.' His personal popularity caused Gladstone to erupt with invective, which received a calm comment from Beaconsfield, who publicly referred to his antagonist as 'a sophistical rhetorician, inebriated with the exuberance of his own verbosity, and gifted with an egotistical imagination that can at all times command an interminable and inconsistent series of arguments to malign an opponent and to glorify himself.' Gladstone did not see himself in this light, and, had he been present, would not have laughed at the Prime Minister's reply to someone who asked him to define the difference between the words 'misfortune' and 'calamity'. 'Well', said Dizzy, 'if Mr Gladstone fell into the Thames, it would be a misfortune; but, if someone pulled him out, it would be a calamity.'

The appalling strain on his enfeebled constitution of the jugglings and junketings at the Berlin Congress had very nearly killed Beaconsfield, and for the remainder of his premiership he struggled against asthma and gout, in addition to Gladstone and the incompetence of his subordinates. He had to stop drinking wine, though at a public dinner, when the food was served up cold, he was heard to say as he sipped the champagne: 'Thank God, I have at last got something warm!' It still amused him to create bishops and deans, because their avowed admiration for him was so much at variance with what they felt, and on hearing that one of his appointments was popular with the clergy he wrote to Lady Bradford: 'It seems a success with all "schools of Church thought", *alias* Church nonsense.'

The errors and disobedience of his Government's representatives in India and South Africa landed the country in two wars, with the Afghans and the Zulus, but once the mistakes had been made Beaconsfield loyally supported those who had made them, ignored public criticism, and both campaigns were successful. He spent as much time as possible at Hughenden among his beeches and his books, enjoying the solitude and telling Lady Bradford, 'I don't want any companion, unless it were you.' The primroses sent him by Victoria showed that he still retained her devotion, but there were some awkward and exhausting periods when she criticised his policy and he had to persuade her that it was really her own.

Tired out, he asked the Queen to dissolve Parliament early in 1880, and while Gladstone raged through Midlothian the Prime Minister rested. A trade depression and a succession of bad harvests helped to bring his rival back to power, and Dizzy viewed the prospect of privacy with unconcern. The one inconsolable person in the realm was Victoria, who wrote him letters which, had they been published, might have caused a revolution in a country that had just sent Gladstone to be her chief adviser.

The spring and summer of 1880 were spent by Beaconsfield writing a novel, *Endymion*, wherein a phrase, 'Time is the great physician', became a common quotation, and a brief duologue illustrated the enigma of his personality:

'Sensible men are all of the same religion.'
'And pray what is that?'
'Sensible men never tell.'

Another passage displayed an aspect of him that made his own political party nervous whenever he opened his lips: 'It was a grand idea of our kings making themselves Sovereigns of the sea. The greater portion of this planet is water; so we at once became a first-rate power.' Like all his novels, *Endymion* reveals a Disraelian dream and has little connection with actuality. As he very well knew, he was only great in action, where his imagination functioned and his sense of reality was acute.

Never bored in the silent tranquillity of Hughenden, he would have liked to resign his leadership of the Party, but they refused to let him go, and soon he started on another novel. With the money made on his last he took the lease of a house in Curzon Street and went to London for the winter months. During the brief periods when asthma left him, gout took its place, and, though he attended many dinners in society and debates in the House of Lords, he weakened as the cold weeks went by. At the end of March he was in bed and the doctors arrived. A bulletin issued by them stated that his health was maintained. 'I presume the physicians are conscious of that. It is more than I am,' he said. Public affairs no longer interested him, though he corrected the proof of his last speech in Parliament, saying, 'I will not go down to posterity talking bad grammar.' The Queen sent primroses picked by herself and letters by special messenger begging him to obey the doctors and do nothing imprudent; but he was no longer able to disobey the first or risk the second. 'I have suffered much', he admitted as he struggled for breath. 'Had I been a Nihilist, I should have confessed all.' Early in the morning of 19 April 1881 he partly raised himself from the bed, drawing up his shoulders as he used to do on rising to address the House. Then he fell back, his words unsaid, and the British people mourned the most original, picturesque and richly gifted personality in their political history.

6

Henry Labouchere

Within three weeks of Beaconsfield's death a proposal to erect a monument in his honour was discussed in the House of Commons. As usual on such occasions, the voices of the speakers were ceremoniously muted, an atmosphere of reverence pervaded the chamber, the facial expressions of those taking part were suitably solemn, and their words took on a mournful dignity. The recently elected member for Northampton, short, placid, with a drawling, displeasing voice, dark hair and white face, rose to add his quota of compliment, his opening phrase striking a responsive chord and drawing murmurs of approbation. 'Lord Beaconsfield', said he, 'possessed rare and splendid gifts.' At these words the House settled into a complacent head-nodding mood. The nods ceased as the speaker proceeded: 'But rare and splendid gifts in themselves are a danger rather than an advantage to the State when the possessor of them does not use them for what is considered by the majority of his fellow-countrymen to be to the public advantage.' Angry glances were directed at the radical member, who went on: 'A statue is granted by a national vote to a politician because his country is grateful to him. I do not consider that the country has reason to be grateful for anything that Lord Beaconsfield did.' Cries of protest were heard from various parts of the House, and when the irreverent fellow sat down it was generally felt that he was 'an outsider' and not 'a sportsman'. From a parliamentary point of view, he remained an outsider and no sportsman for the rest of his life.

His name was Henry Labouchere, and he came of a Huguenot family which had thriven as bankers after the Napoleonic wars. His grandfather had married into the wealthy family of Baring, and the two sons of that alliance were well-off, the elder going into politics and becoming Baron Taunton, the younger joining the family business and marrying the daughter of a Buckingham-shire squire named Du Pré. Their son Henry was born at No. 16 Portland Place, London, on 9 November 1831. His father, John Labouchere, was a stern religious man, strongly puritanical, and there was very little sympathy between parent and child. At the age of six Henry went to a private school at Brighton, where he was thrashed unmercifully by the master for seven years, after which he was caned ritually at Eton for three years, and then received private tuition until he went to Trinity College, Cambridge, in his nineteenth year. Here life became easier, and he spent much time at the Newmarket races and in the company of tipsters and suchlike sportsmen at the various taverns in the neighbourhood. Cambridge did not see much of him because he often went to London when Newmarket had no excitement to offer; and once, when strolling in the Strand, he came face to face with his father, who exploded with indignation and demanded the reason for his absence from the University. Altering his normal expression and looking as little like himself as possible, Henry assured his parent that it was a case of mistaken identity and walked on. But he took care to leave by the next train to Cambridge, which his father also caught. At journey's end he jumped from the carriage and dashed out of the station, being discovered by his irate parent some minutes later surrounded by books, his brow furrowed with studious appli-cation. After registering incredulity over the extraordinary error, and betraying apprehension at the thought that another fellow could be mistaken for himself, he enjoyed an excellent dinner with his much-relieved father at the Lion.

He also laid himself open to misunderstandings with the

University authorities. A proctor caught him one day walking arm in arm through the town with what was then called 'a lady of pleasure'. Asked to account for his company, he introduced her as his sister. The proctor was outraged: 'Nonsense! she's one of the most notorious courtesans in the town.' The young man looked grieved: 'I know that, sir, but is it kind to throw my family misfortunes in my face?' The examiners in particular were suspicious, and one of them asked to see what he so frequently looked at beneath his blotting-paper. He showed some reluctance to exhibit it, but on receiving a peremptory order to do so he produced the photo of a music-hall 'star', explaining that her beauty inspired him to persevere with his work. His career at Cambridge closed abruptly. As he had not attended a single lecture, it was assumed that he would obtain unlawful assistance in the examinations, and one of the pro-proctors believed that a note he wrote to a friend was a crib. He denied this, threw the note on the floor, refused to look for it, handed in the papers he had completed, and walked out. He was admonished and 'sent down'. His father paid his debts, well over £6,000, and he was let loose on the world, wherein he would cause much laughter to many and some tribulation to a few.

Wishing to see as little of him as possible, his father sent him abroad under the conduct of a man who should have been able to keep him in order. But it was an impossible task, and after a period of gambling on the Continent he returned home to face some downright lecturing from his upright father. Each preferring the other at a distance, the young man next started off for South America with letters of introduction to various people who did business with the family firm. But he found life so exciting in Mexico that he decided to go no further south, and passed about two years very agreeably with gamblers, brigands and a travelling circus, a girl in the troupe having taken his fancy. Unable to appreciate the advantage of an adventurous life as a preliminary to serious business, but desirous to keep the home uncontaminated with the youngster's presence, his father managed to get him appointed attaché at the Washington

Embassy, where he extracted fun out of the situation, did as little work as possible, and first earned the friendly distinction of being called 'Labby', by which we shall henceforth know him.

Although he came to the conclusion that the average diplomat was abysmally silly, he decided to remain in the service for the sole purpose of seeing the world and having a good time. From Washington he went on to Munich, Stockholm, Madrid, St Petersburg, Constantinople and other places, his life at each being largely filled with gambling, dancing, love-making and long holidays, though he learned a lot about foreign affairs in the process, amongst other things that the one great object in diplomacy was to talk indefinitely, write interminably, and settle nothing. He fought a duel at Stockholm, and was extremely relieved when the bullets went wide. He met Bismarck at Frankfurt, and, thought him, though his hands were habitually filthy, the only pleasant Prussian he had ever seen. At St Petersburg one day a self-important nobleman called at the Legation and asked to see the Ambassador at once. 'Pray take a chair; he will be here soon', said Labby. 'But, young man, do you know who I am?' and the visitor recited his distinctions. 'Pray take two chairs', said Labby.

He was still amusing himself in diplomacy when news reached him that his father was dying. On arrival home he found that John Labouchere was dead. The butler asked if he would like to see the body. Labby was quite agreeable and entered a room where his father was lying in a coffin. He stood for a few moments gazing down at the face of his dead parent, then turned to the butler and remarked: 'The right man in the right place.' He now had a comfortable income and decided to quit Her Majesty's Service, his manner of doing so being characteristic. Hearing from the Foreign Secretary that he had been promoted Second Secretary at Buenos Aires, he replied that if he could fulfil his duties in South America without leaving Baden-Baden he would be pleased to accept the appointment. But the Foreign Secretary was not pleased to renew the offer.

Back in England he determined to enter Parliament and was

elected for New Windsor. Unseated on a charge of corruption, he was next elected for Middlesex in 1867. At the same time he ventured into theatrical speculation, partly because he had fallen in love with an actress, Henrietta Hodson, who was living apart from her husband and consented to live with Labby instead. This irregular arrangement was duly made known to the electors of Middlesex by the opposite side, and his appearance on the platform was frequently greeted with cries of ' 'Ow's 'Enrietta?' He put a stop to this by opening a meeting with the announcement: 'I wish to convey to you all the gratifying intelligence that Henrietta is quite well.' With a partner Labby opened the Queen's Theatre, Long Acre, in 1867, and their management is notable in stage history for the first appearance together of Henry Irving and Ellen Terry in Garrick's version of *The Taming of the Shrew*, an outstanding failure. Henrietta appeared in several plays and made something of a hit in the name part of *Oliver Twist*, with Irving as Bill Sikes, but Labby soon got tired of losing money and turned his attention to ways of making it. His uncle, Lord Taunton, died in 1869 and owing to the fact that the family fortune had to be inherited by a male Labby became the possessor of a quarter of a million pounds, which he found opportune, having just purchased a quarter-share in the *Daily News*, the circulation of which was declining.

The fortunes of war trebled the sale of the paper, because it so happened that Labby was in Paris when the Franco-Prussian conflict broke out, and his letters describing incidents during the siege of that city were the most amusing ever written under such circumstances. They were sent by balloon or pigeon-post and addressed to Henrietta Hodson to escape the censor. His detachment and common sense helped him to endure with fortitude all the horrors of the siege, though in the course of his humorously narrated experiences he did not pretend to heroism. Describing the bombardment, he said: 'The Panthéon was struck yesterday. What desecration! everyone cries; and I am very sorry for the Panthéon, but very glad that it was the Panthéon, and not me.' He never went to look for danger, remarking that 'to be knocked on the head by a shell merely to gratify one's curiosity appears to me to be the utmost height of absurdity'. In fact he took no more risks that were absolutely necessary to the competent discharge of his duties as a war correspondent, and the phrase 'I reserved investigations for a more quiet moment' adequately expressed his general demeanour when metal was flying about. The tedium and absurdity of war were his constant themes, and in one of his letters he summed up his feelings about the combatants : 'Laugh at the French, abuse them as one may, it is impossible to help liking them. Admire, respect the Prussians as one may, it is impossible to help disliking them.' And he came to the conclusion that the supremacy of the Prussians in Europe would be a social calamity unless the French could civilise them.

The capitulation of Paris released Labby, who was scarcely recognised by his friends on returning to England. He had grown a beard, already streaked with grey, and he looked sixty instead of forty, though he still looked sixty at eighty. He had now discovered his vocation as a writer of light satire on public affairs, which exactly suited the temperament of one who had about as little poetry in his nature as a human being with a good mental equipment can have. In the course of his gambling career he had learnt a great deal about gamblers, and to give them a lively view of their disposition he wrote City articles for *The World*, wherein he exposed the corruption of the financial correspondents of other papers, a policy which was regarded by them as hitting below the belt. As his sceptical attitude to the conduct and motives of human beings was expressed in a tolerant, light-hearted, free-and-easy but utterly insensitive manner, his victims thought that torture was too good for him. He airily exposed the company-promoters, share-manipulators, newspaper-puffers, money-lenders, and all the rest of the swindling world, with a special eye on financial advisers, one of whom, the City editor of *The Times*, whose prestige with readers had been unquestioned for twenty-eight-years, was compelled to retire into private life, while a stockbroker, who could only think in terms of chastisement with a horse-whip, assaulted Labby in the street, and thereby increased the circulation of *The World*. It should be added that the critic of others was not above benefiting himself by judicious speculation founded on inside knowledge, but as he was detached enough to admit it he remained immune from the barbs of his more vulnerable competitors.

Having dealt with the City, he turned his attention to misdemeanours in other walks of life, founded a paper of his own, called it *Truth*, described it as 'another and a better *World*', and put up £1,000 capital, which was never touched, because from the first number in January 1877 it made a handsome profit. He appointed a good assistant, Horace Voules, who soon developed the thick skin necessary for such a job, and began to make every institution, from the Crown to the Treasury, from the Church to the Army, apprehensive on the morning of its weekly appearance. Labby wrote many of the articles in the early numbers, and contributed regularly to the end of his life. He was a first-rate journalist, amusing, provocative, audacious, interested in everything, always readable; and, if only he had been able to endure routine and exercise application, he would have been an ideal editor for this class of paper. But he soon abandoned its direction to Voules, as he got bored with the day-to-day details and duties of the job, preferring talk to work when at the office. Being fearless and uninhibited, he wrote as he spoke and thought. He delighted in the comedy of life, and was amused by the enthusiasms, rages, contradictions and imbecilities of his fellow-creatures. His cynical view of the universe was exhibited quite openly, though he was kind-hearted in an impersonal sort of way. Righteous indignation was as foreign to him as intense conviction, and he was free from cant in a canting age. 'How much £.s.d. does he believe in what he says?' he asked when sniffing humbug in the air. Though a radical in politics, he was also a comedian and made no virtue of his advanced opinions. While believing in social reform, he had little faith in the improvement of human beings. With no reverence for men or their creeds, he spoke and wrote so candidly that people without his humorous impartiality were offended.

Naturally a newspaper run by such a man was not likely to run smoothly, and during his proprietorship *Truth* was on familiar terms with the law. Blackmailers, shady solicitors, questionable doctors, dubious parsons, baby-farmers, women-beaters, directors of companies, newspaper proprietors, charlatans of every description received the attention of *Truth*, and some attempted retaliation. Labby himself was physically assaulted, describing the episodes in his paper with a keen sense of their comedy, and virulently assailed in certain journals, which called forth all his powers as a satirist. He was a famous and popular figure in the law-courts, and usually conducted his own cases. Defending his libels became a sort of hobby, and he enjoyed himself as a cross-examiner. 'I wish they had not put it down for Tuesday', he complained to his solicitor when one of his cases was about to be fought, 'as that's the day when I *write* my libels.'

The only public man for whom he felt something as near admiration as he was capable of feeling was W. E. Gladstone, whom he was the first to call 'the Grand Old Man', but his admiration was qualified with: 'I don't object to Gladstone always having the ace of trumps up his sleeve, but merely to his belief that God Almighty put it there.' And when an enthusiast exclaimed that Gladstone's mission was to bring light, Labby murmured 'Lucifer!' On another occasion he described Gladstone as 'a thimble-rigger'. Nevertheless he believed in Gladstone's reforming zeal; and when the editor and part-owner of the *Daily Telegraph*, Levy-Lawson, switched over from supporting the G.O.M. to attacking him, Labby let fly, explaining that the change of policy was due to the journalist's financial interest in Turkey, a country that Gladstone was vituperating. Following a physical assault and innumerable quips at the expense of the 'Daily Levi', as the editor of *Truth* called the *Daily Telegraph*, the case came before the court, Labby being charged with criminal libel. The hearing lasted for more than a week and the public had good value for their discomfort in the cross-exami-

nation of Levy-Lawson by Labby. The jury disagreed, and Labby
was able to boast that he had discredited Levy-Lawson, who
however was later to be credited with the title of Lord Burnham.

From 1880 to the close of his political career Labby represented
Northampton in the House of Commons, his constituents being
for the most part cobblers who sympathised with his republican
views. His fellow-member for ten years was Charles Bradlaugh,
whose professed atheism enabled Labby, a complete sceptic in
religion, to call himself 'the Christian member for Northampton'.
He soon earned a reputation as 'a character' in the House, which
meant that every time he rose to speak the other members
prepared to laugh, and he usually gave them something to laugh
at, not infrequently on the wrong side of their faces. He had an
unpleasant trick of revealing the realities behind the shams of
political life, and of pricking the vanity of self-important persons.
He was believed to be insincere, for the alternative belief would
have impeached his critics. He did not mind what anyone thought,
but went on expressing his own opinions with such merciless
candour and clarity that, had he been bribable, he could have
asked almost anything for his silence. In his early years he had a
following of about forty fellow-radicals, but in course of time
his uncompromising attitude reduced his disciples to about two.
He never ceased to expose the evil of war, the greed of imperialism, the mammonlike wealth of the Established Church, the
moral humbug of the Nonconformists, the futility of the House
of Lords, and the ludicrous waste of public money when large
sums were voted to members of the Royal Family. His free
opinions were not always to the taste of the side on which he
fought. 'Of course I think our Party is right, but whether we
are or not we've got all the humbug on our side', he said, concluding an argument on the corruption of politicians with: 'The
Tories will go in for any enterprise which they think will land
them on the Treasury Bench – and so will the radicals.' Such
dicta did not endear him to friends or enemies; and when he
remarked that 'The mere denial of the existence of God does
not entitle a man's opinion to be taken without scrutiny on

matters of greater importance', he offended believers and
unbelievers alike, both of whom felt that the affirmation and
denial of the deity were matters of the highest importance.

Though he never ceased to retain the loyalty and admiration
of his cobbler constituents, he aroused the furious enmity of
Court circles; indeed a man who could describe the Duke of
Cambridge as 'standing at the head of his troops, his drawn
salary in his hand' was clearly not seeking for popularity in
such quarters. Queen Victoria called him 'that horrible lying
Labouchere', and the Prince of Wales described him as 'that
viper'. But such judgments were due to his irreverent outspokenness. Wilfred Scawen Blunt testified that 'he was one
of the very few quite honest M.P.s, who always told the truth
and was always amusing', while the Earl of Dunraven said that
'a kinder-hearted man never lived.' The Queen had special
reasons for disliking him. Although he had 'a more sincere
admiration for her than most of the flunkeys who bowed and
scraped before her', yet he felt it excessive that four yachts
should be kept afloat and several palaces kept open for her
convenience. He objected to grants being made to royal persons
on their promotion or marriage; he favoured the abolition of
the Order of the Bath, not to mention all the other Orders; he
grumbled at the cost of transporting and keeping princes and
dukes when they travelled; he criticised the reckless expenditure
on royal festivities; he thought that Her Majesty should
provide for her grandchildren out of her own considerable
income; he even went so far as to censure the behaviour and
musical ability of her late husband the Prince Consort; and, worse
still, in a jubilant moment, he added a verse to the National
Anthem:

> Grandchildren not a few,
> With great-grandchildren too,
> She blest has been.
> We've been their sureties,
> Paid them gratuities,

Pensions, annuities,
God save the Queen!

Little wonder that when Gladstone wished to give the author
of this verse a place in his Cabinet, the Queen would not listen
to the suggestion, and Labby had to reconcile himself to being
'a political leper'. Later on, his wife Henrietta, who had no
sympathy with his lack of ambition, did her best to make the
Foreign Secretary, Lord Rosebery, appoint her husband
Ambassador at Washington, and even managed to persuade
Labby to back her up; but Rosebery had been attacked in *Truth*
and revenged himself by refusing her appeal. Besides, Labby
was much too independent to be given a responsible post; he
would almost certainly have treated diplomatic instructions
with unbecoming levity.

Labby was a curiously impersonal man, and the absence of
sentiment in his nature irritated his wife as much as the absence
of ambition. Though she had retired from the stage, Henrietta
maintained a keen interest in it, and among her achievements
was the 'creation' of Mrs Langtry as an actress. She thereupon
announced her intention of accompanying her protégée to
America; and as her main object in taking this step was to
make her husband miss her, she sacked the domestic staff, put
sheets on the furniture of the living-rooms, and cut the buttons
off his shirts, before leaving; all of which amused Labby, who
was a very abstemious man and lived happily on sandwiches
and sausages at some cheap restaurant during her absence. He
knew that Henrietta would quarrel with Mrs Langtry and fore-
told her early return. The quarrel soon occurred, and Labby was
delighted when she came back, but the lack of surprise in his
welcome was annoying, and the fact that he had been perfectly
comfortable in her absence made her fretful. It is more than
probable that his exasperating equability, his friendly cynicism
and amused toleration, helped to make her a Roman Catholic.
Her conversion did not affect him in the least: it was simply
another of the comical vagaries of life, and he accepted it as he

would have received the information that she had taken to drink or eloped with the butler.

They lived for some years in Queen Anne's Gate, but ultimately came to rest at No. 5 Old Palace Yard, opposite the entrance to the House of Lords, and next to Westminster Abbey, which inspired some verses in *Punch* entitled 'Labby in our Abbey'. Here they gave dinners and receptions to all sorts and conditions of people, actors, politicians, financiers, journalists bishops, barristers, singers, etc. At such functions Labby sometimes told rather risky stories and Henrietta had to keep an eye on him. Once he embarked on a really scandalous bit of gossip to a female guest, who showed signs of discomfort and at length burst out: 'I am sure, Mr Labouchere, you can't be aware that you are talking of my cousin.' Labby was pained: 'My dear madam, surely you don't imagine that I would tell such a story outside the family.'

For the sake of Henrietta he took a house at Twickenham known as Pope's Villa, where she gave pastoral performances of Shakespeare's plays and the host moved about among the guests, dropping such remarks as: 'I think we have every rascal in London here.' Though he pleased his small daughter[1] by rowing her up and down the river, he usually avoided exercise, disliked games, and abhorred all kinds of sport. Food meant as little to him as drink, and he would rather eat a sandwich than the most succulent dish and drink a coffee than the finest wine, just as he preferred taking a bus to a hansom cab and always travelled third class on the railway. His holidays were usually spent at Cadenabbia on Lake Como, where he read, smoked cigarettes, talked to anyone, did nothing, and occasionally hired someone to take him on the lake. His chief pleasure was to sit in the smoking-room of the Commons or the Reform Club, surrounded by a group of members who enjoyed his witty debunking of eminent personalities in public life.

In the last years of the nineteenth century there was plenty of scope for his satire. Financial greed masquerading as imperial

---

1 A natural daughter, not by Henrietta.

James McNeill Whistler:
from a drypoint by Mortimer Menpes

W. S. Gilbert (1891)

good caused several outbursts of patriotism which covered up plunder, culminating in the Boer War of 1899-1902. The Colonial Secretary at that time was Joseph Chamberlain, who had never been forgiven by Labby for splitting the Liberal Party over Gladstone's policy of Home Rule for Ireland, and so hindering the cause of social reform. Chamberlain was therefore the principal villain of the piece, and throughout the South African war he writhed under the ridicule of Labby. But Joseph had big battalions on his side and could afford to treat his opponent with contempt. Over and over again Labby took his life in his hands when he spoke in favour of the Boers at public meetings, and the personal abuse to which he was subjected in newspapers and on platforms would have seriously upset any-one else. But, having a cynical view of humanity, he did not allow the manifestations of mania in wartime, or any other time, to ruffle him, and his calmness in the face of bodily peril was the outward expression of his sanity. 'I do not waste my time in answering abuse', he said; 'I am accustomed to it, and I thrive under it like a field that benefits by the manure that is carted on to it.' Also he was thoroughly in earnest over the war, and the only time Voules ever knew him to lose his temper and use strong language was when the editorial staff of *Truth* begged him to moderate his pro-Boer opinions in writing for the paper, since the sales and advertisements were steadily declining. He said he would ruin his bloody paper and send them all to the devil before ceasing to attack the hell-hound Chamberlain and his gang of financial crooks. Yet he never lost his sense of humour, and when an ambitious young politician named Lloyd George, following a series of British victories, seriously considered the advisability of ceasing to champion the Boers, Labby exclaimed: 'For heaven's sake, don't do anything of the sort! You'd far better stick to your present line. It will pay in the long run.' It did.

Meanwhile *Truth* went on, and so did the libel cases. Labby remained imperturbable. One victim called at Pope's Villa to challenge him to a duel. 'Will you please thank the gentleman very much', he told the servant who brought the message, 'but

N

I am not fighting today. Ask him to call again.' Having no author's vanity, he did not mind how much his articles were edited, saying: 'It has always appeared to me that the making of an article requires two persons, one to write it, the other to cut it down – and generally to cut out what the first man most admires.' He was mischievous but not malicious, and whenever he discovered that he had unwittingly hurt someone he liked he did his best to make amends. Indifferent to his personal appearance, he often looked like a dilapidated bagman, and one of his jackets became a joke in the office: it was disreputable and could be smelt from some distance. At last his wife put it in the dustbin, but he retrieved it. On his occasional visits to the paper he would sit correcting the proof of an article with a chop in one hand and a cigarette in the other. Having finished the chop he took out his teeth, placed them on the table and went on with his work. This upset Voules, who sometimes joined the sub-editor in the next room until it was time for Labby to resume his dentures. But on returning he would find his chief prodding at them with the office scissors or battering them with a ruler to improve their shape. Once the wastepaper-basket burst into flames because Labby had thrown a lighted match into it, but he sat smoking immovably while the staff dealt with the fire. Nothing could agitate him.

He was slily generous. No one ever saw his name on a public subscription list, but he bountifully helped friends in need and did many kind actions by stealth. His critical attitude to public questions and persons gave everyone the impression that he was illiberal by nature. He thought little of Gladstone's successors, telling a friend that 'If you were to take them all together and boil them in a pot, Campbell-Bannerman, Asquith, Morley, Rosebery and Grey, you would not get the worth of a mouse out of them.' These were the new 'liberals', and as Labby had passed the age of seventy by the end of the Boer War, and reduced his following in the House until he could only depend on his own vote, he decided to retire from Parliament. Having bought and 'improved' Michael Angelo's villa near Florence, he announced

his resignation in 1905, to the unspeakable relief of the new
Liberal Prime Minister, Campbell-Bannerman, who felt that
it would now be safe to make the recalcitrant radical a Privy
Councillor. Having no respect of persons, Labby could never be
depended upon to toe the party line or give deference to the
mighty or even lip-service to the Almighty. But he would be
harmless at Florence, and King Edward VII had no objection to
honouring a viper that could no longer sting.

Visitors to his Italian retreat were constant, and he talked as
well as ever, but the death of Henrietta in 1910 shook him, and
after its occurrence his friends thought he looked frail. At the
beginning of 1912 he caught a cold, which brought on bronchial
catarrh, his heart being affected. Though his mind remained
keen, his bodily weakness increased. On 14 January he was dozing
in bed when his future biographer Algar Thorold accidentally
overturned a spirit-lamp on the table. The flash of light roused
Labby, who opened his eyes. 'Flames?' he murmured: 'not yet,
I think.' With a chuckle he closed his eyes for the last time,
expiring just before midnight on the 15th. Thorold, at the end
of his own life, regretted that he had reported this final quip.
Labby would not have shared his regret.

7

James McNeill Whistler

At the dances held in the British Legation at Washington during the early months of 1855 a young man was to be seen in a curious costume, shortness of cash having compelled him to wear his frock-coat which he managed to make as much like a dress-coat as possible by pinning back the skirts. This appealed to the comedic sense of a young attaché, Henry Labouchere, who promptly made friends with the oddly garbed youth. Their friendship was cemented in England many years later, the impudence and irresponsibility of each being equally matched by the other's. Sitting with him in his London club one day, Labby was dealing candidly with notable personalities, much to his friend's amusement. But an old gentleman near-by overheard his observations, strongly objected to their tone, and at last could bear them no longer. Rising with a reddened face, he spoke severely: 'Young man, I knew your grandmother.' Labby rose too, bowed gravely, and said: 'Perhaps, sir, I have the honour of addressing my grandfather.' While his guest gave a high-pitched laugh, the old gentleman stalked off. After that Labby could do no wrong in the eyes of the other, and they never quarrelled, a remarkable circumstance, since his companion, known as James McNeill Whistler, managed to quarrel with all his other friends.

Whistler objected to the place of his birth, the year of his birth and his second baptismal name. He said in a court of law that he had been born at St Petersburg, assured everyone that he was seven years younger than his real age, and changed one of his Christian names for his mother's surname. But his love of inaccuracy must not be indulged by his biographer, who is compelled to state that he was born at Lowell, Massachusetts, on 10 July 1834, and that he was christened James Abbot. His mother's family, named McNeill, had emigrated to America from the island of Skye, his father's from Ireland, but his paternal ancestors were English; and, though he hated to admit it, there was far more of the English eccentric about him than of the Scottish or Irish Celt. Indeed his quarrelsome character was partly the outcome of being a northern American with southern sympathies and a turbulent Gael with the temperament of an irascible Briton.

Some years of his youth were spent in Russia, where his father was the engineer in charge of the railroad then being constructed between St Petersburg and Moscow. On the death of his father the family returned to America, and after the economical up-bringing of a puritanical mother he went to the Military Academy at West Point. Here it soon became clear that he would not make a good soldier, for he was continually absent without leave, careless of discipline and indifferent to the teaching of his professors. Drawing and painting were the only things that interested him, and he proudly proclaimed his ignorance of dates. 'What!' exclaimed the examiner: 'you do not know the date of the Battle of Buena Vista? Suppose you were to go out to dinner, and the company began to talk of the Mexican war, and you, a West Point man, were asked the date of the battle, what would you do?' Whistler was indignant: 'Do? Why, I should refuse to associate with people who could talk of such things at dinner!' His ignorance was unconfined, and his announcement during an examination that 'Silicon is a gas' caused his discharge from West Point in June 1854. At a later period he said that 'If silicon had been a gas, I would have been a general', but it is doubtful if Robert E. Lee, head of the Academy at that time, would have endorsed this view.

His family then made a valiant attempt to get him a job as an engineer at Baltimore. He liked the city so much that in due course it became one of his birthplaces, but his interest in engineering was no keener than his curiosity about silicon and he left for Washington, where he got a job in the Coastal Survey Department, but paid more attention to the social life of the place and usually started work when the day was well advanced, replying to one remonstrance: 'I was not too late; the office opened too early.' By this time he knew that art was his sole interest in life, resisted his family's further attempts to make him adopt a respectable profession, and persuaded them to part with just enough money to keep him in Paris while studying how to paint. They agreed to send him 350 dollars a year in quarterly instalments.

In the summer of 1855 he took up his residence in the Latin Quarter and quickly became popular with a number of young artists who later achieved fame, George Du Maurier, Edward Poynter and Frederick Leighton among them. He drew attention to himself by wearing unusual clothes, and though everyone found him charming he gained a reputation for eccentricity and touchiness. He mixed with the natives of the Quarter, spent most of his time in cafés, formed sexual intimacies with some of the female models, and indulged in many Bohemian sprees. In the time he could spare from these enjoyments he learnt a lot about painting, though he seldom attended the studio where the British students received instruction. He appeared to them excessively lazy, but like all men of unusual temperament he taught himself in his own way, and, when he came into touch with Fantin-Latour, Alphonse Legros and Gustave Courbet, his genius as an artist began to assert itself.

Nearly four years were passed in Paris, with occasional holidays in London at the house of his sister, who had married a surgeon, Seymour Haden, destined in the years ahead for a furious quarrel with his brother-in-law. At last the lure of the Thames made Whistler settle in London, and he began a series of etchings at Wapping, finding beauty in what his contemporaries thought ugly. He lived with a golden-haired Irish girl

who went with him everywhere and was known to all his friends
as Jo, her full name being Joanna Heffernan. She appeared in
some of his pictures, notably as 'The Little White Girl', and
they set up house together in Cheyne Walk, Chelsea, an establishment that was disapproved by his more respectable friends
and relations.

In the early 'sixties several of Whistler's paintings and etchings were exhibited by the Royal Academy, but his most original
work was rejected and he perceived that full recognition could
only come after a long fight against the convention that every
picture should tell a story. But as he enjoyed nothing so much
as a fight, he anticipated the campaign with relish. His friends
at the outset of his life in London included Swinburne and Rossetti,
the last of whom helped him to popularise Japanese prints and
Chinese porcelain in England, and in those early days his
companionship delighted everyone because he had not yet begun
to feel that he was the victim of a conspiracy, a state of mind
eventually caused by his sense of being an alien and by the
irritation felt by an original but egotistical artist whose work
was not in the fashion of the day; for he belonged neither to the
old conventional school of the English nor to the new impression-
istic school of the French. In time he came to regard himself as
an outcast, both artistically and nationally, and since he was
pugnacious by nature he hit out at those who dared to criticise
him, or even qualified their admiration.

He had a full share of vanity as well as conceit, of touchiness
coupled with arrogance. To the question: 'Do you think genius
is hereditary?' he replied: 'I can't tell you; heaven has granted
me no offspring.' Gradually he built up a defensive personality
which resembled no other, and he took care to dress the part.
Even while working in his studio he looked neat and trim, but
out in the streets or lunching at a restaurant he was groomed
to the point of dandyism. In middle life his short, slight, dapper,
perky figure moved daintily along the pavement, with a long
wandlike cane in one hand ('for the critics', he said) and yellow
gloves in the other. He wore a monocle, a tall silk hat, and an

immaculate frock-coat. He took great trouble with the arrangement of his glossy black curly hair, one lock of which was white
and carefully arranged for effect. His conversation was constantly punctuated with a strident 'Ha-ha!' which made people
jump. At parties he told funny stories, usually about himself and
mostly invented as he went along. The best surviving example
was retailed by Robert Ross to the present writer:

'I had no money, and fish was cheap, so I lived on fish. Fish
for breakfast, fish for dinner, always fish. My landlady could
only think in fish. The lodgings reeked of fish. Even the Thames,
which I had beautified, became for me merely the home of fish.
I tried to paint a portrait, but the face of my subject seemed scaly.
Then one day I looked out of my window and up at the clouds
and behold! a mackerel sky. So I looked down. Could I believe
my eyes? At least I could believe my nose. There, in a bowl of
water on my landlady's window-sill, were three goldfish
swimming tauntingly at their ease. I resolved to teach her a
lesson. Soon she would be bringing me a meal of fish. She, too,
should have fish for her meal. I affixed a bent pin to a piece of
string, baited the pin with bread, and let it down from my
window into the bowl beneath. I am not a skilled fisherman, and
I had to play for my fish a long time before they could see the
joke. But at last I was rewarded with a bite. I hooked my first
fish. After that the other two wanted to come up. I helped them
to come. I am a good cook, as you know, and I fried them to a
turn. Then I lowered them, one by one, into the bowl, with a
charming note: "Madam, you have cooked so many fish for me
that I have ventured to cook some for you." She was cured. She
gave me no more fish. She gave me notice instead.'

When Whistler began to make money with his paintings and
etchings he moved to another house on the Embankment, and
by colouring some of the walls yellow and white, others blue,
he commenced a revolution of domestic interior decoration
throughout England. His Sunday breakfasts became famous. As
a rule he cooked and served the food himself, talking ceaselessly
and giving his guests the impression that they were enjoying

a sumptuous repast; whereas their main course usually consisted of a buckwheat cake with treacle or an egg on toast. A bowl of goldfish on the table and some apple-green butter or tinted rice-pudding to harmonise with the plates may have helped the illusion that a feast was in progress, while a good red wine fortified the deception. Asked by a guest one day why the butter was coloured blue in one dish and pink in another, he replied: 'By giving it the delicate tints of Peking and Tokyo, I try to forget that it is churned in London.' Though normally abstemious, he occasionally broke out. Once he dined rather too well at the house of a wealthy art-patron, and after dinner left the table to go upstairs. He managed the ascent with dignity, but returned more expeditiously, falling down a whole flight. Helped to his feet by an anxious host, he asked: 'Who is your architect?' Norman Shaw, he was told. 'I might have known it – the damned teetotaller!' he grumbled.

Frequently hard-up, he yet refused commissions that did not appeal to him. One man offered him a respectable fee for a portrait of himself, but Whistler thought him an unattractive subject and said: 'Yes, I will paint you, but I hope you will not be offended if I make the portrait like.' Hating anecdotal painting, he called his pictures 'symphonies', 'nocturnes', 'harmonies', 'arrangements'. They were intensely individual; and to the average person brought up on works that photographed their subjects or appealed to the more primitive emotions or represented episodes from life, they were incomprehensible. Even his famous portrait of his mother was called 'Arrangement in Grey and Black', and so was his equally striking portrait of Thomas Carlyle, while his charming study of Cicely Alexander came under the heading of 'Harmony in Grey and Green'.

His great period as a painter commenced early in the 'seventies, and about then he changed mistresses. Jo and her son by him left the house and red-haired Maud Franklin was installed in her place. Maud appeared in many of his etchings and paintings thereafter, especially as The Young American in his 'Arrangement in Black and White'. She looked after him more efficiently than Jo had done, managed his affairs and had at least one child, a daughter, by him; but her personality often clashed with his and violent scenes occurred. If he had not depended so much on her business capacity, their liaison of fifteen years would have been abridged.

His haunting impression of Henry Irving as Philip II (1876) did not please the actor; and, when he begged Beaconsfield to sit for him, the ageing statesman told him to run away. A fascinating portrait of this period was of Rosa Corder ('Arrangement in Black and Brown') and he made a powerful study of the prosperous Liverpool shipowner, Frederick Leyland, who had already bought one of Whistler's pictures and frequently asked the artist to stay with his family. But dreadful storms were ahead. Leyland took a London house, 49 Prince's Gate, furnished it magnificently, and engaged Whistler to help with the decorations. But instead of improving the dining-room he transformed it into a sort of peacock's paradise; the walls, woodwork, shutters and ceiling were covered with peacocks – a 'Harmony in Blue and Gold' – the whole being a suitable setting for two of Whistler's pictures. Leyland was horrified and gave Whistler a thousand pounds for his labour instead of the two thousand guineas demanded by the artist, who felt insulted and retaliated by painting a rich and a poor peacock in the place reserved for one of his pictures, under the claws of the rich one appearing the silver shillings which represented the difference between pounds and guineas, since Whistler felt that tradesmen were paid in the first, gentlemen in the second. Later he did a colourful but rather horrible piece of work caricaturing Leyland as 'The Gold Scab'. The unfortunate shipowner suffered for the shortcomings of English critics, who were treating Whistler's pictures as if they were jokes and the artist as if he were a comedian.

One of these critics went too far. John Ruskin viewed the first Grosvenor Gallery exhibition, and wrote of Whistler's 'The Falling Rocket' that he had 'never expected to hear a coxcomb ask two hundred guineas for flinging a pot of paint in the public's face'. Ruskin had enormous influence as an art

critic and this remark had an immediate and deleterious effect
on Whistler's position. At the time he was pawning his portraits
and 'nocturnes' in order to live, while the architect E. W.
Godwin was building for him what came to be known as The
White House in Tite Street, Chelsea. In spite of his poverty he
brought an action against Ruskin, claiming a thousand pounds
for the damage done by the criticism. In the course of his cross-
examination Whistler made one of his finest pronouncements:

'Did it take you much time to paint the "Nocturne in Black and
Gold"? How soon did you knock it off?' he was asked concerning
'The Falling Rocket'.

'I beg your pardon?'

'I was using an expression which was rather more applicable
to my own profession. How long do you take to knock off one
of your pictures?'

'Oh, I knock off one possibly in a couple of days – one day to
do the work, and another to finish it.'

'And that was the labour for which you asked two hundred
guineas?'

'No; it was for the knowledge gained through a lifetime.'

Whistler received a farthing damages, which meant that he
had to pay his own costs. The case ruined him, and he had to leave
his new house in May 1879, some six months after he had moved
in. He gave a few parties there, and copied Sheridan by getting the
bailiffs to wait at table. The night before the sale took place he
wrote in ink above the front door: 'Except the Lord build the
house, they labour in vain that build it. E. W. Godwin, F.R.A.,
built this one.' When he had been made a bankrupt, his pictures
went for a song; and he retired to Venice, where he made many
etchings.

The lack of appreciation shown by his fellow-artists in their
evidence during the Ruskin case hardened and embittered
Whistler, who, since the critics would not accord what was due
to him, determined to assert his claim to be superior to other
men whenever the opportunity occurred; and the persistently
belligerent Whistler, the Master who could bear no rival and

insisted on unqualified adulation, dated from his bankruptcy and appearance in a court of law. The world had mocked at him and ruined him: henceforth he would jeer at the world and help only those who bowed before him; and he began to speak of himself regally in the third person. On his calling for payment of a picture which a dealer had sold, the cheque was given him in a casual sort of way. 'This is careless of you', said he. 'You push the cheque toward me, and you do not realise what a privilege it is to be able to hand it to the Master. You should offer it on a rich Old English salver, and in a kingly way.' Those who began as disciples but in time dared to do things of which he disapproved were obliterated. He knew them no more, and their names were never mentioned in his presence.

Not long after his return from Venice to England the Society of British Artists was founded, and since it would compete with the Royal Academy he took a keen interest in it, becoming President in 1886; but two years of his arbitrary authority and cutting comments set the members by the ears and he was not re-elected, twenty-five of his disciples resigning as a protest, upon which he remarked that 'the Artists have come out and the British remain – and peace and sweet obscurity are restored to Suffolk Street! Eh? What? Ha-ha!' His criticisms of fellow-artists aroused their enmity and his retaliations on the critics made them squirm. Politicians apart, he was probably the most hated famous man of his time. As a rule he was more than a match for any of his self-created antagonists; but when he fell foul of Oscar Wilde he took on someone who was mentally (and physically) twice his size. Whistler's *Ten O'Clock* lecture in February 1885, reviewed in a friendly but humorous style by Oscar, began the trouble. The bare idea of anyone being amusing at his expense was obnoxious to the painter, and a newspaper exchange of repartees gradually developed into an acrimonious battle of personalities, the incomparable superiority of Wilde as a talker adding venom to Whistler's attacks. The poet could not compete with the painter in spite, and Whistler was left with the last word. Swinburne was another friend with whom he quarrelled shortly after delivering his lecture, but as no rivalry in wit was involved this antagonist was let down lightly as a mere 'outsider'.

In 1890 Whistler published his anthology of amusing malice and prim prose, *The Gentle Art of Making Enemies*, a record of his quarrels with one-time friends and of his campaign against critics, whose ludicrous pronouncements were suitably dealt with in pungent phrases. The book was decorated with his well-known signature, a butterfly. But it was a butterfly with a sting, representing his public and private behaviour, for he flitted from one woman to another, as he did from one critic to another, leaving a sharp pain wherever he had settled. He formed a close friendship with the wife of E. W. Godwin, and there were noisy scenes between Beatrice Godwin and Maud, which developed into slanging-matches when Godwin died and his widow spent most of her time in Whistler's studio. It was obvious to everyone who knew them that he and Trixie (as he called her) were in love with each other, and one evening they dined with Henry Labouchere, who brought matters to a head.

'Jimmy, will you marry Mrs Godwin?' asked Labby.

'Certainly.'

'Mrs Godwin, will you marry Jimmy?'

'Certainly.'

'When?'

'Oh, some day', said Whistler.

'That won't do. We must have a date.'

So Labby arranged the wedding at St Mary Abbot's Church, Kensington, in August 1888, and during the ceremony Whistler looked about him apprehensively, afraid that Maud might turn up and enliven the proceedings in a highly irreverent manner. They dashed off to Paris, and when Maud heard the news she collapsed. One of Whistler's disciples, William Stott, at whose house Maud was staying just then, criticised the Master sharply and was knocked down for his pains. Whistler had an unforgiving nature, and on hearing some years later that Stott had expired during an ocean voyage he merely remarked: 'So he died at sea, where he always was.' Following a period when she exasperated Trixie by calling herself 'Mrs Whistler' and living near-by, Maud married a wealthy South American and spent the rest of her life in a comfort she had never known as Whistler's mistress.

Trixie, many years younger than Jimmy, was a dark beauty, and of course became his model, memorably for his picture 'Harmony in Red'. They were a devoted pair and he could hardly bear to be apart from her. He ceased to instigate quarrels, though he remained susceptible to hostility and fancied insults. 'If I died before Jimmy, he would not have a friend left in a week', she declared. They lived for a while in Chelsea, but shortly after a successful exhibition of his pictures they moved to Paris early in 1893. Suddenly people wanted to acquire his 'arrangements' and 'nocturnes', and he actually disposed of 'The Falling Rocket', which Ruskin had priced at a pot of paint, for eight hundred guineas. Thenceforth he could ask almost anything for a picture, and his early works were auctioned for twenty and thirty times as much as he had received for them.

His two years in Paris, with visits to Normandy and Brittany and trips to nearer places, were the happiest of his life. They were also peaceful; but absolute concord did not suit his temperament; he could not live up to his 'harmonies'; and, when he transacted business with a man as quarrelsome as himself, the fur was bound to fly. Sir William Eden, father of a future Prime Minister, was egotistical, dictatorial and prickly, but a lover of beauty. He adored his handsome wife and wanted Whistler to paint her portrait. But he thought the artist's terms, five hundred guineas, excessive, and at length Whistler agreed to do 'a little painting' of Lady Eden for something between a hundred and a hundred and fifty guineas. As Sir William should have foreseen, Whistler regarded the cheque for one hundred guineas which he received for the work as an insult, but instead of returning the cheque he exhibited the picture. Eden brought an action against him, Whistler substituted someone else's head for Lady Eden's, and two legal cases ensued, as a result of which the artist was permitted to keep his picture, the baronet his money. As usual everyone who sided with Eden ceased to be the friend of Whistler, who eventually cleansed his soul of much perilous stuff by producing a dull book called *The Baronet and the Butterfly*, his behaviour being all the more extraordinary because he pursued his vendetta against Eden and the rest, who in his eyes symbolised the conspiracy of the English people against a great artist, while his wife was dying of cancer.

He would not believe that her illness was mortal, and he took her to see innumerable doctors, quarrelling with his medical brother, who had prevented an unnecessary operation by a French doctor, and thereby losing his best friend. Such was the state of his mind that he could not capture the tranquillity essential for his work, much of which he destroyed, though a temporary improvement of her health while they were at Lyme Regis enabled him to produce two fine pictures. Many sleepless nights were spent by her bedside, and when she died at Hampstead in May 1896 he was frantic with grief. He never properly recovered from the blow, and for a while moved about restlessly from one place to another. But after some months he reappeared in public and even occasionally attended an official dinner.

To the end of his life he said hurtful things and did generous actions. He became President of the International Society of Sculptors, Painters and Gravers, the members of which had to be approved by himself, and ran the Company of the Butterfly for the sale of his pictures. Now and then he received a business call at his Fitzroy Street studio, where he received an offer from an American collector: 'How much for the whole lot, Mr Whistler?' 'Five millions.' 'What!?!' 'My posthumous prices. Good-morning.' For a while he paid regular visits to an art school in Paris, his fame attracting many students, and though he was kind to those who were doing their best he dealt effectively with the others. 'Why did you paint a red elbow with green shadows?' he asked one of them. 'I am sure I just paint what I see.' 'Ah! but the shock will come when you see what you paint.' Another young man whose superior manner grated on the Master was examined in this manner:

'Been to College?'

'Yes.'

'I suppose you shoot?'

'Yes.'

'Fish?'

'Yes.'

'Play football?'

'Yes.'

'Then I can let you off painting.'

By the turn of the century Whistler was famous in two hemispheres and comparatively wealthy, with rooms in London and Paris hotels, studios in both cities, and apartments as well. His anglophobia found a new outlet when the Boer War started in 1899; he gloried in Boer victories and exulted in British defeats. Someone happened to remark in his company that the English Commander-in-Chief Sir Redvers Buller was a sound strategist, having retired from a certain engagement without losing a man or a flag or a gun – 'or a minute', Whistler chipped in. During the Boxer Rising in China he expressed a fervent desire that the blue and white porcelain in the palace at Peking would be spared: 'All the Englishmen in the world are not worth one blue China vase.'

His health gradually deteriorated, which he attributed to living so long in the midst of English pictures. He stayed several weeks in Holland and went on a sea-trip to Corsica, but he was tired, out of spirits and disinclined to work. In May 1903 the dying man received the degree of LL.D. from Glasgow University. A steadily weakening heart prevented him from walking, but he still went for drives with his late wife's sister, who lived near-by and attended to his wants. In a room overlooking his beloved Thames, the marvels of which he had unveiled to the world, Whistler died on 17 July 1903, sixty-two years old by his own account, at the age of sixty-nine reckoning from the year of his birth.

8

William Schwenck Gilbert

Wits have one thing in common with bores: they recognise at sight and avoid one another, fearing competition. The wit, like the bore, must have an audience, and dislikes being kept on his toes by a too keen rivalry. A little emulation is helpful, a contest of equals to be deplored. Whistler put up with Wilde only so long as 'the amiable Oscar' played the disciple, and quarrelled with him the moment he showed signs of becoming a master at the same game. There was never the slightest likelihood that W. S. Gilbert would be anything but a thorn in the flesh, and it is not surprising that the two most biting wits of their time kept apart. Evidence of one meeting exists in Gilbert's diary: 'Sunday, 24 Nov. Breakfast with Whistler.' Not another word except that his own wife and Albert Moore were present. The year was 1878. Gilbert and Sullivan's *Pinafore* had been produced that spring, and Whistler's case against Ruskin was about to be heard. No doubt the two wits were on their best behaviour, each trying to outdo the other as a gentleman. But they must instantly have spotted danger signals, and there is no record of another meeting. Some two years after that breakfast Whistler was much too clever to be drawn into controversy over the comic opera *Patience*, even though Gilbert's leading character 'Bunthorne' wore a white lock of hair, called himself

> A greenery-yallery, Grosvenor Gallery,
> Foot-in-the-grave young man,

and sang a ditty which made fun of the Master's well-known tastes:

> Such a judge of blue-and-white and other kinds of pottery –
> From early Oriental down to modern terra-cotta-ry.

The two men had another thing in common besides a slashing wit: they fell foul of their friends on the slightest provocation.

William Gilbert made his entry on life's stage at No. 17 Southampton Street, Strand, London, the date being 18 November 1836, the house being his grandfather's. The Gilberts were Hampshire yeomen until one of them opened a grocery business in London, his son becoming a successful tea-merchant and grandfather of our William, whose godmother's name was Mary Schwenck, hence one of the baby's Christian names, which from boyhood he tried to forget. William's father started life as a naval surgeon, wrote a few books, was caustic, choleric and crotchety by nature, married a Scottish girl, begat a son and three daughters, but failed to create a harmonious home for them, much of their early life being spent in going from one place to another on the Continent. Their mother being repressed, their father oppressive, the children lacked love, and it is difficult to believe that there was ever much sentiment in the relationship of their parents, because when William was thirty years of age he tried to reconcile the two, then living apart, beginning with a formal appeal to 'Dear Mama' and ending with an objurgatory 'Madam'. He failed to bring them together; and it is reasonable to infer that the absence of genuine feeling in his work, as well as the unreality of his themes and the mockery of ageing females, were largely owing to an uncomfortable home life as a child and a deep resentment against his mother for lack of sympathy.

His training as a writer of comic opera began early. At the age of two he was captured by two Neopolitan brigands and redeemed by his parents for the sum of £25. After some tuition at Boulogne, he went to Great Ealing School, where he lightened the boredom of learning by writing verses and drawing cartoons. To the masters he was lazy, to the other boys too masterful.

He enjoyed scribbling sketches and melodramas, daubing scenery for them, acting the leading parts, and bullying the other members of the casts. Being of a competitive nature, he worked hard enough at intervals to end up as head of the school, and went on to King's College, London. While there the Crimean War started. Over six feet tall and full of martial ardour, he began to work for a commission in the Royal Artillery, having taken his B.A. degree. But the war came to a close while his studies were in progress, and instead he obtained an assistant clerkship in the Education Department of the Privy Council Office, where he spent four uncomfortable years at an annual salary of £120, trying to forget his tedious job by joining the Militia, writing songs, studying for the law, and playing practical jokes on the inmates of the Pimlico boarding-house where he lodged, of which a typical example may be given. He liked to give the impression that he exercised some influence in the theatrical world, and one of his fellow-lodgers asked if he could write an order for seats at a play. 'Certainly I could. For stalls or a box?' 'A box, if you please.' Gilbert at once wrote the order; but it was received with laughter at the box-office concerned, and the indignant victim demanded an explanation of Gilbert, who gave it with pleasure: 'You asked me whether I could write you an order for the play. I replied that I could, and I did, but I never said it would be of the least use to you.'

At the end of four years in what he called 'the detestable thraldom of this baleful office' he inherited about £400 from an aunt, and 'on the happiest day of my life I sent in my resignation'. He disbursed the money on the fee for admission to the Bar and for studentship at the Inner Temple, the remainder of his inheritance going to the cost of pupilage in a barrister's chambers and of personal chambers in Clement's Inn. His legal career of four years brought him few clients, little money and no fame. One lady he defended unsuccessfully threw a boot at his head, and a Frenchman whose case he won hugged and kissed him in open court, which made him regret the verdict. Recognising in time that he was not a born barrister, he filled in the hours waiting for imaginary clients by writing farces and making drawings. They were not accepted, so he began to produce articles, poems, skits and parodies, but all were rejected. At length it occurred to him that editors did not bother to look at his things and he determined to send an article and a drawing direct to the proprietor of a newly-launched paper called *Fun*. The proprietor liked both and told his editor, H. J. Byron, to print them. Very soon Gilbert became a regular contributor, and as time went on his *Bab Ballads* were the leading feature in the periodical. (He had been called 'Bab', short for baby, by his parents.) Eventually he published two volumes of them, in 1869 and 1873, and they were quoted and recited at public functions all over the country. What made them unique was a quality that Gilbert himself toned down when he used their themes in his operas: an imaginative perception that human beings and the conditions of their existence on earth are wholly and innately ridiculous, which is the root cause of 'Laughter holding both his sides'. The imperfection of life, a source of sadness in the great poets, is a source of silliness in 'Bab', who created an art of unadulterated absurdity.

Among the friends Gilbert made while writing for *Fun* was Tom Robertson, whose plays (*Society, Ours, Caste, School*, etc.) were put on by the Bancrofts in the 'sixties and revolutionised the British stage with their natural characters, natural situations and natural acting. Robertson was the first of the author-producers, and modern stage-management as we understand it derives from him. Gilbert was allowed to watch rehearsals of the Robertson plays and benefited greatly from the experience. Robertson also advised the lessee of St James's Theatre to ask his friend for a Christmas play, and Gilbert's career as a dramatist opened with the production of *Dulcamara* at the end of December 1866. Once started, nothing could stop Gilbert, who wrote a succession of farces, burlesques, comedies, pantomimes and sketches for music, the number of which made the theatre managers wonder whether he was a man or a syndicate. He visited Paris to spot French plays that could easily be adapted, and incidentally was one of the countless people who left by the last train when the capital was about to be besieged in the Franco-German War of 1870. If all those of whom it is recorded that they left by the last train were bona-fide passengers, the carriages must have stretched from Paris to the coast. Many of his pieces were produced, many scrapped, but the effort of writing them was good training and he never grudged the toil. In later years he thought little of his early essays in dramatic technique, and as none of them has survived his opinion has been endorsed by the public; but he thought a great deal of his serious dramas, mostly in blank verse, which followed those tentatives and which made him the leading playwright of the 'seventies.

In August 1867 he married the pretty fair-haired daughter of an Indian Army officer at St Mary Abbot's Church, Kensington, where in the fullness of time the other stormy wit of the period, Whistler, would be joined in wedlock. Gilbert's bride, Lucy Agnes Turner, was eleven years younger than himself, and to the end of his days their home life was an oasis of peace in a wilderness of war. They had no children, but made up for the lack by having innumerable parties for other people's children. Like so many men who are uncomfortable with their male contemporaries, Gilbert loved animals as well as women and children, and when he could afford it he was surrounded by all three types of fauna.

His serious plays had an element of fantasy that appealed to grown-up children and enjoyed long runs. The first was a blank verse parody of Tennyson's *The Princess*. Then he was commissioned by the manager of the Haymarket Theatre to provide a fairy comedy in iambic pentameter, *The Palace of Truth*, which was followed by *Pygmalion and Galatea* at the same theatre in 1871. The quarrels with actors and actresses who could not or would not do exactly as he told them were a feature of these productions. Another fairy play, *The Wicked World*, was another success. Following one or two excursions into prose drama, he again dropped into verse, and *Broken Hearts* caused several broken friendships at the Court Theatre in 1875. The author quarrelled with the producer, John Hare, the leading actors, Mr and Mrs Kendal, a leading critic, Clement Scott, and a fellow-dramatist, F. C. Burnand. The flare-up with the last two illustrates Gilbert's excessive touchiness. Burnand happened to mention that he was going to see 'Broken Parts'. Scott quoted this in an article, and received a sharp note from Gilbert: 'Burnand's attempt at wit is silly and coarse, and your attempt to bring it into prominence is in the worst possible taste. I am not by any means a thin-skinned man, but in this case I feel bound to take exception to your treatment of me and of my serious work.' Twenty-six years later Scott tried to restore their friendship, but Gilbert still smarted from the quip and declined a *rapprochement*. He revenged himself on his fellow-dramatist many years afterwards when Burnand was editor of *Punch*. At a dinner given by Sir Squire Bancroft someone asked whether that paper ever received good jokes and articles from outsiders. 'Oh, often!' said Burnand. 'They never appear', said Gilbert.

The climate in Gilbert's neighbourhood was always liable to squalls. The next-door noises in Essex Villas, Kensington, interfered with his slumbers, and after an acrimonious correspondence with the tenant he invoked the law. Although the fellow was advised to cease from troubling, it was uncomfortable to live in the vicinity of angry glances, and Gilbert took a house in The Boltons. The purchase of a yacht, the sale of a horse, the unpunctual delivery of letters, the non-payment of a legacy, the uncertain honesty of a male servant: whatever caused him inconvenience resulted in friction, and though his complaints were usually justified their forceful expression made it difficult for the other parties to climb down with dignity. Though proud of his service in the Royal Aberdeen Militia, the time came when he felt it necessary to raise Cain over his mess-bill. To Lord Inverurie, President of the Mess Committee, he wrote: 'I must decline to pay for more messing than I actually enjoyed – if that term can be reasonably applied to the food that was placed before me by the messman.' He queried several items on his account, his complaint being forwarded to the Colonel, whose acid comment provoked Gilbert to write: 'I must decline, after this expression of opinion, to serve under an officer who is so little qualified to command gentlemen.' The case came to the notice of the Commander-in-Chief, who managed to influence matters in a way that preserved Gilbert's self-respect, and the storm blew over. When at length he did resign, after thirteen years of service, he gave as a reason his increasing business as a dramatist.

His stream of plays in the 'seventies included a farcical comedy, *Engaged*, which foreshadowed Wilde's incomparable masterpiece *The Importance of Being Earnest*. An actor who was then making his name, Beerbohm Tree, appeared in a revival of *Engaged*, and two of Gilbert's remarks which amused Tree show how easily the author aroused hostility in those who could not laugh at themselves. Noting that Tree was sweating profusely after the first performance, Gilbert remarked: 'Your skin has been acting at all events.' Tree laughed and said that he ought to have grown a moustache for the part. 'You will be able to grow an enormous moustache before you can play this part', observed Gilbert. But no other player of the time took this kind of thing good-humouredly like Tree, and there was an almighty rumpus between Gilbert and Henrietta Hodson which started with a quip. She played the leading part in one of his comedies and in the course of rehearsal accidently sat down heavily on the stage instead of on a chair. 'Very good, very good', said Gilbert encouragingly: 'I always thought you would make an impression on the stage one day.' She did not think this funny and heated recriminations followed, during which she called him 'a floody bool' and strongly advised him 'to go home and go to bed as that is the best place for you!' He was inflamed, she was incensed, and when he was prevailed upon to apologise by letter she published it in a paper. A few years later she appeared in a revival of his *Pygmalion* and complained of his persecution. He produced a letter from the manager which proved that he had not acted inimically, and she accused him of having forged it.

She issued a pamphlet with a list of her grievances; he countered with a pamphlet proving them baseless. Meanwhile her husband Henry Labouchere kept up a running commentary in *Truth* at Gilbert's expense. Actions for libel pended, but remained pending. The concluding passage between the two wits occurred towards the end of their lives, when Gilbert was unable to obtain accommodation at a hotel in the Italian Lakes which he discovered on inquiry was partly owned by Labby, upon which he declared that he could never understand the other's animosity until it dawned on him that thirty-seven years before he had introduced the editor of *Truth* to his future wife, Henrietta. This made all clear: 'I admit that, quite unwittingly, I did him an irreparable injury, and am disposed to regard his hostility in some measure justified.'

Since financial success meant so much to Gilbert, it gives us the measure of his excessive touchiness in personal relationships, partly owing no doubt to the domestic disharmony of his early years, when we see how again and again he risked the loss of money to appease his pride. The most extreme example of this occurred at the moment of his greatest success. In 1870 he was busy providing sketches for an entertainment at the Gallery of Illustration when the composer Fred Clay introduced him to Arthur Sullivan, whose main ambition was to write grand operas and oratorios. Sullivan was as pliable as Gilbert was the reverse, and the playwright soon imposed his masculinity on the feminine nature of the composer. In the year after their meeting they collaborated in an opera, *Thespis*, which failed, and they were brought together again by an astute man of business, D'Oyly Carte, then directing the Royalty Theatre, who asked them for a one-act piece to follow Offenbach's *La Périchole*. With the appearance of *Trial by Jury* in March 1875 Sullivan's popularity superseded that of Offenbach. Carte then raised the capital for a Comedy Opera Company, and *The Sorcerer* by Gilbert and Sullivan was seen at the Opera Comique in November '77, running for six months. But this was nothing compared with the success of *H.M.S. Pinafore*, which started its career on

25 May 1878, and after a sensational quarrel between Carte and his fellow-directors, which resulted in two versions of the same opera being seen at adjacent theatres, it totalled over seven hundred performances. Carte now formed another partnership, consisted of himself, Gilbert and Sullivan, each of them putting up a share of the capital and dividing the profits.

No copyright agreement then existed between England and America, and *Pinafore* was being performed all over the United States by at least forty companies, everyone concerned making money out of it except the triumvirate responsible for it. 'I will not have another libretto of mine produced if the Americans are going to steal it', announced Gilbert; 'not that I need the money so much, but it upsets my digestion.' So they decided to visit the States, to put on *Pinafore* as it ought to be performed, to produce their next opera there, and to send out companies before the pirates were able to forestall them. They were greeted at Sandy Hook by steamers with bands playing music from *Pinafore*, and they found that everyone in New York could hum or whistle its airs. Gilbert's stage-management made the Americans realise that the various companies they had seen were untrained, and New York went mad over the new opera, *The Pirates of Penzance*, which was launched on 31 December 1879, repeating its American success in London the following April. Unfortunately the irritation aroused in Gilbert by the copyright question, coupled with the general opinion that the tunes in the operas were superior to the words, stimulated perhaps by the exhilarating air of New York, caused him to make several jokes in public at his collaborator's expense, which he thought amusing but which Sullivan found jarring. It was the first hint that the complementary qualities in the partners were liable to mal-adjustment.

But no one could have guessed from their next production that the two were not hand and glove. Gilbert had poked fun at the Church in a Bab Ballad 'The Rival Curates', and it was well-known that he did not care for the clergy. 'I feel like a lion in a den of Daniels', he said on finding himself almost the only layman in a crowd of parsons. But there is a big difference between a comic ballad and a comic opera, and while toying with the theme of the curates in a libretto he suffered a spasm of caution. Would people be moved to mirth by male comics wearing round collars? The thought gave him restless nights. Suddenly the similarity between curates and aesthetes struck him, and as everyone was then laughing at the aesthetic craze he knew he would be on safe ground if he helped to swell the laughter. Quickly he 'rearranged the piece upon a secure and satisfactory basis', and the result, *Patience*, was so successful that Carte transferred it from the Opera Comique to the new Savoy Theatre, which was opened on 10 October 1881 with Gilbert and Sullivan's latest opera. The chief novelties at the Savoy were the lighting of the theatre by electricity and the institution of regulated queues at pit and gallery entrances, where previously people had fought to get in. A new agreement was made between the three partners, Carte claiming £4,000 for the annual rent of the theatre that had been built for him.

Iolanthe followed in 1882, repeating the success of its predecessors, and Gilbert was able to spend a lot of money on furnishing his house in Harrington Gardens, South Kensington, which had been constructed according to his requirements and finished with the censorious correspondence that usually attended his business dealings. He also took a country house near Uxbridge, where he enjoyed tennis on a court large enough for his erratic if powerful style of play. His next libretto, founded on his early play *The Princess*, was in blank verse, with which the performers struggled manfully, some of them losing heart under the author's direction. 'Look here, sir, I will *not* be bullied! I know my lines', cried one of them. 'That may be, but you don't know mine', came the sharp retort. 'I've rehearsed this confounded business until I feel a perfect fool', complained the leading actor George Grossmith. 'Ah, now we can talk on equal terms', said Gilbert. Sullivan, who suffered all his life from kidney trouble, was in agony during rehearsals and had to drug himself with morphia to conduct on the first night of *Princess Ida* (1884), which ran for nine months.

A relative failure was enough to cause a rift in the partnership, which could only exist on a basis of prosperity, and Sullivan announced that he had written his last work for the Savoy. All his friends were telling him that he was wasting his genius on light opera, that he was made for more august creation, and he believed them. He found fault with Gilbert's inhuman plots and demanded greater freedom for his music. There followed a sharp interchange of letters and a meeting. For many years Gilbert had nursed an idea which he had already partly exploited in previous works, viz: that by absorbing a lozenge a person's nature changed to what he or she affected to be. Since the theme was not noticeably lifelike, Sullivan turned it down. They wrangled on paper for a while, and at last each satisfied his conscience by refusing to collaborate in another opera. Carte, who saw vast sums of money slipping through his fingers, almost went mad. He rushed wildly from one of the recalcitrant partners to the other, soothing their resentment, appealing to their cupidity, and explaining that their mutual esteem was only equalled by his for both. Under his treatment they relaxed; Gilbert abandoned his lozenge, and Sullivan agreed to work on the next piece whatever the theme.

The quarrel between the men led to harmony between the words and music of *The Mikado* (1885) which was their greatest success, running for almost two years. As usual Gilbert's production was perfect, his methods at rehearsal being as ruthless as a sergeant-major's, as diligent as an architect's. He was able now to forget work and sail his yacht, while Sullivan could engage in the social round and write an oratorio. At length they turned their attention to another opera, *Ruddigore* (1887), in which Sullivan thought there were too many words, Gilbert thought there was too much music, and the public did not think much of either, for it lasted less than a year. Gilbert had a good opinion of his own contribution to the work, and when many years later George Edwardes, whose musical comedy productions temporarily displaced the Savoy operas in popularity, stated in an interview that *Ruddigore* might have been saved if its librettist had agreed to alterations, Gilbert wrote to the newspaper: 'Mr Edwardes is quite right in supposing that (after polishing up my work to the minutest degree) I have not been in the habit of handing it over to a stage-manager to embellish with alterations and additions at his good pleasure. If I had done so the Savoy pieces would, no doubt, have borne a stronger resemblance to the productions with which Mr Edwardes' name is associated, but that was not the object I had in view.' Gilbert's sensitiveness extended to the title, which some critics thought vulgar, and on being asked by a friend 'How's Bloodygore going?' the librettist sternly corrected him: 'You mean *Ruddigore.*' The other implied that it was the same thing. 'Indeed?' returned Gilbert: 'Then if I say I admire your ruddy countenance (which I do), it means I like your bloody cheek (which I don't).'

Again the lozenge emerged, again Sullivan could not swallow it, and again Gilbert declined to write on anything else. Time passed, tempers cooled, and Gilbert not only started on a totally different theme but wrote a story with human interest that would give the composer almost the scope of grand opera. Sullivan was delighted; and though at first he protested that he must stop writing light stuff and obey his high calling as a serious musician, he set to work on *The Yeomen of the Guard* (1888), which both collaborators considered their best work. Though successful, it did not do as well as their lighter pieces, and it is hardly surprising that Sullivan once more felt that he was made for better things. A violent correspondence ensued, each of them extolling his own virtues and making the most of the other's defects. This went on for some time, but having let off sufficient steam they felt more at ease, and *The Gondoliers* (1889) testified to the calm after the storm. But a tornado lay ahead.

Gilbert believed that Carte was feathering his nest rather too luxuriously on the profits derived from the creative ability of his partners, and there had been a few business brushes between manager and librettist. But when he discovered that Carte had added £500 for new carpets in the front of the house to the preliminary expenses of *The Gondoliers*, which all of them had to share, he was thunderstruck. By their agreement Gilbert and Sullivan were solely responsible for 'repairs incidental to the performance', and if they had to pay for carpets in the auditorium they would also be liable for any improvements made to the interior of the theatre. An angry scene between the two ended in Carte's remark that as Gilbert was dissatisfied with the management he had better cease to write for the Savoy. Naturally Gilbert was galled, and on finding that the composer sided with the manager, who was about to open a new theatre with a grand opera by Sullivan, he could not contain his rage. The succeeding scenes and letters resulted in a law case, Gilbert's refusal to write again for the Savoy, the discovery of serious discrepancies in the theatre accounts, and an embittered correspondence between the collaborators. In the course of the case an affidavit made by Sullivan in effect but wrongfully accused Gilbert of perjury, and this, not the carpet issue, caused all the further misunderstanding between the two men. Sullivan could not retract without injuring Carte, and Gilbert's fury would not abate until the other admitted the false statement.

This state of affairs continued for some time. Sullivan's grand opera *Ivanhoe* did not hit the public taste, and though Gilbert manage to liquefy his lozenge in a comic opera *The Mountebanks* (music by Alfred Cellier) the usual rumpus accompanied the rehearsals. Such circumstances helped towards a reconciliation between the old Savoy partners, though it was not reached until an exchange of letters had enabled each to pocket his pride and maintain his dignity. After much epistolary tribulation they agreed to collaborate once more, and the librettist even travelled to the Riviera for a discussion with the composer. But an attack of gout drove Gilbert to Homburg, whence he wrote to Sullivan: 'My right foot (which I call Labouchere) is very troublesome, and I take a vicious pleasure (not unalloyed with pain) in cramming him into a boot which is much too small for him. My left foot (known in Homburg as Clement Scott) is a milder nuisance, but still tiresome, and would hurt me a good deal if he could.' At the first night of their joint performance, *Utopia Limited* (1893), the audience yelled with pleasure as they shook hands on the stage. But it was only a moderate success, and the old relationship was past repair. Three years later, each having worked with others in the interval, they came together for the last time, and *The Grand Duke* (1896) flopped as decisively as their friendship. Sullivan died in 1900, and Gilbert's feelings softened towards him in retrospect; but Carte was never forgiven, and when he died Gilbert declined to subscribe to a stained-glass window in his memory, explaining that 'the relations that existed between Carte and myself during the last ten or eleven years, and the circumstances that caused those relations, place it out of my power to join in the proposed Memorial.'

The gout inflamed Gilbert's temper. During the 'nineties he was embroiled in several legal cases and fell foul of George Edwardes, who produced one of his operas, *His Excellency* (1895). Comments on his behaviour as a prickly dictator in the theatre made him bring an action against *The Era*, in the course of which, under cross-examination, he scored off Edward Carson. The laughter that greeted some of his replies reduced the court to hysteria. Carson wanted to know if he had quarrelled with Clement Scott:

'Yes, I wrote to Clement Scott nine years ago complaining of a criticism.'

'You said "I am determined not to expose myself again to your insulting gibes"?'

'Yes, no doubt I wrote that.'

'You were cool and calm?'

'Yes, calm and deliberate. I don't know my temperature at the time.'

Gilbert had spoken in an interview of the bad musical comedies then enjoying long runs in London, and on being asked to mention one he referred to the pantomime at Drury Lane Theatre:

'But that only goes on a short time in the year', objected Carson.

'It goes on for a long time in the evening', retorted Gilbert.

'Do you really describe a pantomime as a bad musical comedy?'

'No, but I would describe a bad musical comedy as a pantomime.'

Early in the 'nineties Gilbert bought a modern pseudo-Tudor house, Grim's Dyke, near Harrow, which became his permanent home and a sanctuary for birds and animals. He purchased the site for a theatre in Charing Cross Road, but the work on the foundations exposed subterranean streams, and he said that 'for some time I was in grave doubt whether to continue building or let the fishing'. But the water subsided, and he became proprietor of the Garrick Theatre. He was a regular playgoer, though he drew the line at Shakespeare, saying to George Grossmith: 'If you promise me faithfully not to mention this to a single soul, not even to your dearest friend, I don't find Shakespeare rollicking.' Asserting that Shakespeare was a very obscure writer, he asked a friend to explain a certain passage: 'I would as lief be thrust through a quicket hedge as cry Pooh to a callow throstle.' The friend saw no difficulty at all: a bird-lover would rather be pushed through a thorny hedge than disturb a young feathered songster – 'but I can't for the moment recall the passage; where does it occur? Gilbert replied that he had just invented it and thought it 'jolly good Shakespeare'. Perhaps the funniest thing he ever wrote was a skit on *Hamlet* entitled *Rosencrantz and Guildenstern*, which ranks with Sheridan's parody in *The Critic* and Max Beerbohm's 'Savonarola Brown'.

In the last twenty years of his life Gilbert spent a few weeks annually with his wife on the Continent or making voyages in luxurious steamers. Some of these were undertaken for the sake of his health. 'I had gout all my life till 1900, when rheumatic arthritis came along. They eloped together – the only scandal I ever had in the family.' He went to Egypt for the latter complaint in 1900, and while there his physical helplessness nearly caused him to be 'boiled alive' in a nasty railway smash. However, the

aforesaid elopement soon took place, and in vigorous health he
turned his attention to pretty women with whom he flirted
continuously, though the relationship was apparently never
carried further than 'paddling palms and pinching fingers'.
Kind-hearted when not thwarted, he was at his best with children
and animals, women and birds, all of whom he could pet to his
heart's desire.

Life at Grim's Dyke was a succession of social occasions,
varied by his regular appearances on the local bench of magistrates.
Soon after adopting the role of country gentleman he was asked
by the High Sheriff of the county: 'You have, I believe, studied
the law as a barrister and have a sound knowledge of it?' to which
he replied: 'That is so, but I hope you will not consider it an
impediment', and was made a Justice of the Peace for Middlesex.
Needless to add, his strict code of behaviour caused friction on
the bench, and though a keen motorist himself he was down on
anyone who exceeded the speed limit. Sometimes he went to
London in his car, the driver being restricted to twenty miles
an hour, but most of his visits there were made by the Metropolitan Railway, and the week-end chaos at Baker Street Station
provoked him to write a letter to the Press: 'Saturday afternoon,
although occurring at regular and well-foreseen intervals, always
takes this railway by surprise.'

A last flash of fame both pleased and displeased him in the
years 1906–8, when Carte's widow, Helen, revived the Gilbert
and Sullivan operas at the Savoy. His displeasure arose from the
fact that she did not consult him about the casting of the pieces,
and he informed her that she had subjected him to 'the deepest –
I may say the only – indignity ever offered me during my forty
years' connection with the stage.' He produced the operas while
disapproving of many performers, and he wrote heated letters
to Mrs Carte expressing his sense of outrage at 'the gross
insolence and black ingratitude' with which he had been treated.
He declared that the operas had been 'insulted, degraded and
dragged through the mire' because of the casting and cheap
scenery, and in one of his first-night speeches he assured the

audience that he hoped to be in command of the operas in the near future. So strong were his feelings that he used to pass Helen Carte on the stairs of the theatre taking no notice of her. In another mood he spoke to a friend of the operas that had been thus degraded: 'I have been scribbling twaddle for thirty-five years to suit the public taste.' Asked whether he was not proud of having acquired an estate by his brain, he replied: 'Not at all; it represents the folly of the British public.'

For the winter months he took a furnished London house, where his wife entertained. He continued to scribble what he termed 'light flippery and amusing nonsense', and to feel irritated if anyone slighted it. In 1907 he received a knighthood, which he described as 'a tin-pot, two-penny-halfpenny sort of distinction', 'a mere triviality' and 'an unmeaning scrap of tinsel', adding that 'this indiscriminate flinging about of knighthoods is making me very nervous; it's quite possible they may give one to my butler'. At a banquet in his honour he spoke of the title as 'a commuted Old Age Pension' and suggested that, as a means of national economy, every working man should be knighted at the age of sixty-five. He retained a high opinion of his early plays, which were the journalese of blank verse, and proudly informed someone that 'in the pre-Savoy days I held the foremost position among dramatic authors'. He turned one of them into an opera, *Fallen Fairies*, for which Edward German wrote the music. Produced in December 1909, it failed to draw the public, resulted in furious rows between the librettist and the leading actor, as well as the librettist and the scene-painter, and whitened German's hair. Gilbert's last work to be seen on the stage was a horror-creating episode called *The Hooligan*, depicting the last hours of a criminal in the condemned cell, with which James Welch made something of a sensation as a music-hall 'turn' at the Coliseum in 1911. The playwright never lost his early interest in the law, especially in crime, and legal luminaries were welcome at Grim's Dyke. One of them, a judge, happened to say that he liked all the Savoy operas except *Trial by Jury*. 'He seemed to think', mused Gilbert, 'that in holding the pro-

P

ceedings up to ridicule I was trenching on his prerogative.'

It may have been the relative calm of his later years that made Gilbert say: 'My experience is that old age is the happiest time in a man's life. The worst of it is, there's so little of it.' He was vigorous in body and affable in mind, his chief desire being to forget old quarrels and repair old friendships. Meeting W. H. Kendal, with whom he had not been on speaking terms for thirty-six years, he talked away as if nothing had clouded a lifelong affection. He still bathed regularly in the lake which he had made in the grounds of Grim's Dyke, and on 29 May 1911 he invited two attractive girls to share his sport. Neither could swim well, and one of them called for help when out of her depth. Gilbert shouted words of encouragement, dived in, swam up to her, and said, 'Put your hands on my shoulders and don't struggle.' She complied; but at that moment his heart gave out, and when she reached the bank he was at the bottom of the lake.

He had once expressed a wish that he would die on a summer day in his garden, and the fates were kind.

9

Beerbohm Tree

One of the most famous remarks ever made about a stage performance was Gilbert's summary of Beerbohm Tree's Hamlet as
'funny without being vulgar'. Gilbert denied that he had ever
said this, and Tree declared that himself had invented it, but
there can be little doubt that both of them lied to save their faces.
Evidence that Tree's acting of the part incited the other to
irreverent mirth is supplied in one of Gilbert's letters: 'Do you
know how they are going to decide the Shakespeare-Bacon
dispute? They are going to dig up Shakespeare and dig up
Bacon; they are going to set their coffins side by side, and they
are going to get Tree to recite Hamlet to them. And the one who
turns in his coffin will be the author of the play.'

There were some enthusiasts who preferred Tree's Hamlet to
Henry Irving's, but it was a weird Teutonic conception of the
part, Tree himself having German blood. The Beerbohms had
been timber merchants at Memel on the Baltic Sea since the middle
of the eighteenth century, and one of them married a girl of
Slavonic descent, who produced eleven children, the youngest of
whom, Julius, migrated to London at an early age, became a
corn merchant in the City, and when thirty-nine married a girl
of Yorkshire parentage, Constantia Draper, who bore him three
sons and daughter. Their second son, Herbert, arrived at 2
Pembridge Villas, Kensington, on 17 December 1852. The various
schools he attended in youth made little impression on him, but
the period he spent at his father's old school at Schnepfeuthal in

Thuringia gave him a loathing of education which he never outgrew, owing in large measure to the cruelty of his masters and the futility of enforced instruction.

Julius Beerbohm wished his three sons to enter his business, and they did, Herbert being employed in editing a paper founded by his father, *The Evening Corn Trade List*. But none of them liked the employment. Ernest, the eldest, eventually became a sheep-farmer in South Africa, Julius, the youngest, developed a taste for adventure, explored Patagonia, wrote a book about it, composed poems, and ultimately became a financial gambler, causing brother Herbert much anxiety. As for Herbert, his affection for his father kept him in the City for eight years, though his real interest lay in amateur acting, his mind being full of poetry and empty of corn prices. He was tall and slim and rather limp, having blue eyes, red hair, a diffident manner and a preoccupied air. Absorbed in the theatre, he spent every shilling of his money on playgoing, and borrowed from friends for the same purpose. He imitated the mannerisms of famous actors at smoking concerts and made something of a reputation in amateur performances of widely-different parts, his ability to disguise himself with the aid of make-up and other histrionic tricks being noticed by a few critics.

In time he persuaded his father to let him leave the business and become a professional actor. His mother had died when he was scarcely six, and his father had married his deceased wife's sister, for which purpose the wedding took place in Switzerland, and was now rearing another family, the youngest member of which would one day be known to the world as Max Beerbohm. No doubt his fresh commitment as a family man weakened the opposition of Julius to Herbert's ambition, and on Monday, 20 May 1878, 'Mr H. Beerbohm Tree', that being his adopted stage-name, opened his professional career at the Town Hall, Folkestone. Seven plays were given by the Bijou Comedy Company during the week, Tree appearing in all of them, mostly in leading parts, and on two occasions giving 'by special desire his inimitable Dramatic and Mimictic Recitals', wherein he imitated Irving, Toole, Salvini and other famous actors. After a short season in London, he toured the provinces in several companies and soon made a mark as a 'character' actor. In 1880 he received a good offer from a leading actress, Geneviève Ward, to appear with her in London, and did well in his parts but aroused the jealousy of Geneviève, probably on account of his amorous advances to a younger woman in the company, and was soon on tour again. But his acting had interested certain West End managers and he was engaged to play in two London productions, both parts being lampoons of Oscar Wilde, then being universally caricatured as an aesthete. One manager declined to pay the actor more than £15 a week, which he said 'is every shilling as much as Tree is, or ever will be, worth'. Theatre managers have never been notable for accurate prophecy.

At a Fancy Dress Ball early in 1881 Tree met Maud Holt, a girl of eighteen with a scholastic future, whose interest in Greek and Latin had been side-tracked by a passion for the stage. This was easily deflected into a passion for Tree, who soon reciprocated her feeling. He called at her rooms in Orchard Street and she sang to him. They exchanged poetry, not their own but Browning's, Tennyson's and Shakespeare's. He advised her not to go on the stage unless she felt she *must*. They saw more and more of one another, and in February 1882 he asked her to marry him. After some trepidation at the prospect of union with an actor, she consented. They wrote daily to each other when circumstances prevented their meeting. Occasionally his behaviour caused scenes. He could not help flirting with pretty women, and she could not help feeling annoyed. Apparently he was having an affair with an actress when he asked Maud to be his wife. She discovered this and he had to play the part of a suffering but chivalrous man. He assured her that the other affair would at once be terminated, that he was not worthy of her, but that he would try to live up to her high opinion of him. She melted and all was well. But other misunderstandings followed, and more correspondence. She kept him in a state of emotional fluctuation through the spring of '82, her friends supplying much gossip concerning his gallantries, which caused him to follow her to Aix-les-Bains, where she was nursing an invalid sister, and another temporary breach was succeeded by endearments in the neighbouring woods.

He returned home happy and stayed with his family at Thurnham Court, near Maidstone, where he meditated on Maud and wrote her long letters, all about the beauty of the countryside and their projected nuptials. But the post brought more trouble. His friendship with E. W. Godwin, a notorious Don Juan, vexed her, and she ordered him to break it. This put his back up and he informed her roundly that she must not address him in such terms. He also refused to let her continue her scholastic career, telling her quite frankly that he must have 'a certain authority' over her actions, and that he, not she, would be the bread-winner. Finally he commanded her to 'let the matter drop'. She behaved like a dutiful fiancée, dropped it, and they were married in the church close by Thurnham Court on Sunday, 16 September 1882. Herbert was performing on the evening before and the evening after the ceremony, so they could have no honeymoon, going instead to rooms he had taken at No. 2 Old Burlington Gardens.

Life at first had its ups and downs. When he had a job they could afford to rent good rooms and entertain people; when out of a job they had to take cheap rooms and live inexpensively. Then came success. In March 1884 he played an absurd clergyman, 'the Rev Robert Spalding', in a third-rate farce, *The Private Secretary*, and having built the part up by the invention of burlesque 'business', preposterous catchwords and gags, he handed it over to W. S. Penley, who made a huge success of the show. To display his versatility Tree next appeared as the villain 'Macari' in a thriller, *Called Back*, which established him as a West End actor. He could now mix with all the heads of his profession, from Irving, with whom he got drunk, to Gilbert, who fell in love with Maud. He joined the Garrick Club, became a popular member, and actually began to look for plays before

becoming a manager; for which purpose he journeyed to
Bournemouth to see Robert Louis Stevenson, whose drama
The Hanging Judge was so tedious that Tree had to jab his leg
with Mrs Stevenson's hat-pin in order to keep awake while the
author read it. Some years later he produced two Henley-
Stevenson plays, *Macaire* and *Beau Austin*, but the public showed
no anxiety to see them.

Herbert's engaging social personality won him all sorts of
friends, one of whom, a barrister named Stuart Ogilvie, put up
enough money for the actor to become manager of the small
Comedy Theatre in Panton Street, where he started in April
1887 with a Russian melodrama, *The Red Lamp*, in which he
disguised his face, walk and voice so completely that his admirers
failed to recognise him. The play's success enabled him to take
the Haymarket Theatre that autumn, and here he remained for
ten years. Few of the comedies and dramas he produced have
survived, though his policy of making the pot-boilers pay for
the good work won the commendation of Bernard Shaw. He
put on *Hamlet, The Merry Wives of Windsor* and the first part of
Henry IV, his Hamlet being a quaint edition of himself, his
Falstaff at Windsor a rollicking, enjoyable show, his Falstaff in
Eastcheap remarkably un-Shakespearean. 'Mr Tree only wants
one thing to make him an excellent Falstaff', wrote G.B.S., 'and
that is to get born over again as unlike himself as possible.'
The actor's 'Dr Stockman' in *An Enemy of the People* would have
surprised Ibsen as much as his Falstaff would have perplexed
Shakespeare, but Tree was the first West End manager to spot
the genius of Ibsen and produce one of his plays.

His first considerable success at the Haymarket was *Captain
Swift* by Haddon Chambers, during a rehearsal of which he had
to persuade an actor to utter the word 'bastard', since when
stage characters have been compelled to use less acceptable
words. One of his authors, Henry Arthur Jones, did not take
kindly to his methods at rehearsals, Jones being under the
impression that he knew more than the leading actor about the
play, and a typical scene between them during the preparation

of *The Dancing Girl* caused the author to tear his hair and explode with indignation in the Press:

> H.A.J. No! No!! No!!!
> H.B.T. Don't repeat yourself.
> H.A.J. I must if you won't listen.
> H.B.T. Repetition breeds listlessness. By the time you said your last 'No' I had forgotten what the first was about.
> H.A.J. Very well. I'll be content with one. NO!
> H.B.T. No what?

In later productions of two plays by Jones there were periods when the actor and author, after howling insults at each other, dashed from the stage, the one to his dressing-room, the other into the street. The solicitors of both parties exchanged minatory tirades, the author was expelled from the theatre, and the plays were as short-lived as the patience of the belligerents.

A notable Haymarket success in 1893 was Oscar Wilde's *A Woman of No Importance*. Tree had an unqualified admiration for Wilde's wit and personality, and after the prosperous run of *Lady Windermere's Fan* begged that he might have Oscar's next comedy. Wilde showed no enthusiasm, but liked Tree enough to let him do it. While they were rehearsing Wilde happened to meet Squire Bancroft outside the Garrick Club and they briefly conversed. 'I hear you have written a play for the Haymarket Theatre', Bancroft began, but Wilde corrected him: 'Say rather that the Theatre Royal, Haymarket, has asked me for a play.'

'Well, at any rate, Tree is doing it', Bancroft went on.

'Alas! yes.'

'But won't he be good in his part?'

'Good? No.'

'Surely not bad?'

'Bad? No.'

'Indifferent, then?'

'No, not indifferent.'

'Then what on earth will he be?'

'In the strictest confidence . . but you won't repeat this?'

'Not a word.'

'Then I will whisper it in your deaf ear. Tree will be . . . we must face it manfully . . . he will be Tree.'

He was; but the part suited him so well that he began to speak his own epigrams in the manner of 'Lord Illingworth' in the play, and Wilde noted the fact with amusement: 'Ah, every day dear Herbert becomes *de plus en plus Oscarisé;* it is a wonderful case of Nature imitating Art.'

Maud had played several good parts at the Haymarket and she accompanied Herbert on his first visit to America early in 1895. They had an enthusiastic reception, and the curiosity of the Press inspired Tree with an epigram: 'An American's home is an interviewer's castle.' Innumerable parties and excursions, a visit to President Cleveland, a lecture at Harvard, added to his theatrical performances, exhausted Tree, who spent the first few days of his voyage home in his bunk. But something of vital importance to his future career occurred on his last evening in New York. Instead of going to see Niagara Falls that day he went to see a play that night. His brother Max Beerbohm, who was with him as a salaried private secretary, had seen the dramatic version of George Du Maurier's novel *Trilby* and had thought it bosh. Knowing that Max's intelligence was liable to run away with him, Tree witnessed it, thought it 'hog-wash' but perceived its possibilities with himself as 'Svengali', and bought the English rights.

At home again he set to work on the play, making innumerable alterations and writing new scenes. *Trilby* first appeared at the Haymarket in October 1895, Tree's 'Svengali', a creation of his own, being the hit of the piece, which, constantly revived, was the biggest money-maker of his career as a manager. His ambition now soared far above the acquisition of fortunes on hog-wash. He wanted a large theatre where he could make experiments and satisfy his passion for spectacle. He bought the site of an ancient opera house about to be demolished, and managed to raise enough capital from Lord Rothschild, Ernest

Cassel and other millionaires to erect Her Majesty's Theatre, opposite the Theatre Royal, Haymarket. Tree was the sole proprietor, having to pay £6,000 a year for ground-rent and interest on capital. He was like a child with a new and gorgeous toy, eagerly expecting his friends to admire it. Lunching at the Garrick one day he asked Squire Bancroft to come and gaze at his 'beautiful theatre'. Standing in the colonnade of the Haymarket, Bancroft surveyed Her Majesty's through his monocle. 'Well?' said Tree excitedly. 'A great many windows to clean', was Bancroft's sombre comment.

All seemed to promise well at the opening of the theatre on 28 April 1897, but things went badly at first. His management was saved and firmly established by a superb production of *Julius Caesar* in January 1898. After that he put on a Shakespeare play pretty well every year, each produced with unsurpassable splendour and performed by the best actors of the time. Altogether he did sixteen of Shakespeare's plays, and from 1905 onwards held an annual Shakespeare Festival, reviving from six to twelve of the plays within two or three weeks, each with all the magnificence of the original production, an achievement unique in theatrical history. Unlike his predecessor Henry Irving, he did not disembowel the plays to make the leading actor stand out, but gave as much of the text as possible. When Irving first appeared as Richard III, Walter Bentley made a great hit in the part of Clarence and received an ovation from the audience. The next morning Irving called a rehearsal and cut the part of Clarence to ribbons. Tree on the other hand gave his actors full scope, an idol of the time, Lewis Waller, making the chief hits in several early productions at Her Majesty's; and sometimes the manager chose plays in order to exhibit the accomplishments of his contemporaries.

As an actor Tree could not master Shakespeare's rhetoric and was unsatisfactory in heroic roles. His Shakespearean high spots were 'Malvolio', a great comic creation of his own, hardly as visualised by the author, and Richard II, a moving and picturesque performance whenever Tree took the trouble to act. As he

believed entirely in spontaneity and inspiration, it followed that
he sometimes played superbly, but since inspiration was not
at his beck and call he frequently acted badly. At the top of his
form he towered above his fellows for sheer versatility; below
that he lacked the professional touch and far too often 'walked
through' his parts.

Beyond doubt his love of life interfered with the concentration
so vital to creative work. Acting was Irving's whole existence;
it was but a part of Tree's. There were so many other delightful
things in the world, the relaxed companionship of the club, the
social round, talking, riding, essay-writing, listening to music,
looking at paintings, above all love-making. Tree found pretty
women irresistible, and much disharmony was caused in his
domestic circle. By the end of the century he had set up a second
establishment and was producing a second family. The effect
on Maud might have been expected in one of her puritanical
nature and respectable upbringing. She felt humiliated and
indignant, and there were harrowing scenes between them,
Herbert exasperated beyond endurance, Maud infuriated beyond
articulation. At last he made a home for himself in the dome of
the theatre because he could not endure the strain and attrition of
constant scenes whenever they were together. Sympathising
with her unhappiness, he was constitutionally incapable of
removing its cause. Distressed by his own violent language when
driven to distraction, he hated still more the mendacity with
which he tried to calm her hysterical outbursts, and he declared
that 'of all the laws the marriage law is the most immoral (not
excepting that relating to income tax) for it is productive of
more subterfuge, lying and hypocrisy than any law that governs
us.' As the years went by Maud made the best of an inevitable
situation, and their later relationship was fairly amicable.

A man in his position could not keep his private life wholly
secret from the world, and the possibility of an open scandal
delayed his knighthood, since in those days the men whom the
King honoured had to be domestically beyond reproach. Apart
from Shakespeare, he had produced *Herod*, *Nero* and other plays

by the fashionable poet of the time, Stephen Phillips, Sheridan's *The School for Scandal*, Brieux's *False Gods*, as well as stage versions of Dickens's *Oliver Twist*, Thackeray's *The Newcomes*, Tolstoy's *Resurrection*, and a short story by Kipling, 'The Man Who Was'. In addition he had done a season of plays at Berlin by the request of the Kaiser, who had conferred an order upon him; so it was reasonable to expect that the English Court would recognise his work for the stage, since three less distinguished actors had already been honoured. By 1909 the Lord Chamberlain must have received an assurance that the manager's high artistic achievement would not be nullified by an action in the divorce court; and he became Sir Herbert Tree. 'In order to get on one must stoop to flattery', he once said; 'one must learn to walk backward in order to get forward.' But he had never acted in accordance with this epigram; in fact he had put obstacles in the path of his forward march.

A personal experience must be written in the first person. I made the acquaintance of Tree in 1910 during the exceptionally long run of his super-spectacular *Henry VIII*, and found that he sometimes enjoyed acting in private life as much as he enjoyed it now and then on the stage. His natural absentmindedness, coupled with his love of playing the fool, made his performance extremely entertaining, after I had recovered from the shock of meeting Cardinal Wolsey in the part of a lunatic. Having participated in a bewildering conversation, I was shown a door into the dress-circle and told to return at the close of the play. But as I opened the door he called to me, trotted back along the corridor, drew me into his dressing-room, and asked in a confidential manner: 'Have you ever been to Jerusalem?' I answered in the negative. 'How interesting!' he said, and left me mystified. On my return he indulged in a long monologue, jumping irrelevantly from Shakespeare to winkles, from God to leap-frog, and ending on an autobiographical note: 'Don't confuse love with matrimony . . . Love is more precious than life, but a silver wedding speaks for itself.'

I got a job at his theatre, my first part being in *Julius Caesar* during the annual Shakespeare Festival of 1911, when I was cast for 'Publius', a senile senator who said 'Good-morrow, Caesar' and spoke no more. I devoted so much study to attain the shuffle and squeak of old age that when the moment for my entrance came I momentarily forgot the shuffle in my anxiety to get the squeak. Perceiving my error I halted, and while wondering whether it could be retrieved the actor who played Caesar cut me out of my three words by saying 'Welcome, Publius'. This stunned me, and I replied quite audibly in my natural voice 'Hullo!' Horrified by what I had done, I tottered off the stage and hoped the earth would swallow me. Expecting the sack, I trembled when Tree approached me at the end of the scene. 'What did you say to Caesar?' he asked in a rather fearsome manner. I would have liked to lie, but the truth came out with a blurt and I told him that I had said 'Hullo!' He seemed greatly relieved: 'Oh! I beg your pardon. My mistake. I thought you said "What ho!".' To my amazement I got a small part in *The Merchant of Venice*, the next play in the Festival.

Perhaps because I made a good audience, he seemed to like my company, and I enjoyed several sessions with him, one of them in a taxi-cab. We happened to be leaving the theatre at the same moment, when he took me by the arm, hailed a taxi, pushed me in, and after a little preliminary badinage gave this order to the driver: 'Drive us slowly round and round the West End until we tell you to stop. If you see a man in green trousers, a top hat and spotted waistcoat, blow your horn three times and increase your speed.' At first the driver thought him mad, but on reflection decided he was a detective, and we started off. Tree then abandoned himself to soliloquy, his mind being largely occupied by the tragic fate of an executed murderer, Dr Crippen. I remained practically silent throughout his maunderings, which prompted him to say: 'Don't talk so much . . . Your tongue was given you to hold it.' The episode ended with an enraged driver demanding our names and addresses, his object being to set the law in motion, but I pacified him by disclosing the identity of my companion.

During his somewhat chaotic rehearsals Tree had a habit of making epigrams, and there were sufficient sycophants around him to ensure a good reception for his more fatuous remarks. This, for instance, went with a yell: 'He is an old bore; even the grave yawns for him.' So did this: 'He slept the deep sleep of the unjust.' When he asked, 'Do you say that in the asphalt or the concrete?' the company almost expired; and when he expressed sympathy in the phrase 'My nose bleeds for you', the rehearsal was temporarily suspended. But he frequently brought off neat things, such as: 'In pursuing the phantom of pleasure man loses the substance of happiness.' Or: 'Is life worth living? It depends on the liver.' Or: 'Let sleeping dogs lie, but why let lying dogs sleep?' Or: 'There is only the difference of a letter between the beginning and the end of life – creation and cremation.' His conversation was always entertaining because of his odd manner of speech and the surprising nature of his thoughts. Unfortunately I was not in the production of Bernard Shaw's *Pygmalion* (1914), the rehearsals of which, with Tree's incalculableness, Stella Patrick Campbell's irresponsibility and G.B.S.'s sprightliness, must have provided a series of hilarious exhibitions unique in stage history. Unable in the early days to understand how a man of Tree's frolicsome temperament could have contrived to run such a vast undertaking for so many years, I at length grasped the fact that the theatre business of those days was unlike any other. When successful he made so much money that he could waste it like water, whereas his failures were paid for by those who backed them and his personal expenditure seemed like a flea on the elephant of their debts.

Like many another of his prosperous productions, he took *Pygmalion* off while it was still running to good houses in July 1914 and set off for his annual visit to Marienbad. But the war made him return hurriedly, and a dramatic version of *David Copperfield*, in which he doubled the parts of 'Micawber' and 'Peggotty', did surprisingly well. Soon afterwards he went to Hollywood for a film of *Macbeth*, letting his theatre to Oscar Asche whose *Chu Chin Chow* filled it for over four years. In

1916 Tree had a successful season of Shakespearean and other plays in New York, and on his return home witnessed the show at his theatre, describing it as 'more navel than millinery'. Again he went to America, toured in his Shakespearean repertory, made speeches for the Allies, found he could no longer remain absent from England during the war, and was back in London by May, 1917. An accident to his knee, owing to a fall downstairs, necessitated an operation, which was performed by Sir Alfred Fripp in his nursing home at 16 Henrietta Street, near Cavendish Square. All went well, and on 2 July 1917 Tree sat up in bed to eat his dinner in excellent health and high spirits. But blood clots had formed during the period of rest, and while the nurse was opening the window his heart ceased to beat.

An air-raid occurred while his body travelled to Golders Green, the explosion of bombs and the roar of guns affording an impressive accompaniment to the funeral procession; though the effect was not so striking as Tree could have made it, the ear-splitting din of a mimic thunderstorm in his production of *Macbeth* having made the pedestrians in the street outside scatter in fear of the elements.

10

Oscar Wilde

It was in the late spring of 1892 that Beerbohm Tree met Oscar Wilde at a fashionable function in Belgravia and reopened the question of a successor to *Lady Windermere's Fan*, feeling surprised that the dramatist did not expand with enthusiasm at the prospect of its production at the Haymarket Theatre. 'As Herod in my *Salomé* you would be admirable', said Wilde. 'As a peer of the realm in my latest dramatic device, pray forgive me if I do not see you.' Tree persevered, remarking that his 'Duke of Guisebury' in Jones's *The Dancing Girl* had been highly praised. 'Ah! that's just it', returned Wilde. 'Before you can successfully impersonate the character I have in mind, you must forget that you ever played Hamlet; you must forget that you ever played Falstaff; above all you must forget that you ever played a Duke in a melodrama by Henry Arthur Jones.'

'I'll do my best', said Tree.

'I think you had better forget that you have ever acted at all.'

'Why?'

'Because this witty aristocrat whom you wish to assume in my play is quite unlike anyone who has been seen on the stage before.'

'My God! he must be supernatural.'

'He is certainly not natural. He is a figure of art. Indeed, if you can bear the truth, he is MYSELF.'

This was to a certain extent true, for by that time Wilde had imposed an artificial personality on the outside world, a figure that could never have been visualised by the circle in which his parents had moved.

His father, William Wilde, the most eminent auralist and oculist in Ireland, wrote books on medical science, ancient monuments and the scenery of his native country, lecturing as well on all these subjects. He converted a stable into a hospital and everyone who suffered from ear and eye defects consulted him, not always with success, for Bernard Shaw recorded that he 'operated on my father to correct a squint and overdid the correction so much that my father squinted the other way all the rest of his life'. In 1851 William Wilde married the poetess of the Young Ireland movement, Jane Francesca Elgee, who in 1848 had incited her countrymen to drive the English out of their land. They made a strangely contrasted pair: she was tall, stately, handsome and imperturbable; he was short, undignified, ugly and excitable. Both their sons were born at No. 21 Westland Row, Dublin, Willie in 1852, Oscar on 16 October 1854. The younger had four Christian names: Oscar, Fingal, O'Flahertie, Wills. As he grew up he felt that his godparents had been extravagant and dropped the names one by one, hoping to be known simply as 'The Wilde' or 'The Oscar'. The fame of William Wilde grew, and he was consulted by monarchs. He moved to No. 1 Merrion Square and lavishly entertained doctors, lawyers, writers, archaeologists, foreign notabilities, and the world that revolved round Dublin Castle. He built a house at Moytura on Lough Corrib in Connemara, where the family often spent their holidays, and in 1864 he received a knighthood. A girl who did not survive youth was added to the domestic circle three years after the birth of Oscar.

Outside his own family Sir William Wilde produced a number of natural children, but he provided for their upbringing, and his sexual caprices would merely have been the theme of gossip if Mary Travers, the daughter of a Trinity College professor, had not excited his 'amorous propensities'. When the novelty of the liaison wore off, he tried to calm her with hush-money and expensive presents, but she did not fancy the treatment accorded

Q

to his other discarded women and became a nuisance, following a campaign of anonymous letters and poems with a printed pamphlet which, distributed throughout Dublin, described how 'Dr Quilp' had drugged and violated her. Since he ignored the pamphlet, her next move was to broadcast his letters together with his name and address. Staying at Bray with her children, Lady Wilde was then pestered by small boys who tried to make her buy various tracts which Mary Travers busily disseminated. Provoked at last by the persecution, Lady Wilde sent a strongly-worded letter to Mary's father, and the fat was in the fire. The resulting libel action went against Wilde, damaged his reputation and impaired his character. He died in 1876, twelve years after the scandal.

The early life of Willie and Oscar differed from that of most English children. They had dinner with their seniors and were as familiar with the freedom of speech released by alcohol as their contemporaries across the channel were acquainted with punishment and restraint. They were sent to Portora Royal School, Enniskillen, Oscar arriving there at the age of ten, just in time to hear the opinions of the other boys on the subject of his father's transgressions as revealed in court, but since he was different from most boys in everything else he probably turned the affair into a joke. He disliked games, fighting, bullying, and the usual pastimes of immaturity, but liked books, clothes, flowers, sunsets and solitude. He was bored by learning and never attempted to master what he did not like. 'Nothing that is worth knowing can be taught', he later declared: 'We teach people how to remember, we never teach them how to grow.' But he enjoyed the Greek authors and won the school's Gold Medal. He told amusing stories, which made up for his lack of popularity in other respects, and as he had a kindly, affectionate nature the more turbulent lads soon allowed him to go his own way. Willie and Oscar sometimes spent their holidays with their mother in France, sometimes with both parents at Moytura, where they swam or fished. At the close of his life Oscar recalled that Lough Corrib 'was full of large melancholy salmon, which lay at the bottom of the lake and paid no attention to our bait'. Brother Willie was trained for the Bar, but soon showed an inclination for a different sort of bar, and in time became a somewhat sodden journalist.

In October '71 Oscar gained an 'exhibition' from Portora and an entrance scholarship to Trinity College, Dublin, where his love of the classics enabled him to win many prizes, a 'Foundation' scholarship and the Berkeley Gold Medal for Greek. By nature lazy, he had a phenomenal memory, whatever he read being photographed on his mind, and as he loved Greek he found it easy to outdistance his competitors. One of his tutors was the Professor of Ancient History, John Pentland Mahaffy, who doted on aristocrats as much as he adored Aristotle and taught Oscar the intricacies of snobbery along with the value of hunting and shooting as necessary accompaniments of the cult. None of the ordinary sports and hobbies of his fellow-students appealed to Oscar, who did not find physical exercise essential to muscular development. His bodily strength was as remarkable as his memory, and since young men admire material feats more than mental accomplishments their attitude to him was transformed by an act that he would have thought insignificant, if not vulgar. He wrote a poem and read it aloud at a class symposium. The herculean bully of the circle received it with a sarcastic laugh. Oscar was furious, went up to the fellow, and asked why he had sneered at the poem. The question was rewarded by another laugh, upon which Oscar slapped the bully's face. A fight was instantly arranged. 'No one supposed that Wilde had the ghost of a show', recalled a witness of the episode, 'but when he led out with his right it was like a pile-driver. He followed the surprised bully up with half a dozen crushers and that ended it.' Thereafter Oscar's poetry received the respect usually accorded to pugilism.

As he had done well in his three years at Trinity College, Dublin, his father said that he could finish up at Oxford. He promptly won a demyship at Magdalen College (£95 a year) and in October '74, aged twenty, he arrived at Oxford, where he passed

four entrancing years. Two of the professors at that time influenced him in the only way that an intelligent person can be influenced: they helped him to discover his own nature. John Ruskin
even persuaded him to do something against his nature. In order
to display the dignity of manual labour and to make some of the
undergraduates undertake disinterested work, Ruskin started
road-construction between Upper and Lower Hinksey, and
Oscar became a stone-breaker on that road. But he was not born
for such flinty toil, and his nature only responded to Ruskin's
views on social reform. A greater effect was made on him by the
prose and principles of Walter Pater, who preached what he
dared not practise, the doctrine of living for excitement and
pleasure, for 'any exquisite passion', which he expressed in
language so precious that literary-minded youths were seduced
by it and regarded his essays as a book of revelation. Oscar was
soon under Pater's spell, and what was most artificial in his
writing henceforth can be traced to the effect Pater had on his
tendency to affectation.

He signified contempt for the other professors and did not
engage in the popular pursuits of the University, though he
showed no objection to watching his fellow-undergraduates
exerting themselves on the river or the cricket-field and sometimes allowed a horse to exert itself by riding it. His rooms were
often crowded with fellow-scholars, who talked and drank and
laughed and sang, and already his conversation, good humour and
high spirits were making him popular among the more intelligent
youths. At a later date people invented stories of his effeminate
behaviour at Oxford; but it happens that an athletic contemporary knew of an incident that disposes of them. 'There was
only one man in the college, and he rowed seven in the Varsity
Eight, who had the ghost of a chance in a tussle with Wilde',
recorded Sir Frank Benson, who described what happened on one
occasion. The Junior Common Room at Magdalen determined
to rag Wilde and smash his furniture. Four drunken sportsmen
burst into his rooms, the rest watching from the stairs, ready
to complete the demolition and deal with any attempt to prevent it.

The first of the sportsmen was quickly expelled by a hefty kick, the second followed him with a punch in the wind, the third rejoined his companions by air-transit, and the fourth, a burly fellow as big as Wilde, reappeared in the arms of his intended victim, struggling helplessly. Wilde carried him as easily as a nurse handles a baby to his rooms, buried him beneath a pile of his own furniture, invited the rest to drink his health, and the wretched fellow had the mortification of watching his erstwhile confederates polishing off his wine and spirits. One lesson of that sort was sufficient for the sporting Oxonians.

Oscar did a certain amount of flirting, not only with girls but with Mother Church, and for a while he entertained the idea cf marriage as well as conversion. During long vacations he visited Italy and Greece, his imagination being stirred by Christianity at Rome, by paganism at Athens. Though he always seemed to be reading poetry when not talking, he must have done a certain amount of work at Oxford because in '76 he took a First Class in 'Moderations' in the Honours School, and in '78 a First Class in the Honours Finals, both being considered by the examiners as the most brilliant of their years. He inherited about £4,000 when his father died in '76, won the Newdigate Prize for his poem on Ravenna in '78, and arrived in London that year with the firm intention of making himself known. With his curious nature, the emotional part of him undeveloped, the mental over-developed, fame came to him easily, because his boyish love of exhibition was backed by genius in expression, the combination ensuring the attention of those who loved show as well as those who liked ideas. This odd conjunction of an immature sensibility with a superabundant intelligence, a condition that did not change and may have been due to some glandular defect, explains his social behaviour and his sexual constitution.

In London at that time a number of men were reacting against conventional art and getting known as aesthetes. As nothing arouses comment so certainly as clothes, Wilde decided to dress the part of an aesthete, attending evening parties in a velvet coat, knee-breeches, a soft loose shirt with wide turned-down collar, a large flowing pale green tie, and sometimes carrying a lily or sunflower. Others followed suit, outdid his extravagances, and even appeared in daytime curiously adorned. Oscar himself did not 'walk down Piccadilly with a poppy or a lily in his medieval hand', as suggested in *Patience*. 'Anyone could have done that', he said later. 'The great and difficult thing was what *I* achieved – to make the whole world believe that I had done it.' Much to the annoyance of the other aesthetes who were revolutionising wall-paper, furniture, architecture and painting, Oscar captured the limelight with his costumes and flowers, becoming identified with 'Bunthorne' in Gilbert and Sullivan's opera.

Soon taken up by Society, he made a point of flattering women, knowing that 'no man has any real success in this world unless he has got women to back him'. He wrote sonnets to Ellen Terry, Henry Irving and Sarah Bernhardt, and poems to the beauty of the hour, Lily Langtry, with whom he fancied himself in love. He was caricatured in *Punch* and lampooned on the stage. He talked a great deal of nonsense because he knew that idiotic remarks were repeated far more often than sensible ones. He published a volume of poems, most of which were echoes of other poets, and wrote a drama about Nihilists in Russia, which provided him with a few epigrams for his later comedies. 'It is so exhausting not to talk', says one of the characters, and Wilde was careful not to exhaust himself, his peculiar type of quip already being apparent in his first play. 'We speak the truth to one another here', says the President of the Nihilists. 'How misleading you must find it', replies Prince Paul, the Czar's Prime Minister.

In those days whatever became a craze in England attracted America and Wilde was soon engaged to lecture there, the idea being that he should appear and talk like the aesthete in *Patience*, which had taken the States by storm. He was then a tall handsome fellow, with large limbs, long hair, sloping eyes that seemed to change their colour with his mood, a superb forehead, a weakly sensual mouth. He had been careful to prepare for his arrival by announcing, with journalistic assistance, that he was 'disappointed with the Atlantic Ocean', and by telling the Customs House official that he had 'nothing to declare except my genius'. Instantly he received innumerable invitations and had to exhibit himself everywhere as a sort of zoological specimen. He refused to show himself in the apparel of an aesthete, much to the annoyance of the promoters of his tour, and he did not always please his hosts. 'Wonderful man, Columbus!' said an eager conversationalist. 'Why?' asked Wilde. 'He discovered America.' 'Oh, no! it had often been discovered before, but it was always hushed up.' But the women fell in love with him, and he later complained: 'When I went to America I had two secretaries, one for autographs, the other for locks of hair. Within six months the one had died of writer's cramp, the other was completely bald.'

His opening lecture to a packed audience at Chickering Hall, New York, was something between a hit and a miss. The audience expected fireworks and got philosophy. The tour of leading American cities was financially successful, and the lecturer met a number of interesting people, such as Longfellow, Oliver Wendell Holmes, Louisa Alcott, General Grant, Jefferson Davis, Henry Ward Beecher and Walt Whitman. At Boston sixty youths of Harvard University, with the moblike humour of adolescents, tried to guy the aesthete by dressing like Bunthorne and carrying sunflowers. Wilde got to hear of their intention in advance, made them look silly by appearing in ordinary evening clothes, and completed their discomfiture with humorous references to their presence. Of course he had to visit Niagara, and of course someone exclaimed that they were wonderful waterfalls, receiving his dry comment: 'The wonder would be if the water did not fall.' He crossed the States and gave five lectures at San Francisco, where the youthful members of a club tried to make him drunk, but surprisingly discovered themselves horizontally disposed when he got up to leave. While at Denver he was warned that if he went on to Leadville the tougher inhabitants would probably shoot him or his travelling manager. He replied that nothing they could do to his travelling manager would intimidate him. He went down a mine, where his ability to drink quantities of whisky and smoke strong cigars delighted the miners. 'I opened a new vein, or lode, with a silver drill, the lode being named "The Oscar",' he afterwards related: 'I had hoped that in their grand simple way they would have offered me shares in "The Oscar", but in their artless untutored fashion they did not.' His fame as a drinker became legendary, and many years later Frank Benson heard some cowboys say: 'That fellow is some art guy, but he can drink any of us under the table and afterwards carry us home two at a time.' Wilde came to the conclusion that 'the English have really everything in common with the Americans, except of course language', and enjoyed his visit enormously. Including a short stay in Canada, he remained in America for the whole of 1882.

He returned to England at the beginning of '83 with enough money to take life easily for a time. For a while he settled down in a suite of rooms on the second floor of the Hotel Voltaire in Paris, where he began to write a blank verse play *The Duchess of Padua* and to recreate himself in a fresh part. He met all the notable Frenchmen of the time, Hugo, Zola, Coquelin, Daudet, Dégas, Mallarmé, etc. He also met his future biographer, Robert Sherard, who some years later took him round certain cafés patronised by criminals, drunkenly proclaiming at intervals that anyone who annoyed his friend Monsieur Wilde would quickly regret it. At last Oscar said: 'Robert, you are defending me at the risk of my life.' While at Paris in '83 he polished up his poem *The Sphinx*, but money was running short, and when he heard that Mary Anderson would not produce his blank verse drama he returned to London in May.

A lecture tour in the provinces and Scotland seemed the only way of earning a livelihood, and he undertook it in a mood of boredom. Staying in London between lecture dates, he formed a friendship with Whistler. They were constantly to be seen together at the Café Royal, and were soon on 'Oscar' and 'Jimmy' terms, though Jimmy was Oscar's senior by twenty years, the younger man playing up to the elder. But Wilde's genius as a wit and raconteur made people listen to him when Whistler wanted to talk, and the latter soon found an excuse for getting rid of a disciple who dared to act a leading part in the master's presence. Like every genius in history, Wilde made use of other people's cleverness, and Whistler was irritated when a remark of his own was calmly appropriated by the other. They indulged in a series of amusing newspaper exchanges, but while Oscar remained amiable Jimmy became disagreeable, and their friendship closed with a clever but nasty riposte by the lesser man.

In the later 'eighties Oscar's mother with her son Willie moved to 146 (now 87) Oakley Street, Chelsea, where the receptions of Lady Wilde became fashionable. Oscar had a deep veneration for his mother and made a point of attending them. By that time he was married to Constance Lloyd, a beautiful girl with violet eyes and light chestnut hair. He met her during a lecture tour, and each was instantaneously attracted to the other. Soon they were deeply in love, and their marriage took place in May '84 at St James's Church, Paddington. They went to the Hôtel Wagram in Paris for their honeymoon, and settled down at 16 (now 34) Tite Street, Chelsea. Constance's dowry enabled them to take a lease of the house and transform the interior with the aid of E. W. Godwin and Whistler; but it was vitally important that Oscar should get a job. At first he did some book reviewing, and in 1887 managed to obtain the editorship of a monthly magazine *The Woman's World*, holding it for about three years and contributing literary notes.

During this period his best work was done in the form of fairy tales, which appeared as *The Happy Prince* (1888) and *A House of Pomegranates* (1891), and long essays in leading reviews, called 'The Decay of Lying' and 'The Critic as Artist', which were eventually published in his volume *Intentions* (1891). Having abandoned his editorial job, he produced a novel *The Picture of Dorian Gray*, which had been commissioned by the American firm of Lippincott. It caused a sensation, the critics calling it 'disgusting', 'tainting', 'sickening', 'putrefying', and all the other names reserved for works that made them feel uncomfortable. He followed up the novel with the wittiest essay ever written on a controversial theme, 'The Soul of Man Under Socialism', which would have shut the doors of Mayfair against him if he had not been the most fascinating of talkers. Unfortunately we cannot feel the effect he produced on his listeners because so much depended upon his dramatic pauses, his asides, the sudden gleams of humour, his voice, his compelling character. He was certainly the most versatile and agreeable of famous talkers, for he could charm a mixed company for hours on end and never exhaust their pleasure. Sydney Smith was probably more amusing, but then his listeners were as often as not prostrated with laughter, whereas Wilde mingled gravity and levity in so masterful a manner that the contrast kept people enthralled. We can but dimly sense his incomparable gift with a reported specimen of either kind, not forgetting that each was illuminated all through by his brilliant technique as a talker, by unrecorded interludes, by the spell of his personality.

The first example began with his excuses for arriving late at a luncheon-party, followed by the reason:

'I am, and have been for some time, extremely busy. I have undertaken to write the first volume of The People's Cheap Guinea Series of Great Thoughts, and the subject has occupied every minute I could spare from eating, drinking and sleeping. My contribution to the Series will consist of a small volume of moral essays, which I am hopeful will be purchased by many wealthy persons of restricted means who wish to give their friends little tokens of ill-will at Christmastime. The Archbishop of Canterbury has kindly consented to write a preface expressing his earnest desire that these brief sermons, as I dare to call them, will carry their message of sorrow into many otherwise happy homes. The first essay, on which I am now engaged, deals with the Value of Presence of Mind, and is in the form of an anecdote . . . an incident from real life which was related to me by a well-known actor, still happily amongst us, who owes his very existence to a daring exhibition of coolness in the face of terrible danger.

'He was playing the chief part in a drama which had proved extremely popular in the West End of London. For months there had not been an empty seat in the house, and at every performance the queues for the pit and gallery stretched for miles: indeed they stretched as far as Hammersmith. (I ought to add that the play was being performed *at* Hammersmith.) One evening, at that tense moment when the poor flower-girl rejects with scorn the odious proposals of the wicked marquis, a huge cloud of smoke poured from the wings and the scenery was caught by great tongues of fire. Although the safety curtain was immediately lowered, the audience were terrified and dashed towards the exits. A hideous panic broke out, men shouting and pushing, women screaming and clutching. There was a serious danger that many of the weaker ones would be trampled to death; and in fact some skirts were soiled, several dress shirts were crumpled. At the height of the din the actor of whom I have spoken, who loves and is loved by the flower-girl in the play, came up through the orchestra door, took in the situation at a glance, scrambled on to the stage, stood erect with flashing eyes and upraised arm before the iron curtain, and in a voice which rang like a trumpet through the theatre commanded silence. The audience knew that voice well, and felt reassured: the panic subsided. He told them that there was no longer any danger from the fire, which was now completely under control, but that there was a very real danger from their own fear: their lives depended on keeping their heads: they must return to their seats at once. Feeling thoroughly ashamed of themselves, they did as they were bidden; and when the exits were clear and the seats occupied once more, the actor leapt lightly over the footlights into the stalls and vanished through the first convenient doorway. Then the auditorium filled with smoke; the flames raced in from every side; and not another soul left the place alive.'

Throughout his life Oscar was interested in the character of Jesus and invented all sorts of stories that threw strange lights on the effects of Christ's actions and teachings, one of which he told several times with many variations:

'Christ came to the city and heard the sounds of great rejoicing. He entered a dwelling and saw a man lying drunk upon a couch.

He touched him on the shoulder and asked, "Why do you waste your soul in drink?" The man looked up and answered, "I was a leper once, and you healed me. What else should I do?" He went further into the city and saw a youth following a harlot, and said to him, "Why do you look at this woman with eyes of lust?" The youth knew Him and answered, "I was blind once and you gave me sight. At what else should I look?" So He spoke to the woman: "Why do you walk in the way of sin?" And the woman replied, "You forgave my sins, and the way is pleasant." And He passed out of the city, and saw an old man weeping by the wayside, and asked him why he wept. The old man answered, "Lord, I was dead, and you brought me back to life. What else can I do but weep?" '

Wilde possessed a spiritual faculty that in certain respects resembled that of Christ. Many instances are recorded of his miraculous curative power. He could transform the mental and physical condition of people. 'One met him, feeling depressed', testified Lord Alfred Douglas, 'and in five minutes he had altered the whole aspect of the situation and everything became *couleur de rose*. To repeat the process involved an infinite amount of wit and humour, profundity of thought and deep insight.' One day he called on Graham Robertson, who was suffering from a violent toothache and a bad cold, and could not stand the sight of anyone. Oscar sat down calmly and made Robertson laugh uninterruptedly for an hour and a half, at the conclusion of which the cold and the toothache had completely disappeared. More extraordinary still was the effect he had on Walter Sickert's mother, stricken with grief over the death of her husband. When Oscar called she refused to see him. He persisted. Sobbing in misery she again refused. He said that he would wait until she had changed her mind. 'Then she arose and went into the room where he was waiting, crying as she went', wrote her daughter. 'I saw Oscar take both her hands and draw her to a chair, beside which he set his own; then I left them alone. He stayed a long time, and before he went I heard my mother laughing. When he had gone she was a woman transformed . . .' All Oscar's friends, and many of his acquaintances, bear witness to this supernatural gift, and we know that in the early stages of William Morris's long illness which preceded his death the only person he could bear to see was Wilde. 'I was never so entertained in my life', he told his daughter. 'Indeed the impression left upon us by that aspect of Wilde's nature is one of innate virtue. He was, we may conclude, half-saint, half-satyr.'

Oddly enough his temperament no less than his face were similar to those of another Irishman, Sheridan. They were both essentially kind-hearted, happy and sympathetic, inducing cheerfulness in others; both were easy-going and frivolous, both weak and sensual, submissive to the temptations of the flesh; while the fine eyes and forehead of each were offset by a feeble and disfiguring mouth and jaw. To complete the resemblance, Wilde took up the comedy of manners where Sheridan had left it and produced the wittiest plays to be seen on the English stage since *The School for Scandal.*

A young and energetic actor, George Alexander, had recently become manager of St James's Theatre. He had heard several of Wilde's amusing remarks at parties and particularly enjoyed these:

'Work is the curse of the drinking classes.'

'Whenever I think of my bad qualities at night, I go to sleep at once.'

'I am due at the club: it is the hour when we sleep there.'

'I rely on you to misrepresent me.'

'I never put off till tomorrow what I can possibly do the day after.'

'I would sooner lose a train by the ABC than catch it by Bradshaw.'

'There are a hundred things I want not to say to you.'

Wilde could be as profound as he was superficially funny, but George Alexander would not have appreciated such remarks as these:

'It is the confession, not the priest, that gives us absolution.'

'The sentimentalist is always a cynic at heart. Indeed sentimentality is merely the Bank-holiday of cynicism.'

'Each time one loves is the only time that one has ever loved. Difference of object does not alter singleness of passion. It merely intensifies it.'

'Good resolutions are simply cheques that men draw on a bank where they have no account.'

'Conscience and cowardice are really the same things. Conscience is the trade-name of the firm.'

'Extravagance is the luxury of the poor, penury the luxury of the rich.'

But Alexander had heard enough to convince him that Wilde could write a good comedy, and when he advanced £100 on royalties he felt the matter was settled. But Wilde was excessively indolent, and his memory had to be jogged. 'Don't you want to make money?' Alexander asked. 'I much prefer money that is made for me . . . Ah, I was forgetting . . . yes . . . I suppose I shall have to do something. I owe you a hundred pounds.' 'Oh, don't worry about that!' 'I don't.' At last Alexander received *Lady Windermere's Fan* and liked it so much that he offered to buy it outright for £1,000. Wilde was clearly impressed and after a moment's reflection said: 'I have so much confidence in your excellent judgment, my dear Alec, that I cannot but refuse your generous offer.' At one rehearsal the author suggested that Ben Webster, who played 'Cecil Graham', should wear a green carnation in his buttonhole. 'Why green?' he asked. 'Because it is a charming colour.' 'But there is no such thing as a green carnation.' 'True, but there will be. Nature always copies art, and it is our duty to teach nature how to behave. When the other carnations hear of our wonderful flower, they will droop and die, and next year they will do their best to come up green. Some will overdo it, and it may then be our duty to invent a new colour.' Thenceforth a green carnation became the symbol of Wilde's youthful disciples. The first performance of his first comedy took place on 20 February 1892. Loud cries for the author after the final curtain induced Wilde to take a call, cigarette in hand, and make a short speech which for some reason infuriated the critics.

'Ladies and Gentlemen: I have enjoyed this evening immensely. The actors have given us a charming rendering of a delightful play, and your appreciation has been most intelligent. I congratulate you on the great success of your performance, which persuades me that you think almost as highly of the play as I do myself.'

Anxious to display his versatility, he next wrote a one-act drama in French, and got Sarah Bernhardt to announce *Salomé* at the Palace Theatre, London. But rehearsals had been in progress for three weeks when the Lord Chamberlain refused a licence because biblical characters were introduced, and for once in a way Wilde lost his sense of humour, threatening to become a naturalised Frenchman. But one could make much more money as a writer of witty comedies than of decorative prose, and Wilde pined for the flesh-pots. Deciding to remain an Irishman who had adopted England, he wrote *A Woman of No Importance*, and on the rapturous first-night in April '93 regretfully informed the audience from his box that 'Mr Oscar Wilde is not in the house.'

Two great successes were more than a man of his tastes and adolescent nature could sustain. They went to his head, and luxurious living went to his body, both causing distension. He was followed about by a group of youthful adulators; he ceased to take exercise, and flung money away on cabs and expensive restaurants; he became rather pompous, and his airiest remarks, such as 'It is only by not paying one's bills that one can hope to live in the memory of the commercial classes', were received with howls of glee by his satellites. All this made him defiantly self-assured and wholly irresponsible. In the late 'eighties he had begun to satisfy one aspect of his nature by practising pederasty, and in the 'nineties he flaunted his peculiarity by taking young men, grooms, valets and suchlike, to costly restaurants and by openly visiting a sort of homosexual agency in Westminster. In 1891 he met Lord Alfred Douglas, the extremely good-looking son of the Marquis of Queensberry, and each was instantaneously attracted to the other. Much to the annoyance of the Marquis, who was practically mad, they were constantly in one another's company and frequently spent holidays together. Douglas was enthralled by the conversation of Wilde, who was entranced by the physical appearance of Douglas. Their relationship caused much comment, especially as it was fairly generally known in male society that Wilde had abnormal tastes, though very few people knew that Douglas shared them, and indeed had been saved from disgrace at Oxford by Oscar's timely financial help.

In the years to come Douglas often said that he had helped Wilde to write his comedies. Actually he had been an impediment, preventing Wilde from working and creating emotional scenes which made composition impossible. Between dalliance and agitation Wilde somehow completed his third comedy *An Ideal Husband*, which appeared at the Haymarket Theatre under Lewis Waller's management, Tree being then in America, at the beginning of January '95, and repeated the success of its predecessors. But Wilde now jettisoned all the dramatic tricks that had helped the drama along since the time of Fielding, and while staying at No. 5 Esplanade, Worthing, in September '94 he wrote his masterpiece *The Importance of Being Earnest* in three weeks. It was a work of unadulterated fun, quite unlike anything else ever written for the stage, neither a farce nor a comedy nor a farcical comedy, but an Oscar, unique as the personality of the author. Originally in four acts, George Alexander begged that it should be cut down to three, and after objecting to the curtailment for nearly an hour Wilde finished up by saying:

'Do you realise, Alec, what you are asking me to sacrifice?'

'You will be able to use it in another play.'

'It may not fit into another play.'

'What does that matter? You are clever enough to think of a hundred things just as good.'

'Of course I am . . . a thousand if need be . . . but that is not the

Herbert Beerbohm Tree: *from a charcoal drawing
by John S. Sargent*

Herbert Tree and his brother Max Beerbohm:
from a caricature by the latter headed "Genus Beerbohmiense"

point.' Wilde now became very solemn and portentous: 'The scene that you feel is superfluous cost me terrible exhausting labour and heart-rending nerve-racking strain. You may not believe me, but I assure you on my honour that it must have taken fully five minutes to write.'

Earnest, first seen at St James's Theatre on 14 February 1895, would have eclipsed his earlier comedies if his career had not been extinguished by his own act within two months of its production. The Marquis of Queensberry, whose treatment of his wife and children had been that of a maniac, turned the full blast of his malignancy on to Wilde, his pretended purpose being to save his son, his real purpose to ruin a man whose mental superiority and olympian effrontery made him scream with rage. He had seen red before the publication of an anonymous story called *The Green Carnation*, wherein Wilde and Douglas were cleverly satirised, but after that he saw purple; and when, carrying a bouquet of carrots and turnips, he was refused admission to St James's Theatre on the opening night of *Earnest*, he adopted more forceful tactics, leaving a card at Wilde's club, the Albemarle, on which he wrote 'To Oscar Wilde, posing as a Somdomite', the addition of an 'm' no doubt making it sound more terrible to his distorted fancy. If his was the behaviour of a lunatic, so was Wilde's, who brought an action against him for criminal libel, driven thereto by the equally insane hatred of Douglas for his father.

When Wilde swore to his counsel Sir Edward Clarke that there was no foundation for Queensberry's accusation, he knew perfectly well that he lied, but he never guessed that the defendant would be able to produce any evidence against him except some of his written work and a few private letters to Douglas, which had been stolen by male prostitutes and were now in the hands of blackmailers, one of whom had sent a copy of what the writer thought a prose poem to Tree while *A Woman of No Importance* was being rehearsed. The actor handed it to Wilde, remarking that its contents were liable to be misunderstood. But in his usual light-hearted way Wilde said that if written in

R

verse it could appear in the Golden Treasury. 'Yes, but it is not
in verse', objected Tree. 'That no doubt explains why it is not
in the Golden Treasury', replied Wilde, who treated the whole
business in similar vein when approached by blackmailers, making
them feel foolish, careless of consequences himself. His action
against Queensberry, apart from the irresponsibility natural to
him, may be traced to his belief that he could easily brazen things
out, coupled with a feeling that he was fated to act a tragic role
in life, this being part of a boyish self-dramatisation which he
never outgrew. Add that he was influenced by his devotion to
Douglas, who whipped him up to action whenever he showed
hesitation, and the event became inevitable.

The trial of Queensberry took place in the first week of April
1895. Edward Carson's cross-examination gave Wilde many
opportunities to display his wit on the subject of literature, and
he scored easily. Shortly after his appearance in the witness-
box he happened to run across an actor, Charles Goodhart, in
Piccadilly Circus, where the placards were displaying, the
newspaper boys shouting, his name. Goodhart felt uncomfortable
and spoke of the weather, but Wilde set him at ease: 'You've
heard of my case? . . . Don't distress yourself. All is well. The
working classes are with me . . . to a boy.' Such was his mood
before the second day's hearing. But at the reassembly of the
court it soon became apparent that Queensberry and his friends
had raked London to some purpose, and Wilde's relationships
with certain young men were not so easily explained as passages
in *The Picture of Dorian Gray*. A ruthless cross-examination
by Carson made Clarke advise Wilde to withdraw from the
prosecution; and soon after he did so a warrant was issued for
his arrest, which took place at the Cadogan Hotel in Sloane
Street.

Though still legally innocent, he was refused bail, attacked in
the Press, reviled everywhere, and placed at the mercy of his
creditors, who sold his possessions for a song, his wife and
children having left Tite Street. The English people indulged
in one of their periodic bouts of moral indignation and hate,

their victim being unable to raise money or obtain evidence. Since moral indignation is due to a sense of guilt, and hatred is founded on fear, the casual foreign observer might have assumed that the majority of the male population of England were largely homosexual; but the guilt and fear were mostly caused by their own dissimilar vices. The strange thing is that the indignation and hatred aroused by Wilde persisted for many years, which suggests that those who continued to express such emotions were partly subject to their ostensible cause, since men to whose nature a weakness is wholly alien cannot maintain a feeling of violent hostility to it.

Clarke offered to defend Wilde for nothing, and his action should be remembered along with the sympathy and help of Ernest and Ada Leverson, Adela Schuster, Mrs Bernard Beere, Charles Wyndham, Lady Mount Temple, Ellen Terry, Frank Harris and the Rev. Stewart Headlam. As a rule women are much more civilised than men over lapses from normal conduct, and Wilde would certainly have received assistance from a number of his married female friends if they had not been scared by the moral attitude of their husbands. In spite of much perjured evidence, dragged from the stews, Wilde's first trial ended with a disagreement of the jury; but so great was the public prejudice created against him by the Press that the Government decided on another trial. Granted bail, he failed to gain admission to any hotel, and went to his mother's house in Oakley Street, where for a while he endured the taunts of brother Willie. Then Ada Leverson came to his rescue, and he spent some days in comfort under her husband's roof. His second trial began on 20 May and lasted four days. The jury returned a verdict of 'Guilty', and the judge, whose name was Wills, made the kind of speech to be expected from what Shakespeare calls 'an angry ape', one 'dressed in a little brief authority' and 'most ignorant of what he's most assured'.

Wilde was sentenced to two years' hard labour, and so hideous were the conditions of his captivity that for the first eighteen months he daily longed for death. For six months he was at

Wandsworth Prison, for the rest of the time at Reading Gaol. One day the doctor ordered him, though ill, to get up, and he fainted in chapel, the fall injuring his ear, which never recovered. Having been made a bankrupt, he had to attend the legal proceedings, and on a journey to the law-courts he stood in drizzling rain on a station platform handcuffed to two other convicts, the warders looking as depressed as the prisoners. 'Sir', said Wilde to one of the officials, 'if this is the way Queen Victoria treats her convicts she doesn't deserve to have any.' Nothing could quench his humour for long. The histrionic sense was strong in him, owing to his emotional juvenility, and at one moment he could feel himself a figure of tragedy, at the next laugh at the absurdity of life. About two years before this episode he had spoken with enthusiasm to a lover of Dickens of the master's amazing creative power, almost moving the other to tears, but he could not resist a final quip: 'One must have a heart of stone to read the death of Little Nell . . . without laughing.' When in Reading Gaol he wrote a deeply afflicting account of himself as the object of a laughing, jeering mob at Clapham Junction Station; yet when two Home Office functionaries were sent down to inquire into his condition, as a result of petitions by his friends, they saw him in the infirmary surrounded by other patients, all of whom were convulsed with laughter over the stories he was telling them, while he, in the exercise of his miraculous gift, looked radiant, high-spirited, healthy and happy.

The last six months of his imprisonment were made relatively comfortable by the removal of a brutal governor, Colonel Isaacson, and the substitution of a kind one, Major Nelson; and he was able to write a long letter to Alfred Douglas, parts of which were published by his great friend and literary executor Robert Ross under the title of *De Profundis* five years after his death, though the whole exact transcription, made by Rupert Hart-Davis, appears for the first time in his superbly edited collection of Wilde's letters. In this letter Wilde blamed himself for what had happened to him: 'The one disgraceful, unpardonable, and to all time contemptible action of my life, was to allow myself to appeal to society for help and protection.' But he also exposed Douglas as the malign influence in his life, 'the triumph of the smaller over the bigger nature', and although his accusations were true he censured himself for the weakness which caused his destruction.

The death of his mother during his incarceration was a dreadful blow, and the knowledge that he would not be allowed custody of his sons hurt him deeply; but he signed a deed of separation from his wife, who agreed to pay him £150 a year so long as he avoided Alfred Douglas. His friends visited him whenever possible, Robert Ross, Frank Harris, Robert Sherard, Charles Ricketts, More Adey and others; and he was able in the later months to become friendly with certain warders and convicts. To his great delight he also managed to secure the release of three children, imprisoned for poaching rabbits, by paying their fine. After his release he helped several ex-warders as well as ex-convicts. This was no new thing with him. Generosity in giving was part of his nature, though in his palmy days he had sometimes made a joke of it, as when a beggar stopped him in the street and complained that he had no work to do and no bread to eat. 'Work!' exclaimed Wilde: 'why should you want work? And bread! why should you eat bread?' He placed his hand on the man's shoulder and continued in a kindly if admonitory manner: 'Now if you had come to me and said that you had work to do but couldn't dream of working, and that you had bread to eat but couldn't think of eating it, I would have given you two shillings and sixpence. As it is' – he paused for a moment's reflection – 'I give you half a crown.'

On 19 May 1897 he left Reading Gaol and, having visited Stewart Headlam's house, where he met Ernest and Ada Leverson, he took the boat to France, some of his friends having clubbed together to provide him with means to be at leisure for several months. With Robert Ross and Reginald Turner he remained for a while at the Hôtel Sandwich, Dieppe, having adopted the name of 'Sebastian Melmoth'. Feeling that his friends should take the same precaution, he wrote to Ada

Leverson: 'Reggie Turner is staying here under the name 'Robert Ross', Robbie under the name 'Reginald Turner'. It is better that they should not use their own names.'

Since many people who had once boasted of his acquaintance now ignored or insulted him, a state of outlawry that lasted to the end of his life, he soon left Dieppe and went to stay at Berneval, a village some few miles along the coast, whence he wrote a letter to the *Daily Chronicle* on behalf of a warder who had been sacked for kindness to children. At Berneval he rose early, bathed in the sea, walked in the country, celebrated Queen Victoria's Diamond Jubilee by giving a treat to the village children, and took the Châlet Bourgeat, where he received visitors and composed *The Ballad of Reading Gaol*. But this pastoral life could not last. The days shortened and he got bored. Douglas wrote to him and he responded. He wished to see his sons, but his wife's family opposed the idea, on hearing which, no longer able to bear loneliness, he met Douglas at Rouen. Soon afterwards they went to Naples and stayed in a villa at Posilipo. But lack of funds forced them to separate, Wilde having forfeited his income and Douglas being threatened that his allowance would be discontinued if they remained together. Having written another letter to the *Chronicle* on prison reform, and polished off his ballad, Wilde left Naples.

Soon afterwards he heard of his wife's death at Genoa and knew that he would never again see his two sons. He went to Paris, suggesting to Ross that as he wanted to take rooms a subscription should be opened for 'the sweet sinner of England'. His monthly allowance was resumed with the retreat of Douglas, and occasionally he dined with friends passing through Paris. He could no longer write, ambition being dead in him, and his whole creative ability went into talk. Frank Harris was extremely kind, not only giving him innumerable meals in Paris but asking him to stay for some weeks at the Hôtel des Bains, La Napoule, near Cannes. It was clear to everyone who knew him that the homosexual side of his nature was now dominant; but those who were entranced by his conversation recognised his genius and were too similar or too sensible to pass judgment on his habits.

Having been the guest of Harris for two months at La Napoule, he went to stay with a curious person named Harold Mellor, who had a house at Gland on the shore of Lake Geneva. He remained there for the whole of March, but the society of Mellor drove him to Genoa, and he was back in Paris by May '99. At the Café de la Paix one night he saw the famous actress Ada Rehan with her manager Augustin Daly. Ada longed to bow acknowledgments but 'Mr and Mrs Daly were with me and I could not tell how they would feel about it. You never *do* know with men when they are going to feel very proper and when they are not.' Fortunately Daly was in an improper mood, and Wilde charmed them with his talk. 'We had a lovely evening', Ada declared. A few days later Daly suddenly died. His wife was incapable of action and Ada did not know what to do: 'And then Oscar Wilde came to me and was more good and helpful than I can tell you – just like a very kind brother.'

He still talked wonderfully, his tragic moods lifting under the stimulus of companionship, like the perpetual play of lightning against thunder-clouds, a few friends in a café now taking the place of sparkling receptions in Mayfair and fashionable audiences in St James's. No longer able to luxuriate in success, he dramatised his failure, putting himself in the place of Jesus Christ or Napoleon and declaring that calamity was the inevitable end of great artists.

At the beginning of 1900 he was bribed by Mellor to stay again at Gland, where his host was experimenting with an odd vehicle called 'an automobile', which continually broke down. 'They, like all machines, are more wilful than animals – nervous, irritable, strange things', summed up Wilde. He went to Rome at Mellor's expense and toyed with the notion of entering the Catholic Church but contented himself with receiving the Pope's blessing seven times. Having failed to embrace the faith, he made a success of photography, discovering that 'cows are very fond of being photographed, and, unlike architecture, don't move'. Beerbohm Tree, a thoroughly civilised and large-hearted man, sent him money and wrote: 'I have a lively remembrance of your many acts of kindness and courtesy and was one of those who devoutly hoped that misfortune would not submerge you.' George Alexander, too, after cutting him once on the Riviera, felt ashamed of the act, and in 1900 began to pay him small sums, but this was partly conscience-money, for Alexander had bought the rights of Wilde's comedies for next to nothing when the author went bankrupt.

Oscar returned to Paris, where Jean Dupoirier, landlord of the Hôtel d'Alsace in the Rue des Beaux-Arts, behaved like a real friend, and Wilde remained there for the rest of his life, his unpaid bills being numerous. In August 1900 he dined with Douglas and said that he would not live to see the new century: 'If another century began and I was still alive, it would really be more than the English could stand.' Although he had been treated infamously by many Englishmen, he neither felt nor expressed vindictiveness, dismissing cruel conduct as 'foolish' or 'unimaginative', his attitude to those who had behaved badly being of a saintly nature. One night he was held up by three *apaches*; the situation appealed to his sense of comedy and he invited them into a café, where they paid for his drinks and laughed for two hours at his stories. He announced a momentous discovery to a friend: that alcohol, taken at frequent intervals and in sufficiently large quantities, produced all the signs of intoxication. And when someone brought champagne for his luncheon he said: 'I am dying, as I have lived, beyond my means.'

An operation on the ear which had never recovered from the fall in Wandsworth Prison did not ease the headaches from which he suffered, and, though his friends, Robert Ross and Reginald Turner, did not know it, he was dying of cerebral meningitis. Occasionally the pain became unendurable and morphia injections were administered. At times he thrust his hand into his mouth to prevent himself from crying aloud in agony, and once he took it out to speak bitterly of his bedroom wallpaper. 'It is killing me', he moaned, adding with a sigh of resignation as if he had already succumbed 'one of us *had* to go.' He became speechless, but gave a sign of consent when Robert Ross asked if he should fetch a priest. Received into the Roman Catholic communion, he died on 30 November 1900.

His body, temporarily interred at Bagneux, was moved in 1909 to Père Lachaise Cemetery, where his tomb attracts more pilgrims than that of any other famous person buried there, a refreshing comment on the barbarous generation that had so harshly condemned its rarest spirit.

11

Bernard Shaw

In the year 1886 a bomb was exploded in Chicago killing several policemen. A group of anarchists were charged with the crime, though they declared that the police were responsible, having exterminated their own men by faulty timing. A few of the anarchists were condemned to death, others to life-imprisonment, and a young unknown journalist named Bernard Shaw recorded that he 'tried to get some literary men in London, all heroic rebels and sceptics on paper, to sign a memorial asking for the reprieve of these unfortunate men. The only signature I got was Oscar's. It was a completely disinterested act on his part; and it secured my distinguished consideration for him for the rest of his life.' But though they met on several occasions after that, Oscar Wilde and Bernard Shaw never quite hit it off together. Once Shaw had the experience of listening to Wilde's astonishing discourse; and at the end of his life, on being asked by a newspaper editor what famous man of the past he would like to meet, G.B.S. replied: 'If I craved for entertaining conversation by a first-class raconteur I should choose Oscar Wilde.' Yet their temperaments did not harmonise and they felt awkward in one another's company. Nevertheless Shaw's 'distinguished consideration' for Wilde was proved when the latter went to gaol and his name was not whispered in public. With exceptional daring and complete indifference to popular opinion, Shaw referred on several occasions to 'Mr Oscar Wilde' in the course of his dramatic criticisms, and he was the only person in England who had the courage to do so. He also drew up a memorial for Oscar's reprieve; but as the only person who had backed a similar appeal for the Chicago anarchists was in prison, this one too lacked signatures. At some later date Shaw must have come across an amusing description of a man in *The Picture of Dorian Gray*: 'Ernest Harrowden, one of those middle-aged mediocrities so common in London clubs, who have no enemies but are thoroughly disliked by their friends.' It pleased Shaw to believe that he never made enemies but could not help annoying his friends, so he transferred that part of Wilde's sentence to himself. But Oscar would never have made such an inappropriate remark about G.B.S., whose only enemies had never met him and whose friends were devoted to him.

George Bernard Shaw's birthday, the anniversary of which as an adult he always tried to forget, was on 26 July 1856, at what is now No. 33 Synge Street, Dublin. Owing to the preservation of a letter written by his father to his mother, who was on a visit to relations in July '57, we learn that the one-year-old baby caused as much uneasiness in the domestic circle as the man was later to arouse in artistic and political circles. He howled the place down when he could not get what he wanted, pulled his hat to pieces, expressed his early thoughts on journalism by tearing the newspaper to bits, and was the despair of his nurse. Once he fell out of bed on to his head; but most babies seem to be made of indiarubber and he took it in his bounce. Then he fell backwards off the kitchen table, his head penetrating a window-pane and hitting the iron bar outside. While providing much drama for his family, he remained calm.

For him and his two elder sisters it was a loveless home, in which the affections were starved, the critical sense overfed. Their father, having failed in business, took to drinking; their mother, having failed in matrimony, took to singing. From the first of these the boy learnt how to laugh at life's tragedies, from the second how to appreciate music. An early hatred of poverty was instilled in him by a servant who was supposed to take him for walks in the fashionable squares of Dublin, but took him instead to the squalid tenements of her friends in the slums or to public-house bars. Taught to read and write by a governess and to grasp Latin by a clerical uncle, he went at the age of ten to the Wesleyan Connexional School, but learnt nothing there because the teaching bored him and he had no desire to learn what was taught. He later declared that 'pressing people to learn things they do not want to know is as unwholesome and disastrous as feeding them on sawdust', also that 'those who have been taught most know least'. Having made no progress in two years, he was removed from the Wesleyan and sent to a Roman Catholic school where the pupils were the children of lower middle-class shopkeepers. At once he became a social outcast, being cut dead by all his Protestant pals, who regarded themselves as socially superior to the Catholics. This experience was for him what the blacking-warehouse job was for Dickens, a shameful secret which he kept to himself for the next eighty years. He stuck it for seven months, then struck and went to another Protestant school, where he learnt nothing but recovered his self-respect.

While wasting time at school he busily educated himself in the paths he wished to tread. Before entering his teens he read Dickens, Shakespeare, the Bible, Bunyan and the *Arabian Nights*, and at an age when most boys were struggling with their Latin primers he could whistle several of Mozart's operas. He haunted the National Gallery of Ireland, and learnt to recognise the work of the Old Masters at sight. But his chief pleasure as a boy was derived from the scenery at Dalkey, where his mother had a cottage. 'I was never quite happy as a child', he said, 'except during the summer weeks every year at Dalkey.'

At the age of fifteen he became a clerk in a firm of land agents with a salary of four shillings a week. A year later he was tried for the job of cashier, proved to be eminently capable, was paid eighteen shillings and sixpence a week, and held the post for four years. But though he was good at the work, the work was not good enough for him, and he abandoned it suddenly at the age of twenty, went to London and joined his mother, who had left her husband some years before and was giving lessons in singing.

For the next nine years Shaw was kept by his mother. Efforts by friends to make him earn what was called an honest living were unsuccessful, though he took an occasional job just to oblige them. He had determined to write for a livelihood, and though the articles he despatched were returned by editors with depressing regularity he went on sending them in. A single article earned him fifteen shillings, which was all he got from journalism in nine years. But he also wrote five novels during that time, each of which was rejected by every respectable publisher in England. 'They were the taskwork of my apprenticeship', he told me: 'I wrote them because I knew I had to do something and was incapable of doing anything else. I hated them and felt ashamed of them afterwards, for they reminded me of the dreadful years when I walked the streets of London in shabby clothes without a penny in my pocket. But they taught me my job. Writing gave me no trouble thereafter. And from their fate I learnt the startling consolation which I later put into the mouth of Caesar: "He who has never hoped can never despair".' The novels illustrate his mental development from rationalism to socialism; and in the days ahead one of them, *Cashel Byron's Profession*, was almost a best-seller.

When twenty-five years old Shaw became a vegetarian, and as he neither smoked nor drank alcohol his time and vitality had to be expended in other directions. Though shy and nervous by nature he forced himself to speak in public, and, having been converted to socialism by reading a French edition of Karl Marx, he joined the Fabian Society in 1884. In time he became its 'star' performer on platforms and at street corners, taking part in all the social agitations of the period and achieving great popularity with working-class audiences. The main object of the Fabian Society was to make socialism respectable, and this was done by permeating the Liberal Party with its theories; so successfully in fact that at the close of the century the Liberals won an election on a programme of Fabian socialism. But having come to power the Liberal leaders repudiated Fabianism, and Shaw and Sidney Webb set to work to form the Labour Party, which established itself in Parliament in 1906.

Shaw's earliest activities as a socialist were attended by his strenuous endeavours to earn a living. His education was completed in the Reading Room of the British Museum, which he always called his university, and here he met a writer, William Archer, who forced him into journalism. He began by reviewing books and pictures, and at the age of thirty-two got his first regular job as a critic of music for *The Star*, his salary being two guineas a week. With these articles, signed 'Corno di Bassetto', his irrepressible, irreverent and inimitable personality first burst upon the world, and the volume containing them is as entertaining today as when he first persuaded 'deaf stockbrokers' to read about music. He next received an offer from *The World* to continue the process for five pounds a week, and the initials 'G.B.S.' became famous.

The note of levity in his writing enabled the pundits of the time to call him a charlatan and a clown; but he knew a good deal more about music than any of them, and inwardly they writhed. The leading professors, Alexander Mackenzie, Hubert Parry and Villiers Stanford, all of them to be knighted, were bewildered and exasperated. Mackenzie said that he was 'mad, quite mad', Parry showed signs of apoplexy when speaking of him, but Stanford took his gruel like a man, addressing Shaw at a chance meeting, 'Well, you appear to have been enjoying yourself at our expense', and getting the reply, 'One must have some compensation for being a critic of music'. Shaw admitted that 'I made them all sit up, but instead of being grateful they wanted to lay me out.' Among his many crimes against convention he championed Wagner, then thought a monster of lunacy, and wrote a book about him, *The Perfect Wagnerite*. For six years he sent blasts of fresh air into a department that had previously been monopolised by stuffy pedants, and no critic since his time has dared to be ponderous.

Having infuriated the pedagogues of music, he spent the next three and a half years fluttering the dramatic dovecots. For six pounds a week, under the editorship of Frank Harris, he criticised plays in *The Saturday Review*, ridiculing all the silly fashions in dramaturgy with such devastating humour that he created a public receptive to the play of ideas. He eulogised Ibsen, then considered highly offensive, and wrote *The Quintessence of Ibsenism*. He attacked Shakespeare's plays, which he loved, simply because everyone else was absurdly uncritical of them, and though he admired Henry Irving as an actor he held up to scorn the mangled versions of Shakespeare produced by Irving at the Lyceum Theatre. He slated Arthur Pinero, whose dramas were praised by other critics for qualities they did not possess, and received letters from that author ending 'Yours, with detestation'. Another leading playwright, James Barrie, stopped him in the street with the words: 'Shaw, you ought to be roasted alive, not that even well-cooked you would be to my taste.' His fellow-critic William Archer reproved him for being unpleasant about Sarah Bernhardt, but he explained the difficulty: 'I can never do her justice or believe in her impersonations because she is so like my aunt Georgina', which happened to be a fact. Incidentally I got into hot water for saying that in comparing the acting of Sarah Bernhardt and Eleanora Duse he had been inspired to do his best. 'Blast you! I always did my best', he burst out. 'That was how the quality got into the criticisms. I am an artist, and cannot bear anything that I can better.' This was strictly true, and he rightly turned down my suggestion that I should do a volume of his selected dramatic criticisms for the Everyman Library: 'No. Their quality is so even that you cannot select. It is a case of all or nothing.' The combination of expert knowledge, perpetual gaiety, absolute honesty, idiosyncratic judgment, incessant wit, personal revelation and matchless readability, make his dramatic criticism unique in literature.

The short time he could spare from his literary and sociological labours was passed in philandering with women. Just as Oscar Wilde had no little resemblance to Sheridan, so had Shaw considerable similarity with Swift. All four Irishmen were kind-hearted, but the kindness of Swift and Shaw was sensible and came from the mind, while the kindness of Sheridan and Wilde was sensitive and came from the heart. Swift and Shaw were most alike in their behaviour to the other sex. Both were strangely detached from life, and it may have been this quality that attracted women, who like most creatures long for what they cannot possess. Neither man was attainable, or rather possessable, and each excited women to reckless action. As far as we know Shaw caused more devastation than Swift, but there is an absence of record in the latter case. The point is that the two men seemed to find a pleasure in stimulating feelings they could not or would not gratify, a course which may be traceable to a love of power. Other marks of similarity were their passion for public affairs, their love of influencing events, their use of art for propaganda, and an ability to express their meaning in the clearest, simplest, most direct and forcible prose ever written in English.

We do not know, though we may doubt, whether Swift indulged in chance sexual experiences, but like Shaw he was fastidious by nature and repelled by certain aspects of carnal relationship. Shaw however was more curious than Swift and did not share the Dean's hatred of mankind. Even so sex came to G.B.S., as honour might have come to Falstaff, 'unlooked for'. A young widow named Jenny Patterson 'virtually raped' him on his twenty-ninth birthday. Having lost his chastity, he 'sought her company whenever I could find nothing better to do'. Their intimacy continued for two or three years, after which he got bored with her exigent raptures, and when she made 'a very horrible scene' with his friend Florence Farr he never saw her again. Florence was an actress, and Shaw shared her sexual favours with a dozen other men for some years, allowing many women to fall in love with him without sensual profit to themselves. Annie Besant was one, Edith Nesbit (Mrs Hubert Bland) another, May Morris (William Morris's daughter) a third, and there were several more. His relationship with May Morris had an unfortunate sequel. She believed that he loved her, and in

Oscar Wilde (1890)

George Bernard Shaw (1919)

so far as he was capable of such an emotion he did; but she could not live on his looks, became impatient of his reticence, and married another man. It cannot have been a blissful match because it terminated soon after Shaw went to stay with them. His presence having revived the old feelings in May, he was faced with flight or adultery. He fled.

However tantalising for the women, his amorous experiences taught him a great deal and provided him with much raw material for his plays, the second of which, *The Philanderer*, contains a watered-down version of the scene between Jenny and Florence. His first attempt at drama was called *Widowers' Houses*, a tragi-comedy of slum landlordism, which achieved a single performance by the Independent Theatre at the end of 1892, and had a mixed reception, hoots predominating. An angry note in the cries for 'author' at the final curtain warned him what to expect, and he arrived on the stage taut for trouble. But he had not been a socialist agitator for nothing. The mere sight of him, tall, spare, with a red beard, white face, provocative eyebrows and athletic movements, impressed the audience, while his soft voice and alluring Dublin accent gradually changed the hisses and cat-calls to applause and cheers. No one would consider his next effort, *The Philanderer*; and his third play, *Mrs Warren's Profession* (1893), dealing with female prostitution as an inevitable result of capitalism, was censored in England and caused police-court proceedings in New York. Eight years later the Stage Society, a sort of club unaffected by the censor, gave a Sunday evening performance, which drove the dramatic critics to such a condition of moral panic and protest that the author felt his sermon to be completely justified. He called his first three plays 'unpleasant', and the critics agreed with him wholeheartedly.

It then occurred to him that the West End theatre managers wanted something more palatable, so he wrote three 'pleasant' comedies. *Arms and the Man* (1894) completely fogged the actors, who were so anxious to discover its meaning that they played with deadly seriousness, as a consequence of which it went with a yell of delight and the shouts for 'author' were

s

enthusiastically friendly. He bowed before the storm of gratu-
lation, but being accustomed to a different sort of storm he would
have been bereft of speech if a youngster in the gallery had not
let forth a solitary 'boo', which gave him an opening he quickly
seized upon: 'I quite agree with you, my friend, but what can
we two do against a whole houseful of the opposite opinion?'
This pleasant platform lie went well, but the play did not follow
suit. Amazed to find that they were appearing in a farce, the
actors at once began to play for laughs, and the first-night success
was never repeated. Shaw's next attempt, *Candida* (1894),
perplexed the managers who read it, and at length obtained
two performances by the Stage Society, with a young actor
named Granville Barker in the part of Marchbanks. Some years
later it became popular, but not such a favourite as *You Never Can
Tell* (1896), which again puzzled the managers, one of whom,
Cyril Maude, took the risk of rehearsing the strange piece at the
Haymarket Theatre, two performers throwing up their parts
after the first run-through. Shaw explained to me why he had
found it necessary to withdraw the comedy: 'Allan Aynesworth,
who rehearsed the part of Valentine, was a farcical actor who
hadn't the smallest conception of how to play high comedy. At
my fiftieth attempt to explain how he should handle a scene, he
lost his temper and said "Do it yourself!" I did it. But it was
beyond him; so I advised Maude to abandon the production.'
The Stage Society again came to the rescue and gave two performances of it in '99. Five years later it became the stock
money-maker of the Vedrenne-Barker management.

All this time Shaw had been writing dramatic criticism and
living with his mother in the upper part of a house, No. 29
Fitzroy Square. He now determined to write a play for a particular 'star', and since his description of what happened is an
excellent specimen of his conversational humour it will be
quoted exactly as I received it:

'I wrote *The Devil's Disciple* for William Terriss, then a pet
melodramatic hero at the Adelphi, which was the London home
of melodrama. He and Jessie Millward and Harry Nicholls were

London institutions, and they did their work extremely well. Terriss wanted to tour the world as a "star". He asked me to collaborate with him in a play, the plot to be supplied by him. It was more than a plot: it was all the plots of all the melodramas he had ever played in. At the end of every act he was dragged away to penal servitude through the treachery of the beautiful devil who was the villainess of the piece; and he turned up in the next act as fresh as paint without an attempt to explain this happy change in his fortune. I told him that it would be splendid for the Adelphi, but that in foreign cities, where they would have their own particular native Terriss, they would not stand melodrama from him, but would expect something like Hamlet. So he put his plot in the fire (having several typed copies in his desk) and said "Mr Shaw: you are right."

'So I wrote *The Devil's Disciple* for him, and read it to him in Jessie Millward's flat. He listened in deep perplexity until I had nearly finished the first act, when he said, "Excuse my interrupting you, but is this an interior?" (Melodramas usually begin on the village green.) I said it was. "Right", he said, "now I have it. Go on. You won't mind my interrupting you."

'I went on. When I had read about two pages of the second act, he said, with despair in his face, "Sorry to interrupt you again, but is *this* an interior?" I said it was, and he assured me that I had now set his mind completely at rest, and would I excuse him for interrupting me and fire away. I fired away. When the barrage had lasted two minutes he had fallen into a coma so profound that Jessie and I had to carry him into the next room and give him strong tea before he was thoroughly awake and ashamed of the failure of his effort to live up to the higher drama.

'Nothing more passed between us until he heard that Richard Mansfield had at last conquered New York with a tremendously successful melodrama, and that this was *The Devil's Disciple*. He sent for me hastily to discuss business with him; but before the appointment came off he was stabbed by a lunatic at the stage door of the Adelphi, which, in its old aspect as a temple of melodrama, may be said to have died with him.'

Mansfield's production in New York was Shaw's first stage success, and it occurred at a fortunate moment when overwork as critic, dramatist, vestryman, committee-man and public speaker brought on a breakdown in health, which would certainly have finished him off if he had not married and been nursed back to health by his wife Charlotte, a wealthy Irishwoman whose maiden name was Payne-Townshend. They agreed at the outset that they would not risk the loss of affection by sexual cohabitation; and, though such an arrangement may have been detrimental to Charlotte's health and disposition, there is no doubt that their affection for one another remained unimpaired. She fended him from all sorts of troubles and annoyances; and from the point of view of a man whose activity was excessive outside the bed-room, she was a perfect wife. He gave up dramatic criticism and was hobbling about on crutches when they married, adding a broken arm to a disabled foot during their honeymoon, spent partly at Hindhead and partly at Freshwater Bay Hotel in the Isle of Wight, where on the cliffs near-by he worked hard on an epoch-making play, *Caesar and Cleopatra* (1898-9), which ulti-mately affected not only the drama but fiction, history and biography, though very few practitioners seem to be aware of their debt to him. For three centuries playwrights had been slavishly copying Shakespeare's style of treating historical characters. About thirty years after it was written, Shaw's play had altered all this. With it he revolutionised the art of re-creating historical periods and persons by treating them in a natural and humorous manner. Having recovered from his various accidents, he knocked off a play for Ellen Terry, who could not see herself in the leading part of *Captain Brassbound's Conversion* (1899), until her nurse exclaimed, 'It is you to the life!' Some years later she played it under the Vedrenne-Barker management; but *Caesar and Cleopatra* had to wait longer for a production by Johnston Forbes-Robertson, the actor who had inspired Shaw's portrayal of Julius Caesar.

Tired of trying to reform the stage and please actors, Shaw turned his back on the whole business, and his next play was an essay on philosophy and religion, his own religion of Creative Evolution. *Man and Superman* first appeared in a book (1903) with a long dedicatory letter, a thesis on revolutionary themes and a collection of maxims. The Stage Society performed it in 1905, and then it joined the Court Theatre repertory. Shaw's real chance as a playwright came when Granville Barker, encouraged by the reception of a few afternoon performances of *Candida*, went into management with a business man, J. E. Vedrenne, at the small Court Theatre in Sloane Square, London, and commenced a season of plays on which no West End manager would have risked a penny.

The continued success of the undertaking was due entirely to Shaw, nearly all of whose past plays were produced and whose new plays, *John Bull's Other Island, Man and Superman, Major Barbara* and *The Doctor's Dilemma*, became the talk of the town. Every leading politician went to see them, and the reigning monarch, Edward VII, laughed so heartily at one performance that he broke the chair on which he sat. Shaw produced all his own plays and taught the actors the new technique requisite for his class of work. In effect he created a new type of actor and a new type of audience. People who had never previously been interested in the stage became regular playgoers at the Court, and for three years the Vedrenne-Barker management provided the most original and invigorating series of plays that had been seen in London since the time of Shakespeare. Unfortunately their success went to their heads and they moved to the West End, where the high rents combined with a temporary slump finished their enterprise, and to satisfy the creditors Shaw had to disgorge nearly all the royalties he had earned. But they had created an epoch in theatrical history.

Shaw now took advantage of the position he had won by writing two plays that were simply conversations, which he defined in a letter to me as 'daring experiments in the Aristotelian unities, influenced by Gilbert Murray's translations of the plays of Euripides', in his opinion the noblest feature of the Vedrenne-Barker management at the Court. The first of these Shavian discussions, *Getting Married*, was a modest highbrow success at the Haymarket Theatre. The second, *Misalliance*, was financed by an American manager, Charles Frohman, who was totally mystified by it, shocked by the box-office returns, and said that three performances were three too many.

To show what he could do in the commercial line, Shaw then produced a pot-boiler, *Fanny's First Play*, which ran for nearly two years at a small theatre. He soon made up for that concession to public taste by writing a masterpiece, *Androcles and the Lion* (1913). The hurricane of denunciation which greeted this work from people who mistook church- and chapel-going for Christianity drew the sort of Shavian treatment that usually augmented hubbub: 'I know that most people do not believe that Christians were really killed in the arena at all, and are shocked at the idea of their being callously called to their deaths as numbered turns in a variety entertainment by a vulgar call-boy, instead of simply being painted by Royal Academicians as being politely led up to heaven by angels with palm branches. And it gives me an extraordinary satisfaction when the shrieks of these poor creatures prove that I have brought them face to face for the first time with the grim reality of persecution and their own daily complicity in it, and perhaps hurt their eyes with a flash of the unbearable radiance of real religion.' *Androcles* was followed by Shaw's greatest financial success, *Pygmalion*, done by Beerbohm Tree at His Majesty's Theatre in April 1914, with Mrs Patrick Campbell as the cockney Galatea, a part written for her.

During the war of 1914–18 Shaw became extremely unpopular. He wrote a pamphlet which contained a perfectly sound but completely objective criticism of British foreign policy. In a condition of war hysteria it is always considered unpatriotic to speak the truth. He was denounced on all sides, called a liar, a pro-German, a traitor, and all the other names that are flung at those who keep their heads by those who have lost theirs. Many friends cut him, many acquaintances cursed him; sacks of letters full of abuse arrived at his house; he was expelled from the

Dramatists' Club; one old admirer stated in public that he ought to be tarred and feathered, while others favoured lynching. Shaw remained calm and tolerant, confiding in me that 'War fever is like any other epidemic, and what the patients say or do in their delirium is no more to be counted against them than if they were all in bed with brain fever'. The men who were actually doing the fighting enjoyed his plain speaking, and his public meetings were packed and enthusiastic.

At intervals he turned from the tumult and the shouting to write a comedy in the manner of Tchekov, for whom he had an immense admiration. This was *Heartbreak House*, which, though he assured me he had no favourite among his plays, was the one he felt most strongly about. With the conclusion of hostilities the dementia subsided and the public temperature became normal, or rather subnormal. Those who had thought hanging too good for Shaw were thoroughly ashamed of themselves and mutely invited him to shake hands when next they met. He accepted their proffered friendship in the conviction that, if he spoke his mind in another war, they would demand his death by torture.

While the fight against Germany was in its closing stages he made the first draft of what was to be his testament to the human race, *Back to Methuselah*, wherein his evolutionary theories are shown in stage-action. Believing that the conduct and character of human beings are determined not by their experience but by their expectation of life, he asserted that people could live to almost any age if they so willed it, and that civilisation depended on the fact that everyone could look forward to at least 300 years of life, since men will not bother to improve a world in which they can only survive for a mere half-century or so. The five plays Shaw wrote in order to illustrate his faith were produced by Barry Jackson at Birmingham in October 1923.

But such an undertaking could not possibly pay its way, and the cycle of dramas left the average person exhausted. Shaw recovered his popularity and achieved world-wide fame with his next work, *Saint Joan* (1924), which converted so many people who had previously been hostile to him that in the public estimation he almost became Saint Shaw. He made the best of the universal acclamation by writing *The Intelligent Woman's Guide to Socialism*, a compendium of all his opinions on a subject that had occupied him for over forty years. From the author of *Saint Joan* it was received with a respect not hitherto accorded to the author of *Mrs Warren's Profession*.

In 1925 he was awarded the Nobel Prize for literature, which he refused on the ground that 'the money is a lifebelt thrown to a swimmer who has already reached the shore in safety'. His last wholly successful play, written at the age of seventy-two, was *The Apple Cart*, with which the Malvern Festival in his honour was inaugurated in August 1929. He personally attached more importance to his dramatisation of the Last Judgment, entitled *The Simpleton of the Unexpected Isles*, produced when he was nearly eighty.

At an age when most people prefer to stay at home Shaw started to see the world. He was seventy-five when he visited Moscow and had an interview with Stalin, after which he travelled to South Africa, India, New Zealand, and the United States. Wherever he went his reception was that of a reigning monarch or even a film star. But he was not much impressed by anyone or anything he saw. 'One place is very much like another', he told me, 'and this human being resembles that.' A misadventure in South Africa put him on the track of a black girl's adventures. In the course of a conversation he gave me the details:

'In moments of crisis my nerves act in the most extraordinary way. When utter disaster seems imminent my whole being is instantaneously braced to avoid it: I size up the situation in a flash, set my teeth, contract my muscles, take a firm grip of myself, and, without a tremor, always do the wrong thing. That happened once in Pall Mall. I was bicycling past the National Gallery when a Great Western Railway van emerged from the Haymarket making for Cockspur Street. A lady put up her parasol; the horse shied, turned left, and bolted straight for me on its wrong side. However, I was ready for it. Instead of getting off my bicycle and on to the pavement, as any ordinary human being would have done, I pulled myself together with a supreme effort, went full tilt at that horse, hit it square in the chest, was flung to the ground, and only escaped death by springing up from my ankles and landing an inch or two outside the cart wheels as they passed. The bicycle screamed as it was run over like a spider being torn to pieces. . . .

'My accident in South Africa was more serious. I learnt to drive in 1908 on a car that had its accelerator pedal between the clutch and the brake. That arrangement became automatic for me; and when I changed to cars with the accelerator to the right of the brake I became a deadly dangerous driver in an emergency when I had not my trusty chauffeur next me to turn off the spark when I mistook the pedals. He was unfortunately not with me in South Africa. Well, we were on our way to Port Elizabeth from a pleasant seaside place called Wilderness. I was at the wheel and had done a long drive over mountain passes, negotiating tracks and gorges in a masterly manner, when we came upon what looked like a half mile of straight safe smooth road; and I let the car rip. Suddenly she twisted violently to the left over a bump and made for the edge of the road. I was more than equal to the occasion: not for an instant did I lose my head: my body was rigid, my nerves were of steel. I turned the car's head the other way, and pressed down the wrong pedal as far as it would go. The car responded nobly: she dashed across the road, charged and cleared a bank, taking a barbed wire fence with her, and started off across the veldt. On we went, gathering speed, my foot hard on the accelerator, jerking and crashing over the uneven ground, plunging down a ravine and up the other side, and I should have been bumping over the veldt to this day if Commander Newton, who was in charge of me, hadn't said sternly: "Will you take your foot off the accelerator and put it on the brake." Well, I am always open to reason. I did as he suggested and brought the car to a standstill, the last strand of barbed wire still holding, though drawn out for miles. I was unhurt; but my wife had been rolled about with the luggage in the back seat and was seriously wounded. The Commander rendered first aid; and we finished the journey at Knysna, where she developed a temperature of 108 and was laid up for a month. I bathed every day and wrote *The Adventures of the Black Girl in Her Search for God*.'

In the ordinary way Shaw's notion of recreation was a change of work, and the fable he wrote in South Africa was a mere holiday-task. Back in England his time was spent either in his Whitehall Court flat, where he received many visitors, or in his Hertford-shire home, Ayot St Lawrence, where he worked, walked and attended to his garden. He continued to write plays, prefaces and propaganda, while attending to the publication of a standard edition of his collected works, one volume of which, *Pen Portraits and Reviews*, contains scintillating impressions of people he had known, some of whom are laughed into immortality, as well as a parody of contemporary novel-writing, an inspired mixture of satire, burlesque and insight, such as no one on earth but Shaw could have concocted.

The fungoid growth of European dictators in the 1930s impressed G.B.S., who preferred their activities to the inactivity of Parliamentary government. Hearing from his friend Lady Astor that someone she knew was a typical Englishman with a progressive outlook, he wrote: 'As for the man with "a profoundly liberal mind: an English mind", he must be as great a curiosity as a man with a profoundly peaceful mind: a tiger's mind. All these anti-Mussolinians are idiots.' The funny part of it was that his socialist supporters would have preferred no progressive action at all to any improvement brought about by men hostile to their doctrines, and Shaw was reviled for favouring the social reforms of Hitler and Mussolini, who were at least doing something for their people while the so-called democratic politicians of Great Britain were stuck in the mud, incapable of motion except with the aid of an earthquake. Meeting him in an interval between his various globe-trottings, I said that a careful study of Shakespeare's *Macbeth* was more profitable than a knowledge of economics if one wished to understand these dictators, since Shakespeare knew that power drives men mad. Shaw replied that he would rather have insane people who got things done than inane ones who talked and did nothing.

It was impossible to corner G.B.S., whose platform training had made him a master of riposte. A few examples may be given. Having expressed his opinion that the community were being spiritually starved for lack of religious instruction, he was asked, 'Have we lost faith?' 'Certainly not', he promptly returned, 'but we have transferred it from God to the General Medical Council.' A Swiss woman once made him a proposal: 'You have the greatest brain in the world, and I have the most beautiful body; so we ought to produce the most perfect child.' Shaw countered: 'What if the child inherits my body and your brain?' Knowing that he hated blood-sports and would agree with the sentiment, Lady Astor remarked 'I hate killing for pleasure.' As he said nothing, one of her children probed: 'Do you hate killing for pleasure?' 'It depends upon whom you kill', he answered. At a meeting of some Catholic Socialist Guild he was asked whether he believed in the Immaculate Conception of the Virgin Mary. 'Of course I do', he said with emphasis, and the audience sighed with pleasure. But when he continued: 'I also believe in the Immaculate Conception of my own mother and the mothers of everyone else', the sigh became a gasp.

I once attempted to make him acknowledge the inconsistency of his liberal opinions with his approval of the Soviet Government, but I might have spared my breath. In my biography of him I quoted many sentences from his works which showed that he had done all in his power to make people critical of institutions, antagonistic to persecution whatever the cause, sceptical of authority and healthily rebellious. In spite of which, I said, he had praised and supported the Russian dictatorship, which suppressed free speech, murdered its political opponents, starved its recalcitrant peasants to death, enslaved everyone else, and, generally speaking, made the Robespierres and Marats of the French Revolution seem like a bunch of mealy-mouthed meliorists in comparison. When Shaw read this he said: 'The quotations you've given don't contradict my present attitude towards

Russia. What do you know of the Soviet Government? Nothing whatever. You've simply picked up a lot of hearsay nonsense from the English Press which you believe religiously. Have you ever read a newspaper account of something you happen to know a great deal about?'

'Yes.'

'How true was it?'

'Scarcely a word.'

'And yet you dare to believe the twaddle any journalist cares to invent about Russia because he knows it will please his proprietor, his editor and his readers. Really, Hesketh, I'm surprised at you!'

'But is there no suppression of free speech or shooting of opponents or slave labour in Russia?'

'No more than there is at a time of crisis in England. Just try to tell the truth about this confounded conflict or impede the war effort and see what happens—'

'Ah, well, in wartime things are different.'

'Russia is perpetually at war. She is ringed round with enemies. She can trust no one. Therefore, if she were guilty of the things you say, she couldn't help herself.'

'You'll be telling me next that England's attitude to Communism is the cause of all the horrors that take place in Russia.'

'Prove your horrors before you talk of them.'

'How can I?'

'Exactly.'

'But suppose it could be proved that what I have written there is true, would you still support the Soviet?'

'Yes, because worse things have happened in other countries, especially Germany, and the Russians are trying to create a new and classless society. But don't run away with the idea that my critical sense is suspended where they are concerned. I have criticised freely and openly, and will continue to criticise, their mistakes; but I don't depend upon a hostile Press to tell me what they are. I would as soon expect a completely objective view of a mongoose by a cobra.'

The war that broke out in 1939 found him still capable of sending up the national blood-pressure. He wrote an article which irritated many of those who had been lauding him to the skies a year or two earlier; but he could no more help arousing temper in a crisis than others could help venting it. He was too old now to go on waving a red flag at John Bull, and he lived quietly in his London flat or his country home. I was writing his Life at that time and seeing a good deal of him at both places. He wandered about London visiting the spots he had once known well. His wife died in 1943, and he missed her greatly, though her bad health towards the end had nearly prostrated him.

At the age of ninety he received two honours. Long before that he had been offered a knighthood and a peerage, both of which he had declined, and on being asked whether he would accept the Order of Merit he replied that he had already conferred it on himself. But when in 1946 his native city invited him to become an Honorary Freeman, he accepted, saying that 'Dublin alone has the right to affirm that in spite of my incessantly controversial past and present I have not disgraced her.' He also accepted the offer of St Pancras, which he had served as a vestryman and councillor nearly half a century earlier, to become its first Honorary Freeman. His final completed full-length play, *Buoyant Billions*, was written when he was ninety-two. In the last year of his life he disliked receiving visitors. 'I don't want to see anybody, and I don't want anybody to see me', he exclaimed when I suggested taking one of his lifelong admirers to call on him. 'You don't know what it is to be as old as I am. Do you suppose I want the great G.B.S. to be remembered as a doddering old skeleton?'

But if his physical frame had shrunk his mental capacity had not diminished. Right up to the end he maintained a keen interest in the things that had always interested him, from biology to photography. When past ninety he argued with me about Shakespeare with an energy that a man of forty would have envied; he was busy supplementing the script of the film version of one of his plays; he was carrying on a large private corres-

pondence, besides writing articles for newspapers; and though
he had ceased to swim he continued to sing for his amusement.
One of his many interests cost him his life, a price he was very
willing to pay in his ninety-fifth year. He enjoyed lopping and
pruning his trees, and on a September evening in 1950 he was
busy cutting a branch from one of them when it broke suddenly
and he fell down, fracturing his thigh. The shock to his system
made recovery impossible, and he died early in the morning
of 2 November.

Perhaps no man since Voltaire has had so great an influence
on his age as Shaw. He dealt with every subject so wittily and
entertainingly that people started to think about things which
they had previously dismissed as incomprehensible or boring.
Philosophy, sociology, religion – whatever he touched he brought
to life. By treating serious matters with levity he stimulated his
age. But his most enduring work was done for the theatre. The
union of humour and instruction in his dramatic criticism has no
parallel, and he is the greatest playwright in our language since
Shakespeare. When he started to write for the theatre the British
drama was dominated by the French system of 'well-made'
plays. He destroyed this convention by attacking current morality
and introducing politics, religion and science to a class of
entertainment which had dealt mainly with crime, adultery and
sentimental romance. Every intelligent dramatist since his
day has benefited from his liberating influence.

Yet it is possible that the memory of the man will outlive his
work. As a personality he was unique. His vitality, curiosity,
industry and gaiety; his wit, sanity, good humour and uncommon
sense; his kindliness, toleration, and freedom from envy and
malice; his irrepressible frivolity and fundamental sincerity –
such a compound of qualities in one human being is not likely
to be seen again.

12

Hilaire Belloc

The best thumbnail sketch of Hilaire Belloc was done by Bernard Shaw: 'Like most anti-Socialists, Belloc is intensely gregarious. He cannot bear isolation or final ethical responsibility: he clings to the Roman Catholic Church: he clung to his French nationality because one nation was not enough for him: he went into the French army because it gave him a regiment, a company, even a gun to cling to . . . He combines the intense individualism and land hunger of a French farmer with the selfless Catholicism and scholarship of an Aristotelian cardinal. He keeps his property in his own hand, and his soul in a safe bank . . . He passed through the Oxford rowdyism of Balliol and the military rowdyism of the gunner; and this gave him the super-rowdyism of the literary genius who has lived adventurously in the world and not in the Savile Club. A proletariat of Bellocs would fight, possibly on the wrong side, like the peasants of La Vendée; but the Government they set up would have to respect them, though it would also have to govern them by martial law.'

Before and after the 1914–18 war there were tremendous public tussles between Shaw on the one hand and Belloc or G. K. Chesterton on the other. Their platform debates provided the best intellectual entertainments of the time. Though Shaw could make circles round the other two, they somehow contrived to remain foursquare. It was a battle of giants in which no bones were broken. A complete give-and-take friendship existed

between Shaw and Chesterton, but one always sensed hostility in
Belloc's defensive friendship with Shaw. At any moment it
seemed that the decencies of debate would give way to the
indecencies of abuse on the part of Belloc. At a discussion between
them held in the Savoy Theatre, shortly after the publication
of Belloc's *The Cruise of the Nona*, Shaw magnanimously referred
to the book two or three times in the course of his speech. Each
time he did so Belloc looked at the audience severely and ejaculated
'Buy it!' almost as if Shaw had advised them to borrow it from
a public library. Then there was a contest between Shaw and
Chesterton with Belloc in the chair. Having introduced the
speakers, Belloc said: 'They are about to debate. You are about
to listen. I am about to sneer', and with a savage glance at Shaw
resumed his seat.

A terrific thunderstorm preceded the birth of Hilaire Belloc
on 27 July 1870, and this was followed by the thunder of guns as
the Franco-Prussian War broke out. He was born a Frenchman
at La Celle St Cloud, not far from Paris, his father being French
with an Irish strain, his mother English. It is interesting to
record that the father, Louis Belloc, had been examined before
marriage by a physician of European renown, who had delivered
the verdict that the young man would never become a father
and ought not to consider matrimony, the sequel being that
Louis produced two children, first a daughter who became known
as the writer Marie Belloc-Lowndes, next a son called Hilary
by most of his English friends, both of whom lived healthily to
a sturdy old age. Their mother, Bessie Parkes, descended from
the famous scientist Joseph Priestley, started life in an atmosphere of Unitarianism, fought for progressive causes, became a
Roman Catholic in 1864, fell deeply in love with Louis Belloc
and married him in '67. The war compelled them to quit France
with their two children, and they were among those who left
Paris by that immensely crowded last train before the siege
commenced. They returned after the war to find their home badly
damaged and many of their belongings destroyed or stolen.
Louis Belloc died when Hilary was two years old, and the boy

Shaw, Belloc and Chesterton
*after a public debate between Shaw and Chesterton
with Belloc in the chair*

Hilaire Belloc: *from a portrait*
by James Gunn

spent his early years partly in France, partly in London, mostly in Sussex, where his mother had taken a cottage at Slindon on the South Downs.

He was a precocious child, learning easily, able to illustrate his letters with pictures of persons and places at the age of six. A love of sailing and walking marked his early years and became a lifelong passion. Following some preliminary schooling he went, aged ten, to the Oratory at Edgbaston, where he was at first miserable, the food being bad, the older boys brutal, but his good memory enabled him to collect prizes for mathematics and English. He liked Latin, Greek, history and Mark Twain. Leaving the Oratory in 1887, he fancied a career in the French navy and entered the Collège Stanislas at Paris, but the rigid discipline and constant espionage at that institution repelled him and one term was as much as he could stand. He left abruptly and tried to turn himself into a land agent, for which purpose he worked at Manor Farm, Bury, in Sussex; but the hours were long and gave him little time for the study of his favourite poet, Milton, or for writing his own verses. Having failed to make himself a sailor or a farmer, he thought of being an architect and worked for a while in a London office. Then he tried journalism, but as he held strong republican views the trade of writing to order made no appeal to him. In London he saw much of Cardinal Manning, who told him that 'all human conflict is ultimately theological', though the Cardinal's actions in helping to prevent strikes for higher wages and soothing the ruffled feelings of the working-class seemed to suggest that most human conflict is ultimately the result of hunger.

Marie Belloc was working for the *Pall Mall Gazette* and introduced her brother to the editor, W. T. Stead, who gave Hilary a job in 1889 as 'cycling correspondent in France'. Since he was being paid to take a holiday, he enjoyed it. Not long after his return he had an unforgettable experience. Entering his mother's drawing-room in Great College Street, he saw a girl, Elodie Hogan, and instantly decided to marry her. She was an American Roman Catholic with a call to join a sisterhood.

T

With classic features, a good complexion, strikingly dark-blue eyes, burnished mahogany-coloured hair, her figure and dress lacked distinction. They went about London together, and when she left for America there must have been some agreement between them that marriage was on the cards, though both their mothers were against the match on prudent grounds. Hilary had a will of his own and followed her to California, having borrowed twenty pounds and sold all the prizes he had won. A nasty journey in the steerage and a short stay with relations in Philadelphia absorbed at least half his capital, and his pilgrimage across the continent was accomplished by foot, by winning money at cards, and by selling pictures he made *en route*. He arrived at San Francisco looking like a tramp and did not receive an enthusiastic welcome from Elodie's mother, who sternly opposed his project, the girl herself giving him the impression that her heart was more in favour of a religious life than a domestic one, and making her refusal more definite in a letter which he received on his way home, having recrossed the continent by train. Some years later he wrote: 'There are sights which if one sees them for the first time in boyhood, when one can still feel, are like memories of Heaven; great revelations which build up the mind for the rest of one's life.' Such no doubt were the revelations vouchsafed to him on the way to Elodie, but the visions had now vanished and despair took their place.

Action seemed the only possible tranquilliser, and against his mother's wish he decided to be a conscript in the French army, becoming a gunner in November, 1890. His training took place in Alsace, and at first he found the life 'odious and bewildering'. The orders and insults were hard to bear and the fact that his habits and behaviour were English no doubt incited his superiors to make him eat mud; but in time he became used to the conditions, accepting them automatically. With the experience safely behind him, the usual process of idealising army life began, and, like his *bête noire* Kipling, he acquired the romantic view of war common to many who have done no fighting. He managed to quit the army in ten months, though his memory increased the period in old age, for when I asked how long he had served he replied: 'A year – and a little.' 'How did you manage to get out of it so soon?' 'I pulled strings. I'd a cousin in the French Government.' The trials of military life had one noticeable effect on him. He learnt by heart many of the songs with which the conscripts wiled away the long marches, and sang them lustily in the years ahead.

Towards the close of 1891 he had a piece of good luck. His sister Marie sold her share in a Fund and gave him the money to complete his education at Oxford University. He entered Balliol College at the beginning of 1893 and soon won a Brackenbury scholarship in History. Throughout his time at the University he worked harder and talked faster than any of his contemporaries. His long walks became famous, one of them, from Oxford to London in eleven and a half hours, setting up a record. His achievements on the river, both canoeing and swimming, his running and jumping, his singing, his story-telling and his endless disquisitions gave the impression of a youngster bubbling over with physical vitality and mental gifts much above the normal. He made a considerable reputation as a speaker at the Union, where two notable politicians of the future, F. E. Smith and John Simon, were among his competitors, and eventually he was elected President. Apparently he did not share the high general opinion of F. E. Smith's talents, because on being asked what he thought of the man who later became Lord Chancellor and the first Earl of Birkenhead, he replied: 'Superficial. No brains. A politician . . . Smith wanted to be President of the Union in the summer. That's the important term for people who want to get on. He came to me and begged me to take the Presidency in the Easter term. I didn't mind. I let him have what he wanted.'

In the long vacations Belloc rambled all over the Continent, but in spite of his strenuous recreations he did well in the examinations, winning First Class Honours in June '95. The following month he tried for a Fellowship at All Souls but failed, the failure leaving a mark on him to the end of his days, because success would have meant financial independence. Recalling in the last years of his life what happened, he said: 'Herbert Fisher wanted to get me a Fellowship at New College. And Trinity wanted me, too; but the dons were frightened. They didn't know what I'd do. I might come into the Common Room with a girl over my shoulder.' Asked why he had not been given a Fellowship at his own College, Balliol, he explained: 'That was quite out of the question. Benjamin Jowett, the Master, looked on Catholics as a sect. I would have liked a Fellowship, and if they'd given me a lot of money I'd have taken one. I was married and they weren't paying enough.'

His long waiting for Elodie, with the ups and downs of hope and despondency, came to an end seven years after their first meeting. Recognising at last that she had no call to a sisterhood, she sent the news to Hilary, who overcame the strong opposition of his mother and again crossed the Atlantic, to find Elodie recovering from a serious illness. The strain of the years told upon him and he had a nervous collapse. But her mother was dead and their marriage took place in June 1896. After Belloc had delivered a few lectures in the States, they settled down at Oxford.

Lecturing audiences in the north and coaching students in the south now became his regular job. He formed a lifelong friendship with Maurice Baring, participating in his rowdy parties, when butter was flung at the ceiling, syphons were burst against walls, port was splashed about, a picked reveller was baptised with ink, the conversation was clamorous and the songs were uproarious. Elodie had to accustom herself to Hilary's noisy bibulous parties as well as his insomnia, which made him prowl about the house after midnight. But she could comfort herself with the reflection that he was strong in the Faith and quite capable of breaking a friendship with anyone who attacked or sneered at it. In 1897 they were again in America, where he gave innumerable lectures, and already his light verse was being published. He worried over money, a state that became habitual with him, and considered the Bar as a profession, but dropped it; toyed with the idea later on, but dropped it again. Early in

1900 he moved with Elodie, their son and daughter, to London, where they took the lease of a house at 104 Cheyne Walk, Chelsea.

He now knew that he would have to write and lecture to earn a living, and his book on Danton was his first serious historical study, to be followed shortly by one about Robespierre. With a number of other young journalists who wrote for *The Speaker* he sided with the Boers in their fight for independence, finding a doughty supporter in G. K. Chesterton, to whom he was introduced by E. C. Bentley outside the Mont Blanc restaurant in Gerrard Street, Soho, their friendship being baptised inside the restaurant with several bottles of wine. Although hard at work producing verse, biographies and journalism, he made a pilgrimage to Rome on foot in 1901, his book describing it, *The Path to Rome*, being published the following year and making his reputation as a writer. It contains some of his best descriptive writing and some of his ponderous humour, suggestive of a Dickens who has run to seed. Coincident with its publication he became a naturalised Englishman. Towards the end of his life he reflected on how his life would have passed if he had married a wealthy Frenchwoman of his acquaintance. 'I should probably have been very happy', he said.

But it was not in his constitution to be very happy. His nature was not only divided but sub-divided. There were at least half a dozen Bellocs, each tugging a different way. Insomnia is a sure mark of such division, restlessness is another, and he never ceased to suffer from both complaints. He would have liked to be a soldier, a sailor, a barrister, a statesman, an epic poet, a farmer, a private gentleman and a don. As a consequence of these divergent inclinations, he affected to despise the art of letters, pretending that writers only wrote for money, which was merely another way of saying that he personally ought to have been doing something else. 'Does not any writer who is also reasonably manly prefer any one of man's virtues to an accident of verse or prose?' he asked, without pausing to consider that any one of man's virtues is as much an accident of birth as the ability to write verse or prose, and that a born writer would rather commit murder than follow a different calling. This dubiety of aim resulted in what he called 'that temperament which can only repose in fixed sanctities', a firm authoritative faith being necessary to direct his sceptical and discordant character.

The lack of harmony in his nature was emphasised by his two nationalities. He was an Englishman in France and a Frenchman in England, the romance of one being offset by the realism of the other, which gave the edge of wit to his humorous twists of thought and language. Here is an example: 'Nothing should impede the truth . . . save a substantial sum of money.' One of his carefully reasoned discourses closed with the words: 'What has that to do with the matter? Nothing.' While another began with 'Horace (I think – I won't look it up) . . .' A further illustration: 'You may now think that I have done; but I have not, for I propose to conclude by contradicting myself.' Having laid down certain general laws for attaining perfect proportion in building, he ended thus: 'Consider, then, these canons of a layman, all you architects; apply them to your work; and if I know anything of the attempts to recover the lost spirit of beauty, you will achieve results most hideous and damnable.' Once he tried to describe a particular shade of blue, likening it to 'the mountains in those painters of North Italy . . . the name of whose school escapes me – or, rather, I never knew it.' After explaining where the River Ribble rises, he added 'and a little way off on the other side is Pen-y-ghent, or words to that effect.' Speaking of the address on an envelope, he said: 'It was written in the hand of an educated man. It was almost illegible.' An excellent instance of his disquieting honesty was provided at a public-house off Fleet Street where some of his admirers were listening to his account of an attempt by a group of influential people to silence him on a controversial subject. 'The beasts dared to offer me a bribe of £50!' he exclaimed indignantly, and sounds of outraged feelings arose from those present. 'Now, if they had offered me £500, that would have made all the difference', he concluded. One more example may be given. Belloc had been engaged to address the boys of Harrow School, one of whom, Hugh Kingsmill, told me what happened: 'He was half an hour late, and a lesser man might have had a rough reception. But he strode to the centre of the platform, and in a slightly French accent, which added a note of ferocity to his words, barked out: "I am half an hour late. It is entirely my fault. I do not apologise." He then lectured on London, evoking it in earlier centuries with a rich imaginative power that gave me an impression of genius such as I have received from no other speaker.'

In the early years of the century Belloc's efforts as a writer covered every field. He produced satirical novels, verses, essays galore. He traced the Pilgrim's Way from Winchester to Canterbury and described it in *The Old Road* (1904). And he stood for Parliament as a Liberal in the constituency of South Salford. He was advised by the Roman Catholic clergy that his religion would not help him and that he had better keep it to himself. Robert Speaight, in his *Life of Hilaire Belloc*, quotes his subject's opening speech inspired by this advice: 'Gentlemen, I am a Catholic. As far as possible, I go to Mass every day. This is a rosary' (taking it from his pocket). 'As far as possible, I kneel down and tell these beads every day. If you reject me on account of my religion, I shall thank God that He has spared me the indignity of being your representative.' A man who talked like that did not appeal to British electors in vain, and they brought him in by a substantial majority on 13 January 1906. His maiden speech made him sick, but the bodily sickness caused by his own effort was as nothing compared with the mental sickness resulting from four years spent in the House of Commons. He chucked it at last, having come to the conclusion that the party system was a fraud and that corruption was rife. He tried to get the names of subscribers to political funds made public, but his was a voice crying in the void and by 1910 he perceived that he was wasting his time.

For a while he could not obtain a regular salary on which to keep his family, now consisting of three boys and two girls; but at length he obtained the literary editorship of the *Morning Post*,

a Tory paper. This did not last long because he was too indi-
vidualistic to work in harmony with anyone else and quarrels
with his chief were inevitable. His industry was phenomenal.
He lectured, wrote books, attended Parliament, made speeches
in every part of the country, composed verse, led an active social
life, dealt with a large correspondence, sailed his yacht *Nona*,
supervised alterations and additions to the house he bought in
1906, King's Land, Shipley, Sussex, drank a lot, talked a lot, did
terrific treks all over Great Britain and the Continent, and never
stopped writing essays during dull debates in the Commons, fine
days at sea and jolting journeys by train.

He was at his best as an essayist. Human genius, like the earth
which nourishes it, is good for particular things. The ground on
which a vineyard grows may be valueless for potatoes, and a
man can produce excellent short compositions without being
able to sustain a long work. A distinct charm in an essay is the
expression of the writer's tastes and prejudices, and the strength
of Belloc's add to the attraction of his occasional pieces, in one
of which he suddenly addresses those of his readers who boasted
of 'the island race' and the command of the seas: 'I dislike the
memory of your faces.' In another he breaks off and talks to the
dons: 'I stifle when I think of you.' Such comments would be out
of place in a serious historical work, but they reveal the man, who
could become boring when he gave much space to his bugbears.
The most delightful collection of his essays is *Hills and the Sea*
(1906), his most enjoyable verses are those nonsense rhymes
which made him equally popular in the nursery and the public-
house, and his best work, *The Four Men* (1912), is a series of
impressions, songs and dialogues during a walk through Sussex
by four Bellocs under different names, the sequence being
assembled in a book that will be enjoyed as long as people find
pleasure in walking, talking, drinking, companionship, absurdity,
rousing verse, and what is left of the English countryside. Speaking
of *The Four Men*, Belloc told his daughter Elizabeth: 'I put my
whole heart into that book, but no one cares about it.' Yet he
once informed me that *The Path to Rome* was the only book he

had ever written for love, and when I asked 'Didn't you write
The Four Men for love?' he replied 'No. Money.' '*The Cruise of
the Nona?*' 'Money.' By that time however he had convinced
himself that 'the whole art is to write and write and write and
then offer it for sale, just like butter', which may explain why so
much of his work has melted away.

Having been returned to Parliament for South Salford in 1910,
he decided not to fight the next election, and instead wrote an
attack on the party system aided by Cecil Chesterton, with whom
he started an independent weekly, *The Eye-Witness*, which
exposed the political game and the financial corruption in public
life. But Belloc was temperamentally unfitted to be an editor and
soon handed over the job to Cecil Chesterton, who started an
attack on various public men in connection with the Marconi
Company, which had received a Government contract to establish
stations for wireless telegraphy in Britain. Certain Cabinet
Ministers were involved in share transactions, and the thing
became a public scandal. The result was a court case, a verdict of
'Guilty' against Chesterton and a fine of £100. Belloc then wrote
a book, *The Servile State* (1912), in which both capitalism and
socialism were subjected to acute analysis, and started a series
of monographs on 'British Battles', rushing about Europe to
examine the sites. In the intervals of his limitless labours he
began to bottle his own wine, sent in casks from France.

At the beginning of 1914 he suffered a bereavement from
which he never properly recovered, the death of Elodie, and the
black clothes he wore to the end of his life witnessed to an enduring grief; not unmixed with remorse, for he knew that his
restless vitality, constant carousals, unregulated life, frequent
absences and financial worries had told heavily on her health.
For the rest of his life, though the most gregarious of men, he
felt alone. The war which broke out in August of that year
provided him with enough work to mitigate grief. Murray
Allison, who controlled *Land and Water*, asked him to write
weekly on the progress of hostilities, his articles bringing him
fame and forty pounds a week. When the sales dropped, his

salary was halved, but by then he was getting fifty pounds a week for articles in *The New York American*. He visited the various battle fronts and delivered hundreds of well-paid lectures. Like everyone else, he lost many dear friends during the conflict, including Cecil Chesterton, and his eldest boy was killed shortly before the so-called peace.

From 1919 onwards he dedicated himself to the task of explaining that the Whiggish view of history taught in English schools and universities was false, and the major task of asserting and proclaiming the infallibility of the Roman Catholic Church. Easily able to correct errors in the work of the Whig historians, he thoroughly enjoyed the controversies that ensued. He started a *History of England*, but carried it no further than 1612, probably because it did not sell. Unfortunately his Catholic propaganda entered into the writing of biography, and, while much of his historical writing is well considered, some of his biographical writing is one-sided to the point of absurdity. To praise a stupid monarch like James II because he was a Roman Catholic and to dispraise a soldier of genius like Oliver Cromwell because he never met Catholicism either in arms or diplomacy without defeating it, is to parody propaganda. It is not necessary to like Cromwell as a man in order to admire his qualities as a leader; but, as he had impressed Milton, Dr Johnson, Voltaire, Marvell, Carlyle and Mazarin as a remarkable figure, it was unwise of Belloc to write him off as a bungler, a money-lover, a liar, a sadist, a crook, a cry-baby and a coward, the reader being left with the impression that if Oliver had been less of a funk and more efficient he would have lost all his battles instead of winning them and perished on the scaffold instead of dying in bed in the throes of absolute power. Belloc said of his book on Cromwell that it was 'one of the very few things I am proud to have written', which only shows that a life devoted to propaganda makes it difficult to distinguish between truth and its opposite. But apart from his blurred vision of individuals his feeling for history was strong, his judgment sound, his imagination vivid. His propaganda put heart into his fellow-Catholics, but it was too belligerent and dogmatic to influence those who knew that an institution is as fallible as the people who create it, which means that no institution can be infallible; and he never learnt the simple lesson that propaganda, to be effective, should be administered in small doses, not in large draughts. Belloc seemed to be placing the Church before Christianity, the Sabbath before the man, the institution before the individual for whom it was made. His manner as a lecturer was as uncompromising as his belief. I once heard him describe his method: 'First I tell them what I am going to tell them; then I tell them; and then I tell them what I've told them.'

His physical appearance suited the compulsive nature of his message. Short of stature, thick-set, stoutish, with a stern jaw, a bull neck, massive head, broad shoulders, strong features and high penetrating voice, his speech was clear, forceful and to the point, his manner energetic and aggressive. In private life he was the essence of courtesy to people he liked, inconsiderate to those he disliked. When bored his behaviour was unpredictable and selfish. J. B. Morton records that Belloc made audible remarks in the theatre during the performance of a play and disturbed a row of people by walking out in the middle of a scene. He was capable of bursting into song in the course of a meal to the discomfort of the company, and would sometimes blurt out mundane remarks in the middle of a church service. His own conversation, often a monologue, was a fascinating hotchpotch of satire, nonsense, invective, rabelaisian verses, stories, grousing and fun. But when an informative bore tried to capture the talk, he received merciless treatment. Once a Liberal politician began to recall the uninteresting episodes of his career. Belloc, whose training in the House of Commons had taught him patience, listened with downcast eyes for some minutes, but seized the first opportunity the other's volubility permitted, looked innocently upwards, and asked in his high quick voice: 'Have you heard the story of the male and female contortionists on their honeymoon?' The politician stared in open-mouthed amazement and spluttered 'I – I beg your pardon?' Belloc repeated the question. 'N-no', stammered the other. 'They broke it off,' said Belloc. So did the politician.

Other people's complaints were received with humorous indifference by Belloc, who was always grumbling about something or other, usually lack of money, on which subject he could also be funny: 'Heaven keep us all from great riches – I mean from very great riches.' But he usually reserved his jokes for the laments of his friends, one of whom walked into a Fleet Street pub on a wretched day of wind and rain and spoke severely of the English climate. 'You are always complaining of the climate', remarked Belloc. 'True it rains all day, and there's usually a wind that cuts like a knife, and we scarcely ever see the sun, and most of us will certainly die of pneumonia; but the climate's all right.'

Over his own affairs Belloc was precise to a fault. His incurable restlessness prevented him from staying long in one place, and a stream of directions by telegram or telephone announced the exact times of his departure and arrival and his whereabouts in the interval. One of his friends, Thomas Michael Pope, related an episode at Victoria Station, where Belloc asked the booking-office clerk whether he should travel first or third class to France, detailing his present financial position to help the other to a decision. A queue gathered while Belloc unfolded the facts, which included the cost of his children's education, and an impatient passenger roughly expostulated; but Belloc told him to keep calm and gave him a textbook on trigonometry to study while waiting. This absorption in his personal affairs may explain a curious sentence in one of his essays: 'How a voice perishes! – how we forget the accents of the most loved and the most familiar voices within a few days of their disappearance!' Though he professed a keen appreciation of Mozart's music, this quotation shows that he must have been either tone-deaf or wholly inattentive to the speech of others.

His prejudices and preferences were strongly expressed, so strongly in the case of the Jews that people thought him anti-Semitic. Actually he had merely stated that the Jewish and

Christian cultures were radically dissimilar and that the racial cleavage should be recognised. But he clarified his personal attitude to Hugh Kingsmill and myself when we had a talk with him at King's Land in 1947 : 'It was the Dreyfus case that opened my eyes to the Jew question. I'm not an anti-Semite. I love 'em, poor dears. Get on very well with them. My best secretary was a Jewess. Poor darlings! it must be terrible to be born with the knowledge that you belong to the enemies of the human race.'

'Why do you say the Jews are the enemies of the human race ?' asked Kingsmill.

'The Crucifixion,' answered Belloc.

It struck me that he should have been immeasurably grateful to the Jews for providing the Church with its main mystery and symbol, but I dismissed the notion as inopportune.

For his services to the Faith he was made a Knight of the Order of St Gregory the Great by the Pope, but practically ignored it, regarding titles and honours as ridiculous. Under pressure he accepted a Doctorate of Law from Glasgow University, and for the advantages it secured when travelling in France he wore the ribbon of an officer of the Legion of Honour. But he had long ceased to feel that parliamentary governments could bestow honour on anyone, and welcomed the arrival of the dictators. His misunderstanding of human beings came out when he had a long conversation with Mussolini, who in his opinion was unambitious, sincere, solely anxious to serve the nation. 'What a contrast with the sly and shifty talk of your parliamentarian!' he wrote. The restoration of the crucifix to the Italian schools and the compulsion of the official world to hear Mass no doubt placed Mussolini in a favourable light. Belloc also described General Franco as 'the man who has saved us all'. But the years 1939-45 lay ahead.

Two of Belloc's later works should be mentioned. *The Mercy of Allah* (1922) is an urbanely satirical but withering exposure of the financial racket, while *The Cruise of the Nona* (1925) contains splendid descriptions but too much propaganda to make it wholly acceptable to those who had loved *The Four Men* or

Hills and the Sea or *The Path to Rome*. If, as he confessed, the account of his cruise was written for money, he was going the wrong way to earn it.

Having firmly believed that the Catholic civilisation was the only effective bulwark against barbarism, heresy and atheism, it must have been a dreadful shock for Belloc when Catholic France folded up before the German onslaught, when Catholic Italy joined forces with Germany, and when Catholic Spain sided with Germany, leaving Protestant Britain the sole barrier against savagery during the most critical phases of the struggle that began in 1940. The shock stunned him and no doubt caused the stroke of paralysis which shortly struck him down, though the death of his youngest son on active service in 1941 was the final blow. He had received an intimation of the perils of over-work in September '32, when for several hours he suffered from complete loss of memory. But the merciless downward course began with a slight stroke in January '42, which affected his heart and brought on pneumonia. In the belief that he would die, the Last Sacraments were administered. He pulled through with the timely aid of a glass of wine, but he was never again the man he had been, and he started on the journey 'down the long shadows of declining day', as he once phrased it. The present war and much of the past had been obliterated from his mind, and when J. B. Morton spoke of some discussion in the House of Commons he said: 'Is that bloody nonsense still going on?' On hearing that it was, he said 'Very well', and then, after a pause, added in sinaic tones: 'Tell them from me to go to Hell!' One of them, Winston Churchill, offered him the Companionship of Honour. But in the lingering half-life before him such distinctions were meaningless, and he declined it.

On Sunday, 12 July 1953, he had a seizure in his study while doing something to the fire. A smell of burning brought his daughter Eleanor Jebb to the room, where she found him lying on the floor with some red-hot coal on the carpet, his shirt and vest smouldering, and the place full of smoke. He had been burnt, but more serious was the shock to his system. Taken in an ambulance to a Catholic nursing home at Guildford, he remained partly conscious, partly unconscious, until Thursday, when he won the peace for which he had so continuously sought and so fervently prayed.

Perhaps he would have wished to be remembered for the best verses he ever wrote, which bring to an end the best book he ever wrote, *The Four Men*, the haunting last lines bestowing the kind of earthly immortality which he cherished:

> So, therefore, though myself be crosst
> The shuddering of that dreadful day
> When friend and fire and home are lost
> And even children drawn away –
> > The passer-by shall hear me still,
> > A boy that sings on Duncton Hill.

13

Max Beerbohm

It would be impossible to find two writers who had less in common with one another and were less alike in character and accomplishments than Hilaire Belloc and Max Beerbohm. The first was passionately prejudiced, noisily fanatical, a terrific talker, a great walker, restlessly active and variable in expression; the second was genially tolerant, quietly sceptical, a good listener, a non-walker, physically lazy and uniform in expression. Yet their differences, being complementary, resulted in concord, and they took pleasure in each other's company. Max called Belloc 'a man of many geniuses' but something of a monomaniac, Belloc thought Max sincere and good-hearted. An egotist finds an unobtrusive person pleasantly restful, and Max was both diffident and tactful by nature. His brother Herbert Beerbohm Tree told me that during rehearsals of Wilde's comedy at the Haymarket Theatre several of them used to lunch together at the Continental Hotel in Lower Regent Street (or Waterloo Place), and Max was usually so quiet that Oscar Wilde once said, 'He is jealous of his wit and keeps it to himself', to which Max replied, 'If I did not, it might prove unfaithful to me', a remark that suggests what W. S. Gilbert might have called the maxim of his life. At least Max was grateful for his gifts. A friend of mine once asked him whether he had any hobbies, since none was mentioned in the books of reference. 'I suppose I may claim one hobby of which I have never tired', he replied: 'I enjoy looking at things and

Max Beerbohm

G. K. Chesterton delivering a speech

people, especially people.' And when my friend added that the other had been very lucky throughout his life, Max agreed: 'I have been lucky ... yes ... once.' 'Only once?' 'Once is enough. I was lucky to be born.'

As we have seen, he and Beerbohm Tree had the same father, while their mothers were sisters, Tree's stepmother being his own aunt, so Max and Herbert may be called three-quarters-brothers. Max was the youngest of his father's second family, four sisters having preceded him, and the day he thought lucky was 24 August 1872, the place No. 57 Palace Gardens Terrace, Kensington, though his parents moved to Clanricarde Gardens when he was five, and there he remained till the age of sixteen. It was commonly thought that the Beerbohms were partly Semitic, and when I put the question to Max he said, 'I should be delighted to know that we Beerbohms have that very admirable and engaging thing, Jewish blood.' But he went on to show that two Beerbohm women had married Prussian Generals; and as anti-Semitism was rife in Germany throughout the nineteenth century, such marriages would have been impossible if their family had been even partly Hebraic. He added that if I used this information in my book on Beerbohm Tree, as he hoped I would, 'don't give it as coming definitely from *me*, as it might seem snobbish on my part.'

By the age of seven Max was already drawing soldiers and policemen, moving on to politicians a few years later. At nine years old he went to a school in Orme Square, the master of which, Wilkinson, was 'by far the best teacher I ever had', while his wife gave Max the only lessons he ever had in drawing. He did not profit much from these, but Wilkinson inspired him with a love of Latin and used to play 'touch-last' with him after school hours. His tenth birthday was celebrated at home with champagne-cup, when he drank his own health so liberally that brother Herbert was moved to remonstrance: 'Max, it is bad to be tipsy at ten.' A literary style was apparent in the boy's denial of the charge: 'How can one be tipsy when we are conscious they are not?' It was a proud day for him when, in the absence of an elder brother,

U

he acted as 'best man' (aged ten) at Herbert's marriage.

From Orme Square he went to Charterhouse, where he remained from 1885 to 1890, learning French well from an efficient master, still liking Latin, and whenever possible doing caricatures of his teachers. He hated being a fag as well as being a monitor, and his general feeling for the school was summed up in a phrase: 'My delight in having been at Charterhouse was far greater than had been my delight in being there,' a pleasing euphemism for saying outright that he thoroughly disliked his schooldays there. 'I hope that I shall never experience a more awful emotion', he confessed, than driving to the station after the holidays on the way back to school. 'Boys are not a nice race', he said; 'they are bullies or cowards according to their size', and he detested their games: 'As I hovered in grey knickerbockers, on a cold and muddy field, round the outskirts of a crowd that was tearing itself limb from limb for the sake of a leathern bladder, I would often wish for a nice warm room and a good game of hunt-the-slipper.' At the suggestion of a relative, who usually did the job, he wrote a London Letter for a Scarborough paper in his eighteenth year, and this, coupled with a hint from Herbert that he had better be 'a sort of writer', may have strengthened his inclination in that direction, though he was supposed to be training for the Bar at the University.

In the autumn of 1890 he entered Merton College, Oxford, which was heaven after Charterhouse. He took no part in the sports of the place; and throughout life physical exercise made no appeal to him. He once described golf as 'the most perfect expression of national stupidity', for which reason the game had 'an assured uncheckered future'; and he laughed at 'the notion that a heart strained by climbing is good for the health'. He could discover no charm in the bicycle, saying that it 'gratifies that instinct which is common to all stupid people, the instinct to potter with machinery'. Much more fun was to be derived from caricaturing the dons, and this brought him sufficient fame to attract the attention of William Rothenstein, who visited Oxford in 1893 and did a portrait of Max for his book of 'Oxford

Characters'. Rothenstein thought him 'rather tall' merely because Rothenstein was very short. Max was of medium height, and already he paid considerable attention to his clothes, becoming rather dandified as time went on. His baby-face, heavily-lidded blue eyes with long lashes, broad forehead and sleek black hair with a centre parting seemed to suit his reserved manners and careful diction. He took little part in communal activities, though in view of his future career as a dramatic critic it is interesting to note that at the Merton Debating Society he moved 'that this House views with pleasure the increasing unpopularity of the Drama', his motion being defeated. Occasionally hard-up, he did caricatures for the *Strand Magazine* (1892) and employed his pen by contributing to undergraduate papers.

During the vacations Rothenstein introduced him to the artistic world of London. He met Oscar Wilde ('the most enchanting company in the universe'), Aubrey Beardsley, Reginald Turner, Robert Ross, Lionel Johnson, Charles Conder, Lord Alfred Douglas, and the rest of that circle, his earliest essay appearing in the first number of *The Yellow Book*, which also published a later essay on the year '1880', of which he wrote: 'To give an accurate and exhaustive account of that period would need a far less brilliant pen than mine.' Another essay in the same magazine described how George IV, at the end of his life, laughed and sobbed over the memories recalled by his old coats, and Max's sartorial feelings were expressed in the passage: 'It is pleasant to know that George, during his long and various life, never forgot a coat, however long ago worn, however seldom.' He met many famous figures in the dressing-room of his brother Beerbohm Tree, now manager of the Haymarket Theatre, and usually managed to attend first-nights of the plays thereat, the stalls being 'simply infested with politicians'. He developed a taste for public shows, observing with amusement the various English princes 'whose breasts are all agleam and aglimmer with the symbols of fifty victories at which they were not present'. He enjoyed nearly everything except opera, and was glad to notice that Wagner 'has done undeniably good work in humbling the singers'. Especially he enjoyed the music-halls, and in one of them, the Tivoli, he fell in love with a popular vocalist, Cissie Loftus, who mimicked her contemporaries. He went again and again to watch and hear his goddess, who made him thoroughly dissatisfied with himself. 'I always found myself quite perfect', he declared, but Cissie was now the standard of perfection, and 'if I were not afraid my people might keep it out of the newspapers, I should commit suicide tomorrow.'

He was delivered from his infatuation by Herbert, who took his theatrical company to America in January 1895 and engaged Max as private secretary. The trip was done in good weather but Max was seasick most of the time, his condition being unalleviated by Lionel Brough, a friendly comedian occupying the opposite cabin, who visited him regularly for the purpose of cheering him up with smoking-room yarns; but, as the visit was attended by a powerful aroma from the bar, the patient could have dispensed with the stories. New York harbour struck Max as 'rather fine', and as they drove from the dock the city appeared picturesque with its rough paven streets, 'quite the Nuremburg of the West'. But the appearance changed as they neared Fifth Avenue, and the combination of tall houses, elevated railways, shriekings, whistlings and the clatter of horses' hoofs over the cobbles created a pandemonium which forced Max to describe it as 'a terrible, horrible place'; though he thought the people 'very nice'. They stayed at the luxurious Waldorf on Fifth Avenue and 33rd Street, which Max thought 'a very amusing place, always full of the most interesting people'. He saw a good deal of the dramatist Clyde Fitch, who 'loves my writing, which is a bond. I have never read or seen anything of his, which is awkward'. Four of his short essays were accepted by *Vanity*, the first on Count D'Orsay, and he received a hundred dollars for the lot. He also sold some drawings, and reported to his mother that he looked 'very well dressed'. The weather was so cold 'that one does not seem to realise it'.

Herbert found him endlessly amusing and howled with

laughter when Max suggested an effective line to bring the curtain down on a play. 'Where are you going?' asks the sorrowful heroine. 'I am going to the Thirty Years War', answers the distraught hero. But as a secretary Max was unsatisfactory. The replies to letters received by his brother were so carefully considered and exactly worded that the pile of unanswered ones became unmanageable, and the duty was transferred to someone with a less fastidious style, Max retaining his full salary. Apart from his failure as a secretary, he nearly did his brother a very bad turn. A stage version of George Du Maurier's novel *Trilby* had just been put on and Herbert asked Max to report on it. Max thought it piffle and said it would be a dismal failure in London. Luckily Tree had a free night before leaving New York and went to find out whether his brother had been right. He saw that something could be done with the thing, promptly bought the British acting rights, and turned it into the biggest success of his career.

Max completely recovered from his passion for Cissie Loftus when he got to know a pretty actress in his brother's company named Kilseen Conover, his growing love for whom placed his family in an awkward situation. Back from America they were constantly in each other's company, and she became a frequent visitor at his home, now 19 Hyde Park Place. His mother adored him and would not dream of hinting that neither she nor her daughters cared for Kilseen or thought her worthy of him. One outspoken person got into hot water. This was Herbert's wife, Maud Tree, who thought she was doing the family a good turn by speaking rudely to Kilseen and making her perceive that she was not popular. Maud was rather inclined to interfere in matters that did not concern her, and being an actress herself knew that Max's inamorata was called 'Kill-scene' Conover, a fact she may have mentioned on this occasion. She was quite unprepared for Max's reaction. He wrote her a frigidly furious letter, describing her behaviour as utterly inexcusable and unforgiveable, and saying that henceforth he would cease to regard her as a friend, though he would have to be polite to her whenever they were compelled to meet socially. She attempted to exculpate herself, but a second letter from Max was, if less furious, quite as adamant.

Since his father's death in 1892 Max had been the tin-god of the domestic hearth; his wishes were law; and no one dared breathe a word that might hurt him. Maud's tactlessness therefore caused terror to reign in the household, and 'darling Kilseen' was treated as an empress. Also it happened just then that the entire social world had worked itself into a condition of ethical delirium on account of a glandular peculiarity in Oscar Wilde, and Max's family were greatly relieved that he was spending his time with Kilseen instead of at the Café Royal, where he had previously passed the evenings with the now-undesirable Bohemians who formed Oscar's court. However, all ended happily. Kilseen went on tour, her correspondence with her fiancé cooled, the engagement was broken off, and after a brief interval Max fell in love with another beautiful actress in his brother's company, Constance Collier, of whom his family approved. They became engaged while on holiday at Dieppe; but again a tour interfered with a union. 'Someone more exciting came along,' she told me; in fact the handsome leading man of the company, Julian L'Estrange, carried her off her feet and away from Max, who afterwards felt that marriage to her would have been too exciting for him.

Max's reputation accompanied him from Oxford to London, where his contribution to *The Yellow Book* did not pass unnoticed. He was parodied in *Punch* and interviewed by Ada Leverson, part of their talk being quoted everywhere:

'And what work are you engaged on at present?'

'Oh, I am writing a volume of "Lives of the Brothers of Great Men" – Mr Ralph Disraeli, Mr Jacob Bright, Mr Willie Wilde, and so on.'

'You yourself are a brother, are you not, of Mr Beerbohm Tree?'

'Oh yes. He is coming into the series.'

His first book of essays came out in 1896. It's title, *The Works of Max Beerbohm*, since the author's age was twenty-three, gave him a notoriety which was fortified by the publication of his first book of caricatures the same year. His more frivolous comments, inspired by the sort of nonsense in which Wilde had indulged, were passed from mouth to mouth. Travelling to Croydon by train, he suddenly pulled down the blinds of the carriage. Asked to explain his action, he put his finger to his lips: 'Ssh! Lest I should see the Crystal Palace.' Observing a number of pretty working-girls on holiday at Broadstairs he remarked: 'I don't think the lower orders ought to be attractive – it brings Beauty into disrepute.' His family moved to 48 Upper Berkeley Street, Portman Square, where he had a sky-blue coloured study at the top of the house. Usually he dined away from home, often at Solferino's in Rupert Street, where he joined the disciples of W. E. Henley, calling them 'the Henley Regatta'. For the next decade or so his holidays were mostly spent at Dieppe or at the Berkeley Hotel, Bognor.

Bernard Shaw resigned his position as dramatic critic for *The Saturday Review* in 1898 and suggested Max as his successor. He got the job at £5 a week, called himself 'an intellectual prostitute', and in his opening article expressed his diffidence in following G.B.S. (whose retirement, said he, 'has eclipsed the gaiety of greenrooms') because, unlike his predecessor, he had no well-considered attitude to life and had 'never regarded any theatre as much more than the conclusion to a dinner or the prelude to a supper'. In fact Shaw's pen was a sword with which he slashed at the conventions of dramaturgy, while Max's pen was a feather with which he tickled the dramatists. Normally the malice of Max found expression in his caricatures, the one form of art in which ill-will can pass for good humour, and in his published essays he was careful not to let his talent run away with his tact; but in his theatre criticisms he had little time for caution, and he made enemies by accident. He liked what were known as 'advanced' plays, of which the chief were those by Shaw, though he preferred the G.B.S. comedy to the Shaw philosophy. 'Max only enjoyed my tricks', said Shaw to me.

'When I turned an intellectual somersault, he rolled in his seat, and when I did a bit of cerebral conjuring he had convulsions. He would have liked me best as a music-hall turn, dancing a mental tightrope or producing endless japes by sleight of brain.'

The god of critics and actors and playgoers of that time was Arthur Pinero, but Max thought little of him, saying that he should be condemned 'to perpetual banishment among the penny-a-liners from whom his style is borrowed'. Naturally Pinero thought Max 'not a gentleman' and called him 'a scorpion in the guise of a scholar'. Another famous writer displeased Max, who considered that Rudyard Kipling's genius was too often debased by chauvinism. In later life Max regretted his attacks on Kipling; but harm can never be undone, and had he been able to express his regret in person it may be doubted whether Kipling would have glowed with gratitude.

His dramatic criticism brought Max a wife. A well-known American actress named Florence Kahn came to England with a letter of introduction to him, and he went to see her as 'Rebecca West' in Ibsen's *Rosmersholm*, writing a wholly adulatory notice of her performance. A small thin woman with reddish hair, agreeable features, a refined manner and soulful expression, she had intellectual tastes and wished to lead a simple life. Her disposition and inclinations appealed to Max, who soon threw up his job, married Florence in 1910, and settled down to a quiet life with her at Rapallo in Italy, where they bought a villa and lived happily ever after.

More essays and caricatures had been issued during his time as dramatic critic, and he had finished a novel, *Zuleika Dobson* (1911), inventing a good phrase while polishing it off, a phrase that has been attributed to a score of people, from Dr Johnson to Abraham Lincoln, and is usually quoted thus: 'For those who like this sort of thing, this is the sort of thing they like.' A one-act play founded on his short story, *The Happy Hypocrite*, had also been done in 1900 by Mrs Patrick Campbell as a curtain-raiser to Frank Harris's *Mr and Mrs Daventry*, its reception being so friendly that Max felt bewildered: 'I sit here among the débris of success wondering what on earth can be the matter with my play – why it has appealed to the great heart-disease of the British Public.' However, the public's heart-disease was not fatal enough to make them swallow *Zuleika Dobson*, which he considered 'rather a beautiful piece of work'. The publisher Heinemann must have thought so too, for he advanced £400 on royalties. Max was concerned over its binding and paper, anxious that it should look like a book of essays, 'not like a beastly novel'. American publishers would not be tempted by it, the representative of one firm reporting that 'the author is more highly estimated by himself than by anyone else' and assuring his employers that Max 'has never reached any high standard in his literary work'. Opinions differ sharply on the subject of this story, which contains many amusing sentences, my own favourite being: 'On another table stood Zuleika's library. Both books were in covers of dull gold', and both were railway guides. As a short story it might have been excellent; as a novel of nonsense and satire it does not come off, the joke not being good enough and sustained nonsense ceasing to be funny unless dimly related to reality.

Having officially retired from business, Max saluted some of the contemporaries whose work he admired or disliked in a book of parodies, *A Christmas Garland* (1912), some of which so closely resembled the originals that the caricatures were almost imitations, as in the case of John Galsworthy, whose more extreme forms of evocation were perfectly caught in such phrases as 'that vague, super-subtle scent which boiled eggs give out through their unbroken shells', or 'that peculiar, almost unseizable odour that uncut turquoises have'.

I happened to meet, or rather encounter, Max at about that period. After a rehearsal at His Majesty's Theatre one morning Sir Herbert Tree asked me to go up to his dressing-room and tell his brother Max that he was about to leave for lunch at the Carlton next door and expected to see him there. I found Max standing before a long mirror, regarding himself in an aloof, have-we-been-introduced sort of way. He seemed to be on the point of apologising to his reflection for having been a little too familiar with it. He was alone, and though he noticed my arrival he did not turn round. Being young and nervous I cleared my throat before speaking. He made no attempt to shift his position. 'Are you Mr Beerbohm?' I asked, knowing perfectly well that he was but not knowing how else to open the conversation. He remained silent, and I repeated my question in perhaps too loud a tone. 'Have you a warrant for my arrest?' came the unexpected reply. His immobility got on my nerves and I said, 'No', a little angrily. He gave an affected start and asked, 'Have you brought the handcuffs?' This time my 'No' was almost a shout. 'Then I will come quietly', he said, at last facing me. I now recognised that eccentricity ran in the family, his brother having accustomed me to such behaviour, so I calmed down and delivered the message. 'Sounds like an ultimatum,' he murmured as he went towards the door, adding as he reached the corridor 'Thank you, constable.' I could only suppose that my nervousness had made my manner a trifle too stentorian. When I reported what had happened to Tree later in the day, he said: 'Ah, you should have laughed.'

Max may have been feeling off-colour that morning, though George Alexander, who produced his one-act play, *A Social Success* in 1913, told me that he had never known an author less liable to moods. On the other hand I heard from Robert Ross that Max did not always put a guard on his tongue when something funny occurred to him. For instance, at a dinner-party his neighbours were discussing Margot Asquith, whose memoirs made a sensation in the twenties, and a man remarked that she would be a rattling good sort if only her tongue did not run away with her. 'A pity none of her admirers is public-spirited enough to follow the tongue's admirable example!' quoth Max. This quickly went the rounds and an acquaintance complimented him on it. But Max, aware that his own tongue and Margot's had points in common, suffered a twinge of tact, denied that he had ever said such a thing, and added: 'Furthermore, I don't think it at all clever.'

While serving in the army in 1916 I managed to get an

evening's leave for the purpose of dining with Robert Ross, as
I had innumerable questions to ask him about his great friend
Oscar Wilde. He was a charming and witty companion, and we
discussed everything under the sun, including Max Beerbohm,
whose best caricatures were, said Ross, unreproducible, the
funniest of all having been inspired by an incident which he
vividly recalled for my amusement. In the spring of 1896 Ross
received a wire from Frank Harris, then editing *The Saturday
Review*: 'Will you lunch with me at the Café Royal at 1 o'clock
today – only a few friends to meet the Duc de Richelieu.' On
arriving, Ross found that Harris had forgotten to engage a room,
so about fifty guests, including many notable writers, had to
wait while a large table was placed in the centre of the principal
dining-room, to the inconvenience of the other visitors who were
crowded at small tables against the walls. The lunch began, and
their host was soon chatting away amicably with the Duke on
his right hand. Suddenly the deep booming voice of Harris, which
could be heard above the roar of the loudest traffic, silenced the
din of conversation: 'Homosexuality! No, my dear Duke, I
know nothing of the joys of homosexuality. You must ask my
friend Oscar about that.' Wilde was then in prison, his name
never breathed in public, and the combination of his Christian
name with the unmentionable crime that had caused his downfall
stunned the roomful of people. Not even the clatter of a fork
broke the deathly silence, while every luncher held his breath
and wondered what would happen next. 'And yet', continued
Harris reflectively, in a lower but still resonant voice, 'if
Shakespeare had asked me, I would have had to submit.'

Max Beerbohm was among those present, and produced a
caricature of the back view of a full-length, naked Harris, twirling
his moustaches fiercely and glowering over his shoulder at
Shakespeare, who stands trembling in the corner of the picture,
gazing in terror at his fearful mate with starting eyes, shaking
hands and knocking knees. Written in Max's hand underneath
were the words, 'If Shakespeare had asked me'. Incidentally
Harris pronounced the 'a' in 'asked' short, north-country fashion,

which made it sound funnier. Ross showed me the caricature, and I had to agree that publication would only increase Max's reputation with a very few choice spirits. Ross also let me see another of Max's caricatures that would have been rewarded with social ostracism. A famous nineteenth-century picture by Mary L. Gow depicts Queen Victoria as a girl in her nightdress, with downcast eyes, receiving the Prime Minister and the Archbishop of Canterbury, who come to tell her of the death of William IV and her accession. Max's parody shows Edward VII hurriedly descending the stairs in striped pyjamas to greet Lord Salisbury and Archbishop Temple, bent on a similar errand. But the nub of the entertainment lies in the flounce of a lady's nightdress disappearing round a corner of the landing at the top of the stairs.

Even without this addition Max got into serious trouble when he exhibited, among others, a series of Edward VII cartoons in 1923. The Press slated them, and to his amazement Max found himself labelled with such words as 'stealthy Bolshevist' and 'shameless bounder'. He was accused of a 'dastardly attack on Royalty', of 'infamous bad taste', of Teutonic brutality, and all the other epithets used by the Press when someone displays a lack of herd-instinct. Max instantly withdrew the offending caricatures from the exhibition, because 'they were likely to be misunderstood by the general public and to worry it'. Ultimately, it seems, they were purchased by the Royal Family, kept hidden, and only shown to intimate friends. Max once described himself as a Tory Anarchist: 'I should like everyone to go about doing just as he pleased – short of altering any of the things to which I have grown accustomed.' He had adopted the only political label that an extreme individualist could approve.

Regular trips to England diversified his residence at Rapallo, and he often put up at Paddington station hotel, where he could enjoy solitude incognito; but he remained in England during the two wars, 1914–18 and 1939–45, because he wanted to be 'where the English language is spoken and English thoughts and feelings are expressed'. In the first World War he and his wife stayed for some time with the William Rothensteins at Far Oakridge in the Cotswold country, after which they moved to a furnished cottage nearby, still feeding with the Rothensteins, who noticed that Max navigated the few yards between the two dwellings as if walking in Piccadilly, carefully dressed, carrying stick and gloves, with socks over his shoes in frost or snow in case he should slither and drop his drawings. In winter all the windows of their cottage were closed, and, as if absentmindedly, Max would shut the windows of other people's rooms. During this period he wrote 'Hilary Maltby and Stephen Braxton' as well as 'Savonarola Brown', two of the best things in his best book, *Seven Men* (1919), which contains the quintessence of Max. Returning with his wife to Rapallo after the war, he wrote to Rothenstein: 'I had forgotten how perfect life here could be.'

In 1939 Max received a knighthood. Forty years earlier he had laughed at such distinctions, saying that 'in the future, knighthood may be one of the lighter punishments of the Law. "Forty shillings or a knighthood" sounds quite possible.' And when his brother became 'Sir Herbert' in 1909, he still thought it funny, telling me that 'an old friend of Maud Tree's, whom I met the day after the publication of the Birthday Honours, said that she wanted to write and congratulate Maud, but wasn't sure whether, before the accolade, the envelope ought to be addressed to Mrs Tree, not Lady Tree. "Oh well", I said, "I think there would be no harm in writing *Lady*. I'm sure that in the eyes of Heaven my brother is already a Knight".' But of the many people who ridicule titles, Max was not among the very few who decline them. Although he did not care for the glare of publicity, he enjoyed the halo of renown.

Coming back to England for the second World War, the Beerbohms lived at first in a small Tudor house, Abinger Manor Cottage, Abinger Common, near Dorking. A flying bomb fell too near to be comfortable, and they moved to Flint Cottage, Box Hill, where Meredith had lived. Edinburgh University had already made Max an Honorary Doctor of Laws, and in 1942 Oxford bestowed on him an Honorary Doctorate of Literature.

He delivered the Rede Lecture at Cambridge in 1943, the subject being Lytton Strachey, received an Honorary Fellowship from Merton, his old College, in 1945, and became a popular broadcaster, indulging what he called his 'senile garrulity' to the general pleasure.

In 1944 I ran across him by accident. Staying at the Savage Club while working in the British Museum, I walked into the bar one evening and found it empty except for a solitary member sitting in the corner and sipping a glass of wine. His face seemed familiar, but the barman told me in answer to my whispered question that he was a complete stranger. I had another good look and felt pretty sure that he was Max. As he smiled at me I approached him and said: 'If I am not mistaken, you are Sir Max Beerbohm.' 'You are not mistaken', he replied. I introduced myself, and he at once began to say such nice things about my biography of Bernard Shaw, which had been published a year or two before, that I did not interrupt him. Suddenly he asked whether I liked Shaw very much.

'Is it possible not to like him?' I parried.

'Many people find it possible.'

'But what is there to dislike about him?'

'Everything.'

'Oh come!'

'That is what the people who dislike him say; but I am not of their number.'

'Did you like Wilde as much as Shaw?' I then asked, because I was engaged on a biography of Wilde at the time.

'One cannot compare the two. Wilde was great with his tongue, Shaw with his pen.'

'But as human beings?'

'They were as different from one another as the natives of the same island could be. I preferred Wilde as a companion, Shaw as a character.'

'Has your opinion of Shaw's plays altered since you wrote about them in *The Saturday Review*?'

'Not a lot. But I think his greatest work was his dramatic

criticism, most of which I know by heart. No one has come near him at that job. The rest of us are pygmies in comparison.'

We switched on to other writers, and I asked whether he was thinking of Sir James Barrie when he wrote that 'the more sentimental a man is, the less is he helpful, the more loth is he to cancel the cause of his emotion'. But Max was too cunning to be caught, and asked in mild surprise: 'Was Barrie unhelpful?'

While we were chatting the evening was made hideous by the dismal howlings of an air-raid warning, the flying bombs being then pretty frequent. ' 'Tis the voice of the siren; I heard her complain', misquoted Max as he got up, and with a cheerful *au revoir* he vanished into the din.

In 1947 the Beerbohms retired to Rapallo, where Max received visitors but scarcely ever answered letters, found that he had become too soft-hearted to draw caricatures, endured nightmares, and gazed at the Mediterranean. Florence died in January '51, and he was immersed in misery; but Elisabeth Jungmann, one-time secretary to Gerhart Hauptmann, came to the rescue, and acted thereafter as secretary, housekeeper, hostess and nurse.

In the spring of 1956 Max entered a hospital at Rapallo, suffering from insomnia, inability to take nourishment and a weak heart. He died on 20 May, having married Elisabeth on his deathbed.

14

Gilbert Keith Chesterton

Most socially correct men of forty would perspire at the thought of behaving as they did at the age of fourteen, and it is refreshing to know that Max Beerbohm, as a middle-aged model of propriety, surrendered to an impulse that shocked him on reflection. Walking through the dark streets of London with William Rothenstein, perhaps a trifle lit-up with liquor, they suddenly decided to revive their schooldays by ringing the front-door bells of two stately houses and running away. They barged straight into the arms of a policeman, who would have taken them into custody if they had not suggested that he needed a drink to appreciate their action. It must have been the lurking child in Max that was instantly attracted to the unabashed child in G. K. Chesterton, who, according to Shaw, 'might be trusted anywhere without a policeman. He might knock at a door and run away – perhaps even lie down across the thershold to trip up the emergent householder; but his crimes would be hyperbolic crimes of imagination and humour, not of malice'.

The child Gilbert, who was to win the affection of all who knew him, first appeared in Sheffield Terrace, Campden Hill, London on 29 May 1874, but his parents moved to No. 11 Warwick Gardens when he was about five, and there his youth was spent. His only sister died when he was too young to remember much about her, and his only brother, Cecil, was his junior by five years. An ancestor had squandered what money the family possessed in the time of the Regency; but his son re-established their social standing by selling coal and starting an estate agency, in which Gilbert's father, Edward Chesterton, was a partner, retiring in due course and engaging in various hobbies, one of which, the making of a toy-theatre, enabled Gilbert to enter fairyland. The boy inherited nothing of his father's manual dexterity, but something from his mother, Marie Grosjean, whose Swiss and Scottish ancestry combined to make her practical, commanding and amusing. As a child Gilbert loved fairy-tales and as a man he wrote them, all his stories being fantastic, all his characters fabulous. He was brought up in a tolerant liberal household and allowed to do much as he liked.

He went to school at Colet Court in Hammersmith, then crossed the road at the age of twelve and entered St Paul's School, where he remained for about five years. As a pupil he failed to give satisfaction. Untidy, absentminded, clumsy, living in a world of his own, and unable to take an interest in work or games, he became the butt of masters and boys. He delighted in poetry, the novels of Scott and Dickens, and wandered about in a dreamy fashion, never quite certain of where he was, and conjuring up pictures of Scottish warriors or English oddities. He muttered and laughed to himself, filled his schoolbooks with drawings that obliterated the text, and was quite unable to take the school routine seriously or even to be aware of it. He later referred to his days of pupillage as 'the period during which I was being instructed by somebody I did not know about something I did not want to know'. The High Master of his time, F. W. Walker, had a memorable personality. With a leonine head and a voice like thunder, his roars of rage and mirth echoed through the school and were audible beyond the building. So impressive was he that years later Gilbert pictured him as 'Sunday' in *The Man Who was Thursday*. The tall and gawky lad even managed to move Walker with a prize poem, and Gilbert, then in the sixth form, was ranked with the eighth by order of the High Master, a promotion that disconcerted the youngster.

Gilbert was seen at his best in the Junior Debating Club, which was started by Lucian Oldershaw, who later became his brother-

W

in-law, and strongly supported by Edmund Clerihew Bentley, who was Gilbert's greatest friend and afterwards achieved fame as the inventor of verses known as 'Clerihews'. There were about a dozen members, one of whom, Edward Fordham, told me that after a particularly noisy and troublesome session Gilbert, the permanent chairman, took him aside and in a very gentle but serious manner said that the throwing of buns and slices of cake did not create the right atmosphere for intelligent debates. The Club began with the object of discussing Shakespeare, but it soon took in a hundred other objects, the meetings being held at the houses of the members. A journal was founded, *The Debater*, and Gilbert's first essays appeared in it, mostly on poets, but his later style, thought and actions were apparent in an essay on 'Dragons', written at the age of sixteen. After describing the ancient dragon as resembling 'an intoxicated crocodile', he went on to say that the modern dragon had grown prudent:

'He doesn't see the good of going about as a roaring lion, but seeks what he may devour in a quiet and respectable way, behind many illustrious names and many imposing disguises. Behind the scarlet coat and epaulettes, behind the star and mantle of the garter, behind the ermine tippet and the counsellor's robe, behind, alas, the black coat and white tie, behind many a respectable exterior in public and in private life, we fear that the dragon's flaming eyes and grinning jaws, his tyrannous power, and his infernal cruelty, sometimes lurk.

'Reader, when you or I meet him, under whatever disguise, may we face him boldly, and perhaps rescue a few captives from his black cavern; may we bear a brave lance and a spotless shield through the crashing mêlée of life's narrow lists, and may our wearied swords have struck fiercely on the painted crests of Imposture and Injustice when the Dark Herald comes to lead us to the pavilion of the King.'

A fairly full programme, which he did his best to carry through.

His schooldays began with fighting and ended with friendship. His debating companions were devoted to him and remained his friends for life. He rather enjoyed being stupid in form, doing his

best not to learn Latin; he forgot to do his home-work and sometimes forgot to attend school, for he was discovered wandering
in the playing-field one day when he should have been at his desk
and said that he thought it was Saturday, a full holiday at St Paul's.
Any other boy would have been frequently punished, but somehow punishment seemed unsuitable in his case. I heard him
confess that a master had tried to cane him, 'but the expression
on his face and my own ridiculous posture made me laugh, and
instead of laying it on thick he suddenly appreciated the absurdity
of the situation and desisted'. He wrote a deal of verse in addition
to his essays for *The Debater*, and six lines from a poem called
'Adveniat Regnum Tuum' were remarkable for a boy of sixteen :

> Deep in the heart of every man, where'er his life be spent,
> There is a noble weariness, a holy discontent.
> Where'er to mortal eyes has come, in silence dark and lone,
> Some glimmer of the far-off light the world has never known,
> Some ghostly echoes from a dream of earth's triumphal song,
> Then as the vision fades we cry 'How long, oh Lord, how long ?'

He left St Paul's at the age of seventeen and spent the next
three years at the Slade School for Art, at the same time attending
some lectures on English literature at University College. His
physiological development having been retarded, he now passed
through a somewhat exaggerated period of pubescence, his
rather morbid fancy creating dreadful mountains out of commonplace molehills: 'I had an overpowering impulse to record or
draw horrible ideas and images, plunging deeper and deeper as
in a blind spiritual suicide.' This mildest of young men pictured
the maddest of crimes, and as his companions were 'a good
representative number of blackguards', one of them a diabolist, he
became aware of the seamy side of life. He did no work at the
Slade, but read and thought a great deal, at last emerging from
darkness into light, or, as he put it, 'I was engaged about that
time in discovering, to my own extreme and lasting astonishment,
that I was not an atheist.' From Shakespeare, Scott, Dickens and
Macaulay he moved on to Swinburne, Whitman and R. L.

Stevenson, the last two lifting his vision out of the twilight in which his soul had been straying, giving him a belief in the redemption of the world by comradeship, and influencing his earlier work. For a short while he called himself a socialist, but he never studied economics and soon drifted into Liberalism. Leaving the Slade he worked for a publisher opposite the British Museum, and then joined another publisher, Fisher Unwin, for whom he slaved away at a salary of twenty-five shillings a week.

In 1896 his friend Oldershaw took him to call on the family of Blogg living in Bedford Park, an artistic quarter of London not unlike the garden-cities of the future. The family consisted of a mother and three daughters, one of whom died shortly after, another was eventually married to Oldershaw, and the third, Frances, was secretary of an educational society. Although Gilbert described Frances as 'a queer card', he fell in love with her at once. She was an Anglo-Catholic, quite remote from the artistic circle in which she lived, and to Gilbert she was a sort of goddess. He was too nervous and diffident to speak of his love, though his whole behaviour expressed it, and Frances wondered if he would ever come to the point. At long last he did, as they were crossing the bridge in St James's Park, and he later confessed that he was thoroughly frightened before putting the dread question. Her answer gave him a foretaste of heaven and he seemed to be floating over the earth. He was so fearful of his good fortune that he wrote a long letter breaking the news to his mother, who was making cocoa for him in the same room. Little wonder that she said: 'I always give money to pavement artists, as I am quite certain that is how Gilbert will end.' Indeed the momentary difficulty was to establish himself financially before he could marry Frances, and during their long courtship he wrote poetry to her as well as daily love-letters, which were those of a poet in love with prose. His clothes were still so untidy, his general appearance so neglectful, that Frances's mother asked Oldershaw to tackle him on the subject; and Frances too dropped hints which he treated playfully, assuring her when apart that his boots were on his feet, his laces and buttons done up, his tie was round his neck, his hair brushed, cut and shampooed.

By nature a knight-errant, Gilbert had arrived at the conclusion that individuals were right to fight institutions, that minorities were right to fight their oppressors, and that all fighting against odds was noble. He therefore championed the Boers in their war of 1899-1902 against the British imperialists and financiers; but unlike most of the pro-Boers he was not a pacifist. On the contrary he was a violently patriotic Englishman who thought imperialism the reverse of patriotism and believed it his duty to criticise his country's faults. He was pushed into journalism by friends and began writing for *The Speaker*. Utterly unknown in the autumn of 1899, he sprang into fame early in 1900 with the publication of an anonymous volume of poems, *The Wild Knight*, which included his most famous and oft-quoted verses on 'The Donkey'. One critic said that the work was by John Davidson, who repudiated it; whereupon Gilbert acknowledged it. By the following year he was writing regularly for the *Daily News* and other papers, and it seemed as if he could now depend on a regular income. On 28 June 1901 he and Frances were united at Kensington Parish Church, and when he knelt down the sole of a new shoe exhibited the price ticket. He never lost his boyish love of weapons, carrying a sword-stick and a knife that resembled a dagger wherever he went; and after the marriage service, on the way to the station, he bought a revolver and cartridges with which to protect his wife on the Norfolk Broads during their honeymoon, the first night of which was spent at the White Horse Inn, Ipswich.

Mrs Cecil Chesterton states that their married life opened disastrously because Frances was horrified by the sexual act and refused to consummate their union, that Gilbert, full of self-reproach over his lack of consideration, unburdened himself on the subject to his brother Cecil, and that he remained for the rest of his life an enforced celibate. What actually happened may be conjectured. With his invariable clumsiness and no premarital experience of sex, Gilbert rushed the encounter. In his romantic fancy he may have pictured his wife as an imprisoned maiden who had to be carried away recklessly. Whatever the cause he was too impetuous, and instead of feeling his way he assaulted the shrine. But their deep love for one another must soon have taught him restraint and given her comprehension, for the time came when Frances underwent an operation to make her capable of childbirth, which would not have been necessary if they had not proved her incapacity by frequent experiment. Unfortunately the operation was not fruitful, and they made up for their childlessness by taking an endless delight in the children of their friends.

In the years following his marriage Chesterton became a great Fleet Street figure, quite the most notable since Dr Johnson, and the size of his body grew with his fame. Six feet two inches tall, with small feet, delicately shaped hands and a mass of wavy chestnut hair, he became excessively corpulent, weighing some twenty stone before his fortieth year. He loved company, and journalists gathered together at whatever public-house he frequented to hear his discourse on every conceivable topic. His best sayings were repeated from Charing Cross station to St Paul's Cathedral, and his huge person, covered in a large cloak and wide black sombrero, was known to every cabby in the city, for his habit of taking a hansom for a distance of a few yards, keeping it waiting for hours, and then driving in it for another few yards, made him popular with the jarveys. He talked and thought and wrote under every imaginable circumstance, standing under a lamp-post to finish an article, chatting on the pavement to an acquaintance while the rain streamed down, meditating in the middle of the road while the traffic swirled round him. He seemed to be unconscious of time, place or climatic conditions; he was blithely unaware of his personal appearance; and, as his barber once said, he was always 'head over ears in thought'.

In his speech and writing he ridiculed popular fallacies, pro-duced absurd analogies to drive home his point, and burlesqued any argument by carrying it a step further. For instance, he once referred to the type of modern philosopher or journalist who threw off some preposterous assertion in a parenthesis, as though it were too obvious to be discussed. He illustrated this method by quoting someone who had written: 'In two hundred years' time (when the individual consciousness is merged in the communal) . . .', which, said he, was as if himself had written: 'In 1649 King Charles I was condemned to be executed by a Council presided over by Bradshaw (whose mother was a walrus) . . .' or 'My home is in Beaconsfield, which is seven miles from High Wycombe and four miles from Gerrards Cross (where I ate ninety negroes) . . .' He followed these examples with a specimen of the kind of thing then being said by those who opposed Home Rule for Ireland: 'England is bounded on the east by the North Sea, on the south by the English Channel, and on the west by Ireland (whose inhabitants are incapable of governing themselves) . . .'

His first home with his wife was in Edwardes Square, Kensington, but they soon left that for No. 60 Overstrand Mansions, Battersea, afterwards settling down at Beaconsfield in Buckinghamshire. Soon he was writing a weekly causerie for the *Illustrated London News*, and his articles appeared in all sorts of papers. Every little group or society asked him to lecture or debate, and his evenings were constantly taken up with public disputation. He had a thin high-pitched voice, and his lecturing was not impressive; but the battle of debate roused him, and no one but Shaw could beat him at that game. Humour and wit bubbled out of him and he roared with laughter at his own jokes, whether spoken or written. His Anglo-Catholic wife brought many clergymen into his life, and he enjoyed discussion on theology as much as he revelled in Fleet Street vulgarity. Frances had to keep an eye on his personal appearance and check his absent-mindedness, for he was quite capable of dining at the House of Commons with a boot on one foot and a slipper on the other, and equally capable of sending her a telegram: 'Am in Market Harborough. Where ought I to be?' She wired back 'Home', knowing that she could direct his movements more easily in person. He and his brother Cecil argued about every-thing interminably, sometimes for twelve hours at a stretch, and not even Frances could tear them apart; though as a rule it pleased him to obey her, for he knew that she alone had his interests at heart.

His high spirits and apparent happiness were infectious. For him the commonplace was always miraculous, and so every hour of the day gave him something to wonder at, or to laugh at, and always to enjoy. His brief comments amused everyone including himself. Here are a few:

'Man is a biped, but fifty men are not a centipede.'

'The word "good" has many meanings. For example, if a man were to shoot his grandmother at a range of five hundred yards, I should call him a good shot, but not *necessarily* a good man.'

'I would tell a man who was drinking too much "Be a man", but I would not tell a crocodile who was eating too many explorers "Be a crocodile".'

After a meeting at which he had discussed racial characteristics, a woman came up to him and simpered: 'Mr Chesterton, I wonder if you can tell me what race I belong to?' Carefully adjusting his glasses and peering at her, he replied: 'I should certainly say, madam, one of the conquering races.'

Following the success of the female enfranchisement move-ment, he declared: 'Twenty million young women rose to their feet with the cry *We will not be dictated to*, and promptly became stenographers.'

Hundreds of ideas, flung away by him, were appropriated and used by other journalists. As he sat in a tavern with a bumper of burgundy, his talk was torrential, and when alone he scribbled away unceasingly, whether in tea-shops, public-houses, cabs, omnibuses, trains or streets. His mind was so full that he found it almost impossible to remember appointments, and he frequently wrote to explain why he had failed to turn up. Once he called on a publisher at the exact hour agreed upon, but he spoilt the effect by handing the man a letter explaining elaborately why he could not keep the appointment.

His stories, like himself, were so full of ideas that they gave the impression of being written by an absentminded man, one whose mind was elsewhere. The first to make him popular with the reading public was *The Napoleon of Notting Hill* (1904), written at the urge of poverty. With ten shillings in his pocket, he left a harassed wife for Fleet Street, where, after a shave, he went to the Cheshire Cheese and ordered a luncheon which included all his favourite dishes and a bottle of red wine. Feeling thoroughly braced he called on John Lane the publisher, gave a synopsis of the story he wished to write, and said that he could not begin it without twenty pounds in his pocket. Lane did not like parting from money, especially at short notice, and promised to send it in a few days. 'If you want the book', said Chesterton, strengthened by wine, 'you will have to give it to me today.' Lane disbursed; and when finished, with his usual indifference to money, Chesterton sold the book outright for a hundred pounds. As in his other fantasies, *The Man Who was Thursday* (1908), *Manalive* (1911) and *The Flying Inn* (1914), the last of which contains a quantity of rousing verse, Chesterton's Napoleon fights for the liberty of individuals to lead their own lives in their own way against the soul-destroying influence of monopolies and laws made by the few for the control of the many. In his stories we hear for the last time the cry of human beings for the freedom increasingly denied them by cranks, reformers and financiers. The people in his tales are the embodiments of ideas, for he was interested in opinions, not personalities, and life appeared to him as a conflict between good and evil, not as the clash of actual characters. His pockets were always stuffed with detective stories and tales of bloody combat. Like Don Quixote he pictured himself engaged in an endless battle against diabolic forces, the sword-stick, the revolver and the bowie-knife which he always carried being the protective armour of an incurably romantic nature. It would have been a dreadful day for him if he had ever drawn a drop of real human blood.

Because he lived solely in a world of ideas, he could not help filling his books with his own thoughts, and the personality of G.K.C. found expression under such titles as *Robert Browning* (1903), *Charles Dickens* (1906), *George Bernard Shaw* (1909), *William Blake* (1910), *William Cobbett* (1925) and *Robert Louis Stevenson* (1927). The ground he held in common with those writers was described perceptively and luminously, but outside that territory he was at sea. Many instances could be given of his failure to understand their peculiarities, but we must content ourselves with one example of misreading in his book on Shaw, and one of misreporting. 'Chesterton's book is a very good one in itself', Shaw said when I touched on the subject. 'It has little to do with me, as G.K.C. has never made any study of my works, and in one place actually illustrates my limitations by telling the world something I should have made one of the characters say in *Major Barbara* if I could have transcended those limitations: the joke being that it is exactly what I did make the character say, as Chesterton might have found had he taken the trouble to open the book and refer to the passage. But if you leave me out of account, you will find, I think, that the book is full of good things, and very generous into the bargain.'

The case of misreporting occurred in G.K.C.'s *Autobiography* (1936), wherein he stated that at a male party held in a vast tent in a Westminster garden, the festivities including the boiling of eggs in Beerbohm Tree's top hat, Shaw alone remained sober, and at one point got up, sternly protested, and stalked out. 'Chesterton's memory played him a trick,' Shaw told me. 'I usually avoided all social gatherings for men only, as men would not enjoy themselves decently in the absence of women. All that about a tent in Westminster, and boiling eggs in a top hat, if it really took place, is quite new to me. I wasn't there. But there was a male party in the house of a friend in Westminster at which I sat next Chesterton. After dinner, they began throwing bread at one another; and one of them began making smutty speeches. They were actually drunk enough to expect a contribution from me. I got up and went home. You must remember that I am a

civilised Irishman, and you cannot civilise an Englishman, nor
an English woman either, except superficially. When I first saw
an assembly of respectable and sober English ladies and gentlemen going Fantee, and behaving like pirates debauching after
a capture, I was astounded. I am used to it now; but it is not
possible for me to take part in such orgies.'

Against such *gaffes* as these, due to a lack of perception
where personalities were concerned, Chesterton could sometimes
say in a phrase what other historians would take a chapter to
explain, as in his *ShortHistory of England* (1917), where the real
cause of the Civil War was shown to be a quarrel, not between
the people and the King, but between the squirearchy and the
monarchy: 'There was no village Hampden in Hampden village.'
Again, in his book on Cobbett, the attitude to the poorer classes
of the Whig territorial aristocracy in the eighteenth and early
nineteenth centuries was put succinctly: 'They were more
interested in pheasants than in peasants: that was an aitch they
were most careful not to drop.'

Shaw fully appreciated Chesterton's historical work, and in
spite of their dissimilar natures they were very fond of one
another, often exchanging visits after G.K.C.'s removal from
Battersea to Beaconsfield in 1909. Frances was wise to rescue her
knight from the Fleet Street tourney, for he drank too much and
gave away all his money. He needed a nurse, a valet, an accountant
and a protector, and she now took control of him, giving him a
sense of stability. Expenditure was restricted on his visits to
London, and he found it impossible to stand a round of drinks
on half a crown, but his friends were eager to keep his glass
replenished. Like everything else, money was for him an abstract
idea, not a concrete counter, and he had a poor opinion of people's
acquisitiveness. 'To be clever enough to get all that money, one
must be stupid enough to want it', says 'Father Brown' in one
of the stories which G.K.C. began to write around that delightful
little priest soon after the move to Beaconsfield. Although some
of his poems like 'The Ballad of the White Horse' and 'Lepanto'
contained lines that were quoted by all sorts of people, his

most popular productions were the 'Father Brown' detective stories, a series of fairy-tales which contain the one sleuth in literature not dimly descended from Dupin or Bucket or Cuff or Holmes. He could splash his colours all over these yarns, and make his paradoxes seem like the deductions of logic.

Frances and Gilbert were happy at Overroads, their first house at Beaconsfield, but happier still when they bought a field and built a studio on it, from which evolved a house called Top Meadow, where they could entertain all their friends, perhaps the most welcome being Father John O'Connor, who provided a few hints for 'Father Brown', Hilaire Belloc, who brought several of his books to be illustrated by G.K.C., and Maurice Baring, who later helped him to become a Roman Catholic. The paper started by Belloc in 1911 and then edited by Cecil Chesterton received contributions from G.K.C. It began as *The Eye-Witness*, became *The New Witness* in 1912, and created a sensation over the Marconi affair. Cecil's attacks shook the authorities; and when he was found guilty of criminal libel but fined instead of being imprisoned, his friends regarded it as a triumph. Indeed the whole business smelt a bit fishy, and Cecil's action was justified.

The outbreak of war in 1914 made many people aspire to heroism, and especially the romantic G.K.C., but a broken right arm that had never recovered prevented him from lifting it above his shoulder, which disqualified him from the infantry, the fact that no horse could carry a man of his weight put the cavalry out of the question, and he mournfully confessed his only value to his country: 'I might possibly form part of a barricade.' Overwork brought on a breakdown in health towards the close of 1914, and for many weeks he hovered between life and death. On recovering he took over the editorship of *The New Witness* from Cecil, who managed to join the army in 1916. It was a dreadful blow when Cecil died in hospital shortly after the conclusion of the war, and Gilbert, with his knight-errant's idealisation of action, always declared that Cecil had been killed 'in the trenches' or had 'died fighting in the Great War'. Undoubtedly the conditions of active service had caused Cecil's death, but Edward

Fordham assured me that the only time he had ever known G.K.C. anything but open and honest was over his brother's end, insisting that he had perished in battle. As we have seen, he was a little shaky on facts, particularly in regard to persons, and no doubt he honestly believed what his fancy pictured. But he was steady enough on one point in connection with the war. Years before it started Belloc had convinced him that Prussia was the real menace to civilisation; and in this they were right, for the financiers and politicians quickly undid all that our soldiers had done, and within a generation Prussian savagery, organised by a monomaniac, was again let loose on the world.

Gilbert and his wife visited Palestine and Italy soon after the war, and then went on a lecture tour of the United States. On Sunday, 30 July 1922, Father John O'Connor received Gilbert into the Roman Catholic Church, the ceremony taking place in the chapel of the Railway Hotel at Beaconsfield. Ever since writing a book on *Orthodoxy* (1908) G.K.C. had been drifting in that direction, and would have reached his destination sooner if he could have taken Frances with him; but her conversion followed in 1926. Just as a realistic sceptical mind like Belloc's needed direction, so did a romantic mystical mind like Chesterton's need anchorage. 'Catholicism gives us a doctrine, puts logic into our life', he wrote, '. . . it is a base which steadies the judgment . . . To be a Catholic is to be all at rest! . . . The Church of England does not speak strongly. It has no united action. I have no use for a Church which is not a Church militant, which cannot order battle and fall in line and march in the same direction.' The chivalrous warrior and the man who craved for certitude had at last found his spiritual home. Many of his admirers thought that conversion had changed his character. But no one's character ever changes fundamentally, though some circumstances will bring out aspects that are innate, other circumstances other aspects. The most we can say is that G.K.C.'s character was diluted, his individuality watered down, by baptism in the Faith.

Frances was out of sympathy with his editorial duties, which indeed wore him out, but loyalty made him carry on the torch lit by his brother. He was not a good editor because the technical side of the business bored him; but he was wonderfully patient, he never got rattled, and everyone on the staff loved him. He hated personal quarrels and animosity, doing his utmost to avoid giving judgment between angry disputants. In 1926 he reluctantly allowed the paper to be re-named G.*K.'s Weekly*, and out of that the Distributist League came into being, its object being to preach the distribution of property, an idea originally formulated by Belloc as an antidote to capitalism and socialism. Chesterton worked hard for it, lecturing and debating in all parts of the country, and incidentally sacrificing a good deal of the money earned from his books to keeping the paper afloat, much to his wife's discomfort. Following his grave illness he was compelled to restrict his wine-drinking, but he never attempted to lessen his labours, and it was a fortunate day for him when Dorothy Collins became his secretary, for she arranged his affairs in every department, from income-tax returns to social and speaking engagements. Frances, too, was overjoyed by the coming of a perfect secretary, and soon Dorothy Collins was an adopted daughter, accompanying them everywhere, driving them about on holidays, and organising everything. Frances suffered from arthritis of the spine and was not always capable of attending to her husband's wants, though he still shouted for her when he wanted a tie to be tied or a bootlace to be done up.

They again visited America in 1930-1 and G.K.C. lectured all over the States. His physical clumsiness seems to have impressed the Americans as much as his mental alertness and they were concerned over his difficulty in getting into and out of motor cars. Someone suggested that he should do it sideways. 'I have no sideways', said he. Particularly impressed in New York by the advertising signs that flickered on Broadway, he thought of them as fairy-lights, crying: 'What a paradise of beauty this would be for anyone who couldn't read!' Frances was ill at Chattanooga in Tennessee, and Gilbert at once cancelled all his lectures. His agent was in despair and begged Dorothy Collins to accompany him. Frances got better, and he agreed to

continue his tour with Dorothy in attendance, but the cancellat-
ions had cost him several hundreds of pounds. Incomparably
better as a talker than as a lecturer, he suddenly won a new
popularity in the early 'thirties by proving himself an ideal
broadcaster.

The last year of his life was saddened by fierce personal
quarrels between members of the paper's staff, and increasingly
he sought solace at home, where he loved entertaining children,
throwing his dagger about the lawn, making passes at the
flowers with his sword-stick, practising shots with a bow and
arrow, and playing with his dog. One little girl was told by her
mother that she was going to visit a very great and clever man,
from whom she could learn a lot. After the tea-party the child
explained what she had learnt from the great and clever man: 'He
taught me how to throw buns in the air and catch them in my
mouth.' In much the same casual way he wrote stories and essays,
throwing ideas into the air and leaving his secretary to catch
them on paper. Whenever Dorothy Collins told him that money
was needed he would say: 'Very well. Let us write a "Father
Brown" story', and start it at once. Fortunately he never heard
that his last 'Father Brown' story was declined by the editor
to whom it was sent. It would have distressed him to know that
he was written out and that the story was too bad to be published.

Early in 1936 it became clear to Frances and Dorothy that he
was failing, and a motor-trip abroad was advisable. They went
to Lourdes and Lisieux, and he seemed better. Driving them
home from the English coast, Dorothy said 'Oh, sing something!'
G.K.C. promptly obliged and sang extracts from the Gilbert
and Sullivan operas for an hour or so, interspersing them with
nonsense and chit-chat. When they got back he tried to work
as usual, but his mind had lost its usual clarity and he fell asleep
at intervals. He was soon laid up with a weak heart, and had
periods of unconsciousness. The thought of death had terrified
him in the past, and when he pricked his finger or felt slightly ill
his wife and secretary had to console him that all was well. But
when he knew that he was dying, he was not in the least afraid.

On 13 June 1936 Frances and Dorothy entered his room to see that he was comfortable. He opened his eyes and said: 'Hullo, my darling! Hullo, my dear!' They were his last words, and next day his heart ceased to beat.

I heard from Dorothy Collins that the coffin in which he lay was so big that it could not be got through the door of the bedroom, and that windows were removed for its egress. This reminded me of a talk I once had with him about my favourite character in literature. I said that Shakespeare had been wrong to kill Falstaff, who was deathless, and G.K.C. played with this idea: 'You are quite right. Falstaff was merely shamming death, as he had done at the battle of Shrewsbury. But when they came to fetch his body, they could not get it down the narrow stairs; so they removed the roof and hoisted him up. When they had got him so far, his spirit took him further, and he soared upwards until he was out of sight; and the gravedigger who had talked to Hamlet stared at the sky muttering: "Is he to be buried in Christian burial that wilfully seeks his own levitation?"'

Nearly a decade before his death the passing of G.K.C., one of the most lovable personalities in the history of English letters, had been celebrated in a 'Premature Epitaph' by Colin Hurry:

> Place on his hand the jewel, on his brow the diadem,
> Who in an age of miracles dared to believe in them.

> Chesterton companion
>   His companions mourn.
> Chesterton Crusader
>   Leaves a cause forlorn.
> Chesterton the critic
>   Pays no further heed.
> Chesterton the poet
>   Lives while men shall read.
> Chesterton the dreamer
>   Is by sleep beguiled;
> And there enters heaven
>   Chesterton . . . the child.

Chief Sources

NOTE: *I have only included the original sources, those which convey much previously unknown information of value about my subjects; but innumerable other books containing less significant biographical data have been consulted, as well as all the published works and letters written by the wits concerned. In the cases of Sydney Smith, Disraeli, Labouchere, Whistler, Gilbert, Tree, Wilde, Shaw, Belloc, Beerbohm and Chesterton, I have been able to add personal knowledge or private information to the printed authorities.*

JONATHAN SWIFT

Literary Correspondence of Dean Swift, 1741.
Remarks on the Life and Writings of Jonathan Swift by Lord Orrery, 1751.
Observations upon Lord Orrery's Remarks (Anon.) by Dr Delany, 1754.
The Memoirs of Mrs Letitia Pilkington, 3 vols., 1754.
Essay upon the Life of Swift by Deane Swift, 1755.
Life of Swift by Hawkesworth, 1755.
Life of Swift by Dr Johnson (in *Lives of the Poets*).
Life of Swift by Thomas Sheridan, 1785.
Life of Swift by Walter Scott, 1814.
The Closing Years of Dean Swift's Life by W. R. Wilde, 1849.
Life of Swift by John Forster (1667-1711), 1875.
The Life of Jonathan Swift by Henry Craik, 2 vols., 1894.
Unpublished Letters edited by Birkbeck Hill, 1899.
The Life and Friendships of Dean Swift by Stephen Gwynn, 1933.
In Search of Swift by Denis W. Johnston, 1959.

SAMUEL JOHNSON

The Life of Samuel Johnson, LL.D. by James Boswell.

The Journal of a Tour to the Hebrides with Samuel Johnson by James Boswell.

A Journey to the Western Islands of Scotland by Samuel Johnson.

Letters of Anna Seward, 1784–1807 edited by A. Constable, 6 vols., 1811.

Johnsonian Miscellanies (including Mrs Piozzi's Anecdotes, Arthur Murphy's biography, and much else) edited by George Birkbeck Hill, 1897.

Diary and Letters of Madame D'Arblay (Fanny Burney), 6 vols., 1904.

The French Journals of Mrs Thrale and Dr Johnson edited by Moses Tyson and Henry Guppy, 1932.

Thraliana: the Diary of Mrs Hester Lynch Thrale (later Mrs Piozzi), 1776–1809, 2 vols., edited by Katharine C. Balderston, 1942.

Samuel Johnson by Joseph Wood Krutch, 1945.

The Letters of Samuel Johnson collected and edited by R. W. Chapman, 3 vols., 1952.

Young Samuel Johnson by James L. Clifford, 1955.

Letters of James Boswell collected and edited by Chauncey Brewster Tinker, 2 vols., 1924.

The Private Papers of James Boswell from Malahide Castle edited by Geoffrey Scott and Frederick Pottle, 18 vols., 1928–34.

Boswell's London Journal, 1762–3 edited by Frederick A. Pottle, 1950.

RICHARD BRINSLEY SHERIDAN

Memoirs of the Public and Private Life of R. B. Sheridan by John Watkins, 2 vols., 1817.

Memoirs of the Life of Richard Brinsley Sheridan by Thomas Moore, 1825.

Sheridaniana, 1826.

Memoir of Mr Sheridan by William Smyth, 1840.

The Croker Papers edited by L. J. Jennings, 3 vols., 1885.

Lives of the Sheridans by Percy Fitzgerald, 2 vols., 1887.

Sheridan by W. Fraser Rae, 2 vols., 1896.

The Creevey Papers edited by Sir Herbert Maxwell, 2 vols., 1903.

Sheridan by Walter Sichel, 2 vols., 1909.

Sheridan: a Ghost Story by E. M. Butler, 1931.

Harlequin Sheridan by R. Crompton Rhodes, 1933.

Creevey by John Gore, 1948.

Betsy Sheridan's Journal edited by William LeFanu, 1960.

SYDNEY SMITH

A Memoir of the Reverend Sydney Smith by his daughter, Lady Holland, with a selection from his letters, edited by Mrs Austin, 2 vols., 1855.

Memoirs, Journal and Correspondence of Thomas Moore edited by the Right Hon. Lord John Russell, M.P., 8 vols., 1856.

Memorials of His Time by Henry, Lord Cockburn, 1856.

The Life and Letters of the Rev. Richard Harris Barham by his Son, 2 vols., 1870.

The Life and Times of Henry, Lord Brougham written by Himself, 3 vols., 1871.

Diary, Reminiscences and Correspondence of Henry Crabb Robinson, 2 vols., 1872.

Archibald Constable and his Literary Correspondents: a Memorial by his Son, Thomas Constable, 3 vols., 1873.

Monographs: Personal and Social by Lord Houghton, 1873.

The Life and Letters of Lord Macaulay by G. O. Trevelyan, 1881.

The Greville Memoirs, vols. 3 and 5, 1888.

Rogers and His Contemporaries by P. W. Clayden, 2 vols., 1889.

The Life, Letters and Friendships of Richard Monckton Milnes (first Lord Houghton) by T. Wemyss Reid, 1890.

The Life and Times of Sydney Smith, based on Family Documents and the Recollections of Personal Friends by Stuart J. Reid, revised edition, 1896.

Sydney Smith by George W. E. Russell (English Men of Letters), 1904.

The Smith of Smiths by Hesketh Pearson, 1934. (With an Introduction by G. K. Chesterton.)

The Letters of Sydney Smith edited by Nowell C. Smith, 2 vols., 1953.

BENJAMIN DISRAELI

Personal Recollections of the Earl of Beaconsfield by the Duchess of Rutland, 1881.

Home Letters of Benjamin Disraeli, 1885.

The Croker Papers, 1885.

The Greville Papers, 1874–85.

Personal Reminiscences of the Right Hon. Benjamin Disraeli, Earl of Beaconsfield by Henry Lake, 1891.

The Life of Benjamin Disraeli, Earl of Beaconsfield by W. F. Monypenny and G. E. Buckle, 6 vols., 1910–20.

Benjamin Disraeli by the Right Hon. Sir Edward G. Clarke, 1926.

Letters of Benjamin Disraeli to Lady Bradford and Lady Chesterfield edited by the Marquess of Zetland, 2 vols., 1929.

Letters of Benjamin Disraeli to the Marchioness of Londonderry, 1938.

Dizzy by Hesketh Pearson, 1951.

The Young Disraeli by B. R. Jerman, 1960.

HENRY LABOUCHERE

The *Daily News*, 1870–1.

The Diary of a Besieged Resident in Paris, 1871.

Hansard, 1880–1905.

Edmund Yates: His Recollections and Experiences, vol. 2, 1884.

The Life of Henry Labouchere by Algar Labouchere Thorold, 1913.

Portraits of the Seventies by G. W. E. Russell, 1916.

The Life of Sir Charles Dilke by Stephen Gwynn and Gertrude M. Tuckwell, 2 vols., 1917.

The Diary of a Journalist by Sir Henry Lucy, 3 vols., 1920-3.

The Life of Sir William Harcourt by A. G. Gardiner, 2 vols., 1923.

The Letters of Queen Victoria, second and third series, edited by G. E. Buckle, 1928-32.

Memoirs of an Old Parliamentarian by the Right Hon. T. P. O'Connor, 2 vols., 1929.

Lord Rosebery by the Marquess of Crewe, 2 vols., 1931.

My Diaries by Wilfred Scawen Blunt, 1932.

The Life of Joseph Chamberlain by J. L. Garvin, vols. 2 and 3, 1933-4.

Labby: The Life of Henry Labouchere by Hesketh Pearson, 1936.

JAMES McNEILL WHISTLER

London and Provincial Press, 26-7 November, 1878.

The Gentle Art of Making Enemies by J. McNeill Whistler, 1890.

The Baronet and the Butterfly by J. McNeill Whistler, 1899.

Recollections and Impressions of James A. McNeill Whistler by Arthur Jerome Eddy, 1903.

Whistler as I Knew Him by Mortimer Menpes, 1904.

With Whistler in Venice by Otto H. Bacher, 1908.

The Life of James McNeill Whistler by E. R. and J. Pennell, 1908.

Memories of James McNeill Whistler by T. R. Way, 1912.

The Whistler Journal by E. R. and J. Pennell, 1921.

Whistler: the Friend by Elizabeth Robins Pennell, 1930.

Whistler by James Laver, 1930.

Men and Memories by William Rothenstein (1872-1900), 1931.

Time Was by Graham Robertson, 1931.

The Tribulations of a Baronet by Timothy Eden, 1933.

The Life and Opinions of Walter Richard Sickert by Robert Emmons, 1941.

The Pre-Raphaelite Tragedy by William Gaunt, 1942.

The Man Whistler by Hesketh Pearson, 1952.

WILLIAM SCHWENCK GILBERT

Rutland Barrington by Himself, 1908.

Piano and I by George Grossmith, 1910.

Old Days in Bohemian London by Mrs Clement Scott, 1919.

W. S. Gilbert: His Life and Letters by Sidney Dark and Rowland Grey, 1923.

Recollections of a Savage by Edwin A. Ward, 1923.

Studio and Stage by Joseph Harker, 1924.

The Gilbert and Sullivan Journal, 1926-35.

Gilbert and Sullivan by A. H. Godwin, 1926.

Sir Arthur Sullivan: His Life, Letters and Diaries by Herbert Sullivan and Newman Flower, 1927.

Gilbert, Sullivan and D'Oyly Carte by François Cellier and Cunningham Bridgeman, 1927.

The Story of Gilbert and Sullivan by Isaac Goldberg, 1929.

The Life and Reminiscences of Jessie Bond as told by Herself to Ethel Macgeorge, 1930.

Me and Mine by Mrs Alec Tweedie, 1932.

Gilbert and Sullivan by Hesketh Pearson, 1935.

Gilbert by Hesketh Pearson, 1957. (The first full Life, founded on family documents.)

BEERBOHM TREE

Herbert Beerbohm Tree by Mrs George Cran, 1907.

Herbert Beerbohm Tree: Some Memories of Him and His Art collected by Max Beerbohm, 1920.

Days and Ways of an Old Bohemian by Major Fitzroy Gardner, 1921.

Oscar Asche by Himself, 1929.

Harlequinade by Constance Collier, 1929.

The Life and Letters of Henry Arthur Jones by Doris Arthur Jones, 1930.

Ellen Terry's Memoirs with additions by Edith Craig and Christopher St John, 1933.

Both Sides of the Curtain by Elizabeth Robins, 1940.

Haymarket: Theatre of Perfection by W. Macqueen-Pope, 1948.

Bernard Shaw and Mrs Patrick Campbell: Their Correspondence edited by Alan Dent, 1952.

Beerbohm Tree by Hesketh Pearson, 1956. (The first Life of Tree, founded on family documents.)

OSCAR WILDE

The Life of Oscar Wilde by Robert Harborough Sherard, 1906.

Oscar Wilde: The Story of an Unhappy Friendship by Robert H. Sherard, 1908.

Bibliography of Oscar Wilde by Stuart Mason (Christopher Millard), 1914.

The Trembling of the Veil by W. B. Yeats, 1926.

The Romantic '90s by Richard Le Gallienne, 1926.

The Autobiography of Lord Alfred Douglas, 1929.

My Memoirs by Sir Frank Benson, 1930.

Men and Memories by William Rothenstein, 1872-1900, 1931.

Time Was by W. Graham Robertson, 1931.

My Diaries by Wilfred Scawen Blunt, 1932.

Recollections of Oscar Wilde by Charles Ricketts, 1932.

Aspects of Wilde by Vincent O'Sullivan, 1936.

Sir George Alexander and the St James's Theatre by A. E. W. Mason, 1935.

Oscar Wilde Discovers America by Lloyd Lewis and Henry Justin Smith, 1936.

Oscar Wilde: The Man – the Artist by Boris Brasol, 1938.

Self-Portrait taken from the Letters and Journals of Charles Ricketts, R.A. collected and compiled by T. Sturge Moore, edited by Cecil Lewis, 1939.

The Life of Oscar Wilde by Hesketh Pearson, 1946.

The Letters of Oscar Wilde edited by Rupert Hart-Davis, 1962.

BERNARD SHAW

Shaw's Prefaces to *Immaturity* (1931), *The Irrational Knot* (1905), *London Music in 1888-9* (1937), his *Sixteen Self Sketches* (1949), his *William Morris as I knew Him* (1936) and his *Pen Portraits and Reviews* (1932) contain autobiographical material.

George Bernard Shaw: His Life and Works by Archibald Henderson, 1911.

Shaw by J. S. Collis, 1925.

Frank Harris on Bernard Shaw, 1931.

Ellen Terry and Bernard Shaw: A Correspondence edited by Christopher St John, 1931. (With preface by Bernard Shaw).

Bernard Shaw: Playboy and Prophet by Archibald Henderson, 1932.

Bernard's Brethren by C. M. Shaw, 1939.

Letters to Florence Farr by Bernard Shaw, 1946.

G.B.S. 90: Aspects of Bernard Shaw's Life and Works edited by S. Winsten, 1946.

Days with Bernard Shaw by Samuel Winsten, 1948.

The Real Bernard Shaw by Maurice Colbourne, 1949.

Thirty Years with G.B.S. by Blanche Patch, 1951.

Bernard Shaw and Mrs Patrick Campbell: Their Correspondence edited by Alan Dent, 1952.

Bernard Shaw: His Life, Work and Friends by St John Ervine, 1956.

Advice to a Young Critic (Letters by G.B.S.) 1956.

Bernard Shaw's Letters to Granville Barker edited by C. B. Purdom, 1956.

The *Cornhill Magazine*, Summer 1956: 'The Nun and the Dramatist' (Letters between Dame Laurentia McLachlan and Bernard Shaw).

To a Young Actress: The Letters of Bernard Shaw to Molly Tompkins, 1961.

Bernard Shaw: His Life and Personality by Hesketh Pearson (complete edition with Postscript), 1961.

HILAIRE BELLOC

Hilaire Belloc by C. Creighton Mandell and Edward Shanks, 1916.

I, too, have lived in Arcadia, by Mrs Belloc-Lowndes.

Hilaire Belloc by Renée Haynes, 1953.

Hilaire Belloc by J. B. Morton, 1955.

Testimony to Hilaire Belloc by Eleanor and Reginald Jebb, 1956.

The Life of Hilaire Belloc by Robert Speaight, 1957.

MAX BEERBOHM

Max Beerbohm in Perspective by Bohun Lynch, 1920.

Men and Memories by William Rothenstein, 3 vols., 1931, 1932, 1939.

Frank Harris by Hugh Kingsmill, 1932.

Sir Max Beerbohm: Man and Writer by J. G. Riewald, 1953.

Conversation with Max by S. N. Behrman, 1960.

GILBERT KEITH CHESTERTON

The Debater, Journal of the Junior Debating Club (St Paul's School), 3 vols., 1891-3.

G. K. Chesterton: A Criticism (Anon.) by Cecil Chesterton, 1908.

G. K. Chesterton: A Portrait by W. R. Titterton, 1936.

Autobiography by G. K. Chesterton, 1936.

Father Brown on Chesterton by John O'Connor, 1937.

The Laughing Prophet by Emile Cammaerts, 1937.

Chesterton: As Seen by his Contemporaries by Cyril Clemens, 1939.

Those Days by E. C. Bentley, 1940.

The Chestertons by Mrs Cecil Chesterton, 1941.

Gilbert Keith Chesterton by Maisie Ward, 1944.

Return to Chesterton by Maisie Ward, 1952.

Index